D1111367

The Innovator's Dilemma

THE MANAGEMENT OF INNOVATION AND CHANGE SERIES
Michael L. Tushman and Andrew H. Van de Ven, Series Editors

Emerging Patterns of Innovation: Sources of Japan's Technological Edge
Fumio Kodama, with a Foreword by Lewis M. Branscomb

Crisis & Renewal: Meeting the Challenge of Organizational Change
David K. Hurst

Winning through Innovation: A Practical Guide to Leading Organizational Change and Renewal
Michael L. Tushman
Charles A. O'Reilly III

Imitation to Innovation: The Dynamics of Korea's Technological Learning
Linsu Kim

The Innovator's Dilemma: When New Technologies Cause Great Firms to Fail
Clayton M. Christensen

The
Innovator's
Dilemma

When New Technologies Cause Great Firms to Fail

CLAYTON M. CHRISTENSEN

Harvard Business Review Press
Boston, Massachusetts

The web addresses referenced in this book were live and correct at the time of the book's publication but may be subject to change.

Paperback ISBN: 978-1-63369-178-0

Library of Congress Cataloging-in-Publication Data

Christensen, Clayton M.
 The innovator's dilemma : when new technologies cause great firms to fail / Clayton M. Christensen.
    pages cm
  ISBN 978-1-4221-9602-1 (hardback)
 1. Creative ability in business.   2. Industrial management.   3. Customer services.   4. Success in business.   I. Title.
  HD53.C49 2013
  658—dc23

                                                          2013020203

The paper used in this publication meets the requirements of the American National Standard for Permanence of Paper for Publications and Documents in Libraries and Archives Z39.48-1992.

Contents

In Gratitude

Although this book lists only one author, in reality the ideas it molds together were contributed and refined by many extraordinarily insightful and selfless colleagues. The work began when Professors Kim Clark, Joseph Bower, Jay Light, and John McArthur took the risk of admitting and financing a middle-aged man's way into and through the Harvard Business School's doctoral program in 1989. In addition to these mentors, Professors Richard Rosenbloom, Howard Stevenson, Dorothy Leonard, Richard Walton, Bob Hayes, Steve Wheelwright, and Kent Bowen helped throughout my doctoral research to keep my thinking sharp and my standards for evidence high, and to embed what I was learning within the streams of strong scholarship that had preceded what I was attempting to research. None of these professors needed to spend so much of their busy lives guiding me as they did, and I will be forever grateful for what they taught me about the substance and process of scholarship.

I am similarly indebted to the many executives and employees of companies in the disk drive industry who opened their memories and records to me as I tried to understand what had driven them in the particular courses they had taken. In particular, James Porter, editor of *Disk/Trend Report,* opened his extraordinary archives of data, enabling me to measure what has happened in the disk drive industry with a level of completeness and accuracy that could be done in few other settings. The model of the industry's evolution and revolution that these men and women helped me construct has formed the theoretical backbone for this book. I hope they find it to be a useful tool for making sense of their past, and a helpful guide for some of their decisions in the future.

During my tenure on the Harvard Business School faculty, other colleagues have helped refine this book's ideas even more. Professors Rebecca Henderson and James Utterback of MIT, Robert Burgelman of Stanford, and David Garvin, Gary Pisano, and Marco Iansiti of the Harvard Business School have been particularly helpful. Research associates Rebecca Voorheis, Greg Rogers, Bret Baird, Jeremy Dann, Tara Donovan, and Michael Overdorf; editors Marjorie Williams, Steve Prokesch, and Barbara Feinberg; and assistants Cheryl Druckenmiller, Meredith Anderson, and Marguerite Dole, have likewise contributed untold amounts of data, advice, insight, and work.

I am grateful to my students, with whom I have discussed and refined the ideas put forward in this book. On most days I leave class wondering why I get paid and why my students pay tuition, given that it is I who have learned the most from our interactions. Every year they leave our school with their degrees and scatter around the world, without understanding how much they have taught their teachers. I love them and hope that those who come across this book will be able to recognize in it the fruits of their puzzled looks, questions, comments, and criticisms.

My deepest gratitude is to my family—my wife Christine and our children Matthew, Ann, Michael, Spencer, and Catherine. With unhesitating faith and support they encouraged me to pursue my lifelong dream to be a teacher, amidst all of the demands of family life. Doing this research on disruptive technologies has indeed been disruptive to them in terms of time and absence from home, and I am forever grateful for their love and support. Christine, in particular, is the smartest and most patient person I have known. Most of the ideas in this book went home on some night over the past five years in half-baked condition and returned to Harvard the next morning having been clarified, shaped, and edited through my conversations with her. She is a great colleague, supporter, and friend. I dedicate this book to her and our children.

Clayton M. Christensen
Harvard Business School
Boston, Massachusetts
April 1997

Preface

In 1990 I began asking the two questions that would eventually help shape this book. First, "Why is success so difficult to sustain?" And second, "Is successful innovation really as unpredictable as the data suggests?" By that time I'd been a strategist at the Boston Consulting Group, where I'd had unusual opportunities to see at every level how companies competed, and I had cofounded CPS Technologies to commercialize advanced-materials technology developed in MIT labs. But neither career path had yet to fully answer those two questions that were keeping me up at night.

So, at thirty-eight, with the support of my wife and months before our fifth child was born, I became a doctoral student and made those questions my life's work. I'm happy to say I got the answer to the first, and—with the continued help of tremendous colleagues drawn to the subject over the last two decades—I'm still homing in on the second. In this new edition of *The Innovator's Dilemma*, I'll show you some of the exciting new research we've conducted since the book was first published two decades ago.

Why is success so difficult to sustain? This was, and still is, an important question, because when you look across the sweep of business history, most companies that once seemed successful—the best practitioners of best practice—were in the middle of the pack (or, worse, the back of it) a decade or two later. And we discovered something unsettling and counterintuitive. What often causes this lagging behind are two principles of good management taught in business schools: that you should always listen to and respond to the needs of your best customers, and that you should focus investments on those innovations that promise the highest returns. But these two principles, in practice, actually sow the seeds of every successful company's ultimate demise. That's why we call it the innovator's dilemma: doing the right thing is the wrong thing. This dilemma rears its head when a type of innovation that we've termed *disruptive technology* arises at the low end of the market, in the simplest, most unassuming applications. Explaining this paradox is the purpose of this book.

Incidentally, another scholar who subsequently joined me in the study of this phenomenon, Michael Raynor of Deloitte Research, has noted that disruptive technology is probably the cause behind the "creative destruction" that economist Joseph Schumpeter observed to be the primary engine of economic progress more than half a century ago. I think Michael is right.

And what about that second question, the one about successful innovation really being as unpredictable as the data suggests? Here's an illustration that I think helps show what I mean: all venture capitalists convince themselves—to various degrees—that the companies they're investing in will succeed. Otherwise they wouldn't invest in them in the first place, right? But they are correct in only 10 to 20 percent of the investments they make, so they have structured their whole industry on hedging their bets against the alleged unpredictability of innovation. (The amounts of their financial commitments, for example, vary greatly depending on statistical assessments of the risks involved.) The track record of innovators inside established companies is roughly the same.

But think about it: if we could determine that innovation is *inherently* unpredictable—and not just a risk to manage like venture capitalists do—then it would lead us down a *very* different path, and research done by my colleagues and me seems to be indicating that this is, in fact, the case. For example, before World War II, if you were in the business of drilling for oil, 90 percent of the wells you drilled would be dry. Just like a venture capitalist's, your instincts told you there might be oil in those places, but you spent 90 percent of your working life drilling dry holes. In the subsequent seventy-five years, however, geological researchers have developed theories that tell them what data to seek about structures deep in the earth, and those theories help them give meaning to that data. Now they can predict with much more accuracy whether oil is present *before* they start drilling. There's no guaranteed guide to oil drilling yet, but today over 60 percent of the wells drilled strike oil.

Today, my colleagues and I are striving to bring to innovators, entrepreneurs, and the people who invest in them the same kinds of useful theories that those geologists brought to oil drilling. We want to help them know which pieces of information they need to collect, and how to interpret that information, so that they can become predictably successful at a rate that wasn't possible in the past. And I'm thrilled to report that, since this book was first published, we have made substantial progress with these theories.

It might seem audacious to assert that hard-headed, data-driven, results-oriented managers can benefit from using theories—indeed, the terms *theory* and *theoretical* connote *impractical* in modern business speak. But theories are statements of cause and effect—which actions yield which results, and why. As such, a good theory is consummately practical. The truth is, every time managers take an action or make a plan, they do it with the belief that if they take the actions they envision, they'll get the results they need. So managers are in fact voracious consumers of theory. The problem—the reason why succeeding at innovation has seemed so unpredictable—is that researchers to date haven't provided a body of theory that is valid and reliable enough to give innovators a solid sense of whether there is "oil down there" before they start drilling.

Some who have read this book have been bothered that the examples I used to illustrate the effects of disruption are all drawn from the past. But perhaps that's because those readers have been misled as to what theory actually is, and how it is built. Let me explain. Data *only* exists about the past. Theory must be derived, therefore, from careful observation of the past; then by categorizing those observations and correlating those categories with the outcomes of interest; then by understanding what *causes* those outcomes; and finally by showing how that causal mechanism can produce different results in different circumstances. Theory is then improved by using it to *predict*: retrospectively to predict what should have happened in the past, and prospectively to predict what will happen in the future. That being said, the theory of disruption continues to yield predictions that are quite accurate, in an astounding range of industries and applications—from satellites and national defense to computers and telecommunications; from retailing software to national economic development; and from health care to education.

Hundreds of students, consultants, investors, executives, and academics have joined with me to continue testing the theory of disruption and to research the problems of innovation. In many ways this book has become a common platform of understanding upon which we have gathered, and I'm incapable of expressing how grateful I am for all they have taught me since the first publication of this book. I can think of no professional pursuit more rewarding than joining with such kind, selfless, and intelligent people in the pursuit of light and truth.

Countless articles and books have been written on this shared platform. I invite you to dig into this body of work, some of which is listed under my name on the Harvard Business School website. In doing so, I hope you will notice that *The Innovator's Dilemma*, published two decades ago, is the *last* piece for which I was the sole author. All subsequent scholarship has been with dozens of wonderful colleagues—a tribute to how greatly so many people have contributed to this body of understanding we have been working to build.

The great historian of science, Thomas Kuhn, taught us that the key to improving any theory is to surface anomalies—events or phenomena that the theory *cannot* explain. It is only by seeking to account for outliers—exceptions to the theory—that researchers can improve the theory. That's why I need you to join me as a researcher. After you've read this book, put the theory of disruption on like a set of lenses and search for things in your past and present experience for which the theory cannot yet account. Then let me know about the anomalies, so that we can get to work improving the theory to resolve them.

Clayton M. Christensen
Kim B. Clark Professor of Business Administration
Harvard Business School

Introduction

This book is about the failure of companies to stay atop their industries when they confront certain types of market and technological change. It's not about the failure of simply any company, but of *good* companies—the kinds that many managers have admired and tried to emulate, the companies known for their abilities to innovate and execute. Companies stumble for many reasons, of course, among them bureaucracy, arrogance, tired executive blood, poor planning, short-term investment horizons, inadequate skills and resources, and just plain bad luck. But this book is not about companies with such weaknesses: It is about well-managed companies that have their competitive antennae up, listen astutely to their customers, invest aggressively in new technologies, and yet still lose market dominance.

Such seemingly unaccountable failures happen in industries that move fast and in those that move slow; in those built on electronics technology and those built on chemical and mechanical technology; in manufacturing and in service industries. Sears Roebuck, for example, was regarded for decades as one of the most astutely managed retailers in the world. At its zenith Sears accounted for more than 2 percent of all retail sales in the United States. It pioneered several innovations critical to the success of today's most admired retailers: for example, supply chain management, store brands, catalogue retailing, and credit card sales. The esteem in which Sears' management was held shows in this 1964 excerpt from *Fortune*: "How did Sears do it? In a way, the most arresting aspect of its story is that there was no gimmick. Sears opened no big bag of tricks, shot off no skyrockets. Instead, it looked as though everybody in its organization simply did the right thing, easily and naturally. And their cumulative effect was to create an extraordinary powerhouse of a company."[1]

Yet no one speaks about Sears that way today. Somehow, it completely missed the advent of discount retailing and home centers. In the midst of today's catalogue retailing boom, Sears has been driven from that business. Indeed, the very viability of its retailing operations has been questioned. One commentator has noted that "Sears' Merchandise Group lost $1.3 billion (in 1992) even before a $1.7 billion restructuring charge. Sears let arrogance blind it to basic changes taking place in the American marketplace."[2] Another writer has complained,

> Sears has been a disappointment for investors who have watched its stock sink dismally in the face of unkept promises of a turnaround. Sears' old merchandising approach—a vast, middle-of-the-road array of mid-priced goods and services—is no longer competitive. No question, the constant disappointments, the repeated predictions of a turnaround that never seems to come, have reduced the credibility of Sears' management in both the financial and merchandising communities.[3]

It is striking to note that Sears received its accolades at exactly the time—in the mid-1960s—when it was ignoring the rise of discount retailing and home centers, the lower-cost formats for marketing name-brand hard goods that ultimately stripped Sears of its core franchise. Sears was praised as one of the best-managed companies in the world at the very time it let Visa and MasterCard usurp the enormous lead it had established in the use of credit cards in retailing.

In some industries this pattern of leadership failure has been repeated more than once. Consider the computer industry. IBM dominated the mainframe market but missed by years the emergence of minicomputers, which were technologically much simpler than mainframes. In fact, no other major manufacturer of mainframe computers became a significant player in the minicomputer business. Digital Equipment Corporation created the minicomputer market and was joined by a set of other aggressively managed companies: Data General, Prime, Wang, Hewlett-Packard, and Nixdorf. But each of these companies in turn missed the desktop personal computer market. It was left to Apple Computer, together with Commodore, Tandy, and IBM's stand-alone PC division, to create the personal-computing market. Apple, in particular, was uniquely innovative in establishing the standard for user-friendly computing. But Apple and IBM lagged five years behind the leaders in bringing portable computers to market. Similarly, the firms that built the engineering workstation market—Apollo, Sun, and Silicon Graphics—were all newcomers to the industry.

As in retailing, many of these leading computer manufacturers were at one time regarded as among the best-managed companies in the world and were held up by journalists and scholars of management as examples for all to follow. Consider this assessment of Digital Equipment, made in 1986: "Taking on Digital Equipment Corp. these days is like standing in front of a moving train. The $7.6 billion computer maker has been gathering speed while most rivals are stalled in a slump in the computer industry."[4] The author proceeded to warn IBM to watch out, because it was standing on the tracks. Indeed, Digital was one of the most prominently featured companies in the McKinsey study that led to the book *In Search of Excellence.*[5]

Yet a few years later, writers characterized DEC quite differently:

> Digital Equipment Corporation is a company in need of triage. Sales are drying up in its key minicomputer line. A two-year-old restructuring plan has failed miserably. Forecasting and production planning systems have failed miserably. Cost-cutting hasn't come close to restoring profitability. . . . But the real misfortune may be DEC's lost opportunities. It has squandered two years trying halfway measures to respond to the low-margin personal computers and workstations that have transformed the computer industry.[6]

In Digital's case, as in Sears, the very decisions that led to its decline were made at the time it was so widely regarded as being an astutely managed firm. It was praised as a paragon of managerial excellence at the very time it was ignoring the arrival of the desktop computers that besieged it a few years later.

Sears and Digital are in noteworthy company. Xerox long dominated the market for plain paper photocopiers used in large, high-volume copying centers. Yet it missed huge growth and profit opportunities in the market for small tabletop photocopiers, where it became only a minor player. Although steel minimills have now captured 40 percent of the North American steel market, including nearly all of the region's markets for bars, rods, and structural steel, not a *single* integrated steel company—American, Asian, or European—had by 1995 built a plant using minimill technology. Of the thirty manufacturers of cable-actuated power shovels, only four survived the industry's twenty-five-year transition to hydraulic excavation technology.

As we shall see, the list of leading companies that failed when confronted with disruptive changes in technology and market structure is a long one. At first glance, there seems to be no pattern in the changes that overtook them. In some cases the new technologies swept through quickly; in others, the transition took decades. In some, the new technologies were complex and expensive to develop. In others, the deadly technologies were simple extensions of what the leading companies already did better than anyone else. One theme common to all of these failures, however, is that the decisions that led to failure were made when the leaders in question were widely regarded as among the best companies in the world.

There are two ways to resolve this paradox. One might be to conclude that firms such as Digital, IBM, Apple, Sears, Xerox, and Bucyrus Erie must *never* have been well managed. Maybe they were successful because of good luck and fortuitous timing, rather than good management. Maybe they finally fell on hard times because their good fortune ran out. Maybe. An alternative explanation, however, is that these failed firms were as well-run as one could expect a firm managed by mortals to be—but that there is something about the way decisions get made in successful organizations that sows the seeds of eventual failure.

The research reported in this book supports this latter view: It shows that in the cases of well-managed firms such as those cited above, *good* management was the most powerful reason they failed to stay atop their industries. Precisely *because* these firms listened to their customers, invested aggressively in new technologies that would provide their customers more and better products of the sort they wanted, and because they carefully studied market trends and systematically allocated investment capital to innovations that promised the best returns, they lost their positions of leadership.

What this implies at a deeper level is that many of what are now widely accepted principles of good management are, in fact, only situationally appropriate. There are times at which it is right *not* to listen to customers, right to invest in developing lower-performance products that promise *lower* margins, and right to aggressively pursue small, rather than substantial, markets. This book derives a set of rules, from carefully designed research and analysis of innovative successes and failures in the disk drive and other industries, that managers can use to judge when the widely accepted principles of good management should be followed and when alternative principles are appropriate.

These rules, which I call *principles of disruptive innovation*, show that when good companies fail, it often has been because their managers either ignored these principles or chose to fight them. Managers can be extraordinarily effective in managing even the most difficult innovations if they work to understand and harness the principles of disruptive innovation. As in many of life's most challenging endeavors, there is great value in coming to grips with "the way the world works," and in managing innovative efforts in ways that accommodate such forces.

The Innovator's Dilemma is intended to help a wide range of managers, consultants, and academics in manufacturing and service businesses—high tech or low—in slowly evolving or rapidly changing environments. Given that aim, *technology*, as used in this book, means the processes by which an organization transforms labor, capital, materials, and information into products and services of greater value. All firms have technologies. A retailer like Sears employs a particular technology to procure, present, sell, and deliver products to its customers, while a discount warehouse retailer like PriceCostco employs a different technology. This concept of technology therefore extends beyond engineering and manufacturing to encompass a range of marketing, investment, and managerial processes. *Innovation* refers to a change in one of these technologies.

THE DILEMMA

To establish the theoretical depth of the ideas in this book, the breadth of their usefulness, and their applicability to the future as well as the past, I have divided this book into two parts. Part One, chapters 1 through 4, builds a framework that explains why sound decisions by great managers can lead firms to failure. The picture these chapters paint is truly that of an innovator's dilemma: the logical, competent decisions of management that are critical to the success of their companies are also the reasons why they lose their positions of leadership. Part Two, chapters 5 through 10, works to resolve the dilemma. Building on our understanding of why and under what circumstances new technologies have caused great firms to fail, it prescribes managerial solutions to the dilemma—how executives can simultaneously do what is right for the near-term health of their established businesses, while focusing adequate resources on the disruptive technologies that ultimately could lead to their downfall.

Building a Failure Framework

I begin this book by digging deep before extending the discussion to draw general conclusions. The first two chapters recount in some detail the history of the disk drive industry, where the saga of "good-companies-hitting-hard-times" has been played out over and over again. This industry is an ideal field for studying failure because rich data about it exist and because, in the words of Harvard Business School Dean Kim B. Clark, it is "fast history." In just a few years, market segments, companies, and technologies have emerged, matured, and declined. Only twice in the six times that new architectural technologies have emerged in this field has the industry's dominant firm maintained its lead in the subsequent generation. This repetitive pattern of failure in the disk drive industry allowed me first to develop a preliminary framework that explained why the best and largest firms in the early generations of this industry failed and then to test this framework across subsequent cycles in the industry's history to see whether it was robust enough to continue to explain failures among the industry's more recent leaders.

Chapters 3 and 4 then deepen our understanding of why the leading firms stumbled repeatedly in the disk drive industry and, simultaneously, test the breadth of the framework's usefulness by examining the failure of firms in industries with very different characteristics. Hence, chapter 3, exploring the mechanical excavator industry, finds that the same factors that precipitated the failure of the leading disk drive makers also proved to be the undoing of the leading makers of mechanical excavators, in an industry that moves with a very different pace and technological intensity. Chapter 4 completes the framework and uses it to show why integrated steel companies worldwide have proven so incapable of blunting the attacks of the minimill steel makers.

WHY GOOD MANAGEMENT CAN LEAD TO FAILURE

The failure framework is built upon three findings from this study. The first is that there is a strategically important distinction between what I call *sustaining* technologies and those that are *disruptive*. These concepts are very different from the incremental-versus-radical distinction that has characterized many studies of this problem. Second, the pace of technological progress can, and often does, outstrip what markets need. This means that the relevance and competitiveness of different technological approaches can change with respect to different markets over time. And third, customers and financial structures of successful companies color heavily the sorts of investments that appear to be attractive to them, relative to certain types of entering firms.

Sustaining versus Disruptive Technologies

Most new technologies foster improved product performance. I call these *sustaining technologies*. Some sustaining technologies can be discontinuous or radical in character, while others are of an incremental nature. What all sustaining technologies have in common is that they improve the performance of established products, along the dimensions of performance that mainstream customers in major markets have historically valued. Most technological advances in a given industry are sustaining in character. An important finding revealed in this book is that rarely have even the most radically difficult sustaining technologies precipitated the failure of leading firms.

Occasionally, however, *disruptive technologies* emerge: innovations that result in *worse* product performance, at least in the near-term. Ironically, in each of the instances studied in this book, it was disruptive technology that precipitated the leading firms' failure.

Disruptive technologies bring to a market a very different value proposition than had been available previously. Generally, disruptive technologies underperform established products in mainstream markets. But they have other features that a few fringe (and generally new) customers value. Products based on disruptive technologies are typically cheaper, simpler, smaller, and, frequently, more convenient to use. There are many examples in addition to the personal desktop computer and discount retailing examples cited above. Small off-road motorcycles introduced in North America and Europe by Honda, Kawasaki, and Yamaha were disruptive technologies relative to the powerful, over-the-road cycles made by Harley-Davidson and BMW. Transistors were disruptive technologies relative to vacuum tubes. Health maintenance organizations were disruptive technologies to conventional health insurers. In the near future, "internet appliances" may become disruptive technologies to suppliers of personal computer hardware and software.

Trajectories of Market Need versus Technology Improvement

The second element of the failure framework, the observation that technologies can progress faster than market demand, illustrated in Figure I.1, means that in their efforts to provide better products than their competitors and earn higher prices and margins, suppliers often "overshoot" their market: They give customers more than they need or ultimately are willing to pay for. And more importantly, it means that disruptive technologies that may underperform today, relative to what users in the market demand, may be fully performance-competitive in that same market tomorrow.

Many who once needed mainframe computers for their data processing requirements, for example, no longer need or buy mainframes. Mainframe performance has surpassed the requirements of many original customers, who today find that much of what they need to do can be done on desktop machines linked to file servers. In other words, the needs of many computer users have increased more slowly than the rate of improvement provided by computer designers. Similarly, many shoppers who in 1965 felt they had to shop at department stores to be assured of quality and selection now satisfy those needs quite well at Target and Wal-Mart.

Figure I.1 The Impact of Sustaining and Disruptive Technological Change

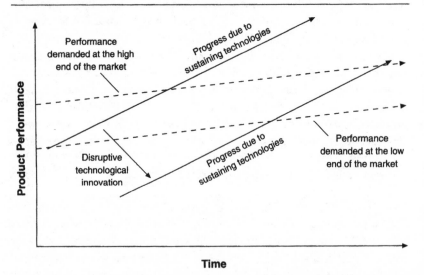

Disruptive Technologies versus Rational Investments

The last element of the failure framework, the conclusion by established companies that investing aggressively in disruptive technologies is not a rational financial decision for them to make, has three bases. First, disruptive products are simpler and cheaper; they generally promise lower margins, not greater profits. Second, disruptive technologies typically are first commercialized in emerging or insignificant markets. And third, leading firms' most profitable customers generally don't want, and indeed initially can't use, products based on disruptive technologies. By and large, a disruptive technology is initially embraced by the least profitable customers in a market. Hence, most companies with a practiced discipline of listening to their best customers and identifying new products that promise greater profitability and growth are rarely able to build a case for investing in disruptive technologies until it is too late.

TESTING THE FAILURE FRAMEWORK

This book defines the problem of disruptive technologies and describes how they can be managed, taking care to establish what researchers call the *internal* and *external* validity of its propositions. Chapters 1 and 2 develop the failure framework in the context of the disk drive industry, and the initial pages of chapters 4 through 8 return to that industry to build a progressively deeper understanding of why disruptive technologies are such vexatious phenomena for good managers to confront successfully. The reason for painting such a complete picture of a single industry is to establish the internal validity of the failure framework. If a framework or model cannot reliably explain what happened within a single industry, it cannot be applied to other situations with confidence.

Chapter 3 and the latter sections of chapters 4 through 9 are structured to explore the external validity of the failure framework—the conditions in which we might expect the framework to yield useful insights. Chapter 3 uses the framework to examine why the leading makers of cable excavators were driven from the earthmoving market by makers of hydraulic machines, and chapter 4 discusses why the world's integrated steel makers have floundered in the face of minimill technology. Chapter 5 uses the model to examine the success of discount retailers, relative to conventional chain and department stores, and to probe the impact of disruptive technologies in the motor control and printer industries. Chapter 6 examines the emerging personal digital assistant industry and reviews how the electric motor control industry was upended by disruptive technology. Chapter 7 recounts how entrants using disruptive technologies in motorcycles and logic circuitry dethroned industry leaders; chapter 8 shows how and why computer makers fell victim to disruption; and chapter 9 spotlights the same phenomena in the accounting software and insulin businesses. Chapter 10 applies the framework to a case study of the electric vehicle, summarizing the lessons learned from the other industry studies, showing how they can be used to assess the opportunity and threat of electric vehicles, and describing how they might be applied to make an electric vehicle commercially successful. Chapter 11 summarizes the book's findings.

Taken in sum, these chapters present a theoretically strong, broadly valid, and managerially practical framework for understanding disruptive technologies and how they have precipitated the fall from industry leadership of some of history's best-managed companies.

HARNESSING THE PRINCIPLES OF DISRUPTIVE INNOVATION

Colleagues who have read my academic papers reporting the findings recounted in chapters 1 through 4 were struck by their near-fatalism. If good management practice drives the failure of successful firms faced with disruptive technological change, then the usual answers to companies' problems—planning better, working harder, becoming more customer-driven, and taking a longer-term perspective—all *exacerbate* the problem. Sound execution, speed-to-market, total quality management, and process reengineering are similarly ineffective. Needless to say, this is disquieting news to people who teach future managers!

Chapters 5 through 10, however, suggest that although the solution to disruptive technologies cannot be found in the standard tool kit of good management, there are, in fact, sensible ways to deal effectively with this challenge. Every company in every industry works under certain forces—laws of organizational nature—that act powerfully to define what that company can and cannot do. Managers faced with disruptive technologies fail their companies when these forces overpower them.

By analogy, the ancients who attempted to fly by strapping feathered wings to their arms and flapping with all their might as they leapt from high places invariably failed. Despite their dreams and hard work, they were fighting against some very powerful forces of nature. No one could be strong enough to win this fight. Flight became possible only after people came to understand the relevant natural laws and principles that defined how the world worked: the law of gravity, Bernoulli's principle, and the concepts of lift, drag, and resistance. When people then designed flying systems that recognized or harnessed the power of these laws and principles, rather than fighting them, they were finally able to fly to heights and distances that were previously unimaginable.

The objective of chapters 5 through 10 is to propose the existence of five laws or principles of disruptive technology. As in the analogy with manned flight, these laws are so strong that managers who ignore or fight them are nearly powerless to pilot their companies through a disruptive technology storm. These chapters show, however, that if managers can understand and harness these forces, rather than fight them, they can in fact succeed spectacularly when confronted with disruptive technological change. I am particularly anxious that managers read these chapters for *understanding*, rather than for simple answers. I am very confident that the great managers about whom this book is written will be very capable on their own of finding the answers that best fit their circumstances. But they must first understand what has caused those circumstances and what forces will affect the feasibility of their solutions. The following paragraphs summarize these principles and what managers can do to harness or accommodate them.

Principle #1: Companies Depend on Customers and Investors for Resources

The history of the disk drive industry shows that the established firms stayed atop wave after wave of sustaining technologies (technologies that their customers needed), while consistently stumbling over simpler disruptive ones. This evidence supports the *theory of resource dependence*.[7] Chapter 5 summarizes this theory, which states that while managers may *think* they control the flow of resources in their firms, in the end it is really customers and investors who dictate how money will be spent because companies with investment patterns that don't satisfy their customers and investors don't survive. The highest-performing companies, in fact, are those that are the best at this, that is, they have well-developed systems for killing ideas that their customers don't want. As a result, these companies find it very difficult to invest adequate resources in disruptive technologies—lower-margin opportunities that their customers don't want—until their customers want them. And by then it is too late.

Chapter 5 suggests a way for managers to align or harness this law with their efforts to confront disruptive technology. With few exceptions, the only instances in which mainstream firms have successfully established a timely position in a disruptive technology were those in which the firms' managers set up an autonomous organization charged with building a new and independent business around the disruptive technology. Such organizations, free of the power of the customers of the mainstream company, ensconce themselves among a different set of customers—those who *want* the products of the disruptive technology. In other words, companies can succeed in disruptive technologies when their managers align their organizations *with* the forces of resource dependence, rather than ignoring or fighting them.

The implication of this principle for managers is that, when faced with a threatening disruptive technology, people and processes in a mainstream organization cannot be expected to allocate freely the critical financial and human resources needed to carve out a strong position in the small, emerging market. It is very difficult for a company whose cost structure is tailored to compete in high-end markets to be profitable in low-end markets as well. Creating an independent organization, with a cost structure honed to achieve profitability at the low margins characteristic of most disruptive technologies, is the only viable way for established firms to harness this principle.

Principle #2: Small Markets Don't Solve the Growth Needs of Large Companies

Disruptive technologies typically enable new markets to emerge. There is strong evidence showing that companies entering these emerging markets early have significant first-mover advantages over later entrants. And yet, as these companies succeed and grow larger, it becomes progressively more difficult for them to enter the even newer small markets destined to become the large ones of the future.

To maintain their share prices and create internal opportunities for employees to extend the scope of their responsibilities, successful companies need to continue to grow. But while a $40 million company needs to find just $8 million in revenues to grow at 20 percent in the subsequent year, a $4 billion company needs to find $800 million in new sales. No new markets are that large. As a consequence, the larger and more successful an organization becomes, the weaker the argument that emerging markets can remain useful engines for growth.

Many large companies adopt a strategy of waiting until new markets are "large enough to be interesting." But the evidence presented in chapter 6 shows why this is not often a successful strategy.

Those large established firms that have successfully seized strong positions in the new markets enabled by disruptive technologies have done so by giving responsibility to commercialize the disruptive technology to an organization whose size matched the size of the targeted market. Small organizations can most easily respond to the opportunities for growth in a small market. The evidence is strong that formal and informal resource allocation processes make it very difficult for large organizations to focus adequate energy and talent on small markets, even when logic says they might be big someday.

Principle #3: Markets that Don't Exist Can't Be Analyzed

Sound market research and good planning followed by execution according to plan are hallmarks of good management. When applied to sustaining technological innovation, these practices are invaluable; they are the primary reason, in fact, why established firms led in every single instance of sustaining innovation in the history of the disk drive industry. Such reasoned approaches are feasible in dealing with sustaining technology because the size and growth rates of the markets are generally known, trajectories of technological progress have been established, and the needs of leading customers have usually been well articulated. Because the vast majority of innovations are sustaining in character, most executives have learned to manage innovation in a sustaining context, where analysis and planning were feasible.

In dealing with disruptive technologies leading to new markets, however, market researchers and business planners have consistently dismal records. In fact, based upon the evidence from the disk drive, motorcycle, and microprocessor industries, reviewed in chapter 7, the only thing we may know for sure when we read experts' forecasts about how large emerging markets will become is that they are wrong.

In many instances, leadership in sustaining innovations—about which information is known and for which plans can be made—is not competitively important. In such cases, technology followers do about as well as technology leaders. It is in disruptive innovations, where we know least about the market, that there are such strong first-mover advantages. This is the innovator's dilemma.

Companies whose investment processes demand quantification of market sizes and financial returns before they can enter a market get paralyzed or make serious mistakes when faced with disruptive technologies. They demand market data when none exists and make judgments based upon financial projections when neither revenues or costs can, in fact, be known. Using planning and marketing techniques that were developed to manage sustaining technologies in the very different context of disruptive ones is an exercise in flapping wings.

Chapter 7 discusses a different approach to strategy and planning that recognizes the law that the right markets, and the right strategy for exploiting them, cannot be known in advance. Called discovery-based planning, it suggests that managers assume that forecasts are wrong, rather than right, and that the strategy they have chosen to pursue may likewise be wrong. Investing and managing under such assumptions drives managers to develop plans for learning what needs to be known, a much more effective way to confront disruptive technologies successfully.

Principle #4: An Organization's Capabilities Define Its Disabilities

When managers tackle an innovation problem, they instinctively work to assign capable people to the job. But once they've found the right people, too many managers then assume that the organization in which they'll work will also be capable of succeeding at the task. And that is dangerous—because organizations have capabilities that exist independently of the people who work within them. An organization's capabilities reside in two places. The first is in its processes—the methods by which people have learned to transform inputs of labor, energy, materials, information, cash, and technology into outputs of higher value. The second is in the organization's values, which are the criteria that managers and employees in the organization use when making prioritization decisions. People are quite flexible, in that they can be trained to succeed at quite different things. An employee of IBM, for example, can quite readily change the way he or she works, in order to work successfully in a small start-up company. But processes and values are not flexible. A process that is effective at managing the design of a minicomputer, for example, would be ineffective at managing the design of a desktop personal computer.

Similarly, values that cause employees to prioritize projects to develop high-margin products, cannot simultaneously accord priority to low-margin products. The very processes and values that constitute an organization's capabilities in one context, define its *dis*abilities in another context.

Chapter 8 will present a framework that can help a manager understand precisely where in his or her organization its capabilities and disabilities reside. Drawing on studies in the disk drive and computer industries, it offers tools that managers can use to create new capabilities, when the processes and values of the present organization would render it incapable of successfully addressing a new problem.

Principle #5: Technology Supply May Not Equal Market Demand

Disruptive technologies, though they initially can only be used in small markets remote from the mainstream, are disruptive because they subsequently can become fully performance-competitive within the mainstream market against established products. As depicted in Figure I.1 (on page xx), this happens because the pace of technological progress in products frequently exceeds the rate of performance improvement that mainstream customers demand or can absorb. As a consequence, products whose features and functionality closely match market needs today often follow a trajectory of improvement by which they overshoot mainstream market needs tomorrow. And products that seriously underperform today, relative to customer expectations in mainstream markets, may become directly performance-competitive tomorrow.

Chapter 9 shows that when this happens, in markets as diverse as disk drives, accounting software, and diabetes care, the basis of competition—the criteria by which customers choose one product over another—changes. When the performance of two or more competing products has improved beyond what the market demands, customers can no longer base their choice upon which is the higher performing product. The basis of product choice often evolves from functionality to reliability, then to convenience, and, ultimately, to price.

Many students of business have described phases of the product life cycle in various ways. But chapter 9 proposes that the phenomenon in which product performance overshoots market demands is the primary mechanism driving shifts in the phases of the product life cycle.

In their efforts to stay ahead by developing competitively superior products, many companies don't realize the speed at which they are moving up-market, over-satisfying the needs of their original customers as they race the competition toward higher-performance, higher-margin markets. In doing so, they create a vacuum at lower price points into which competitors employing disruptive technologies can enter. Only those companies that carefully measure trends in how their mainstream customers *use* their products can catch the points at which the basis of competition will change in the markets they serve.

LESSONS FOR SPOTTING DISRUPTIVE THREATS AND OPPORTUNITIES

Some managers and researchers familiar with these ideas have arrived at this point in the story in an anxious state because the evidence is very strong that even the best managers have stumbled badly when their markets were invaded by disruptive technologies. Most urgently, they want to know whether their own businesses are targets for an attacking disruptive technologist and how they can defend their business against such an attack before it is too late. Others, interested in finding entrepreneurial opportunities, wonder how they can identify potentially disruptive technologies around which new companies and markets can be built.

Chapter 10 addresses these questions in a rather unconventional way. Rather than offering a checklist of questions to ask or analyses to perform, it creates a case study of a particularly vexing but well-known problem in technological innovation: the electric vehicle. Positioning myself in the role of protagonist—as the program manager responsible for electric vehicle development in a major automobile manufacturing company wrestling with the mandate of the California Air Resources Board to begin selling electric vehicles in that state—I explore the question of whether electric vehicles are in fact a disruptive technology and then suggest ways to organize this program, set its strategy, and manage it to succeed. In the spirit of all case studies, the purpose of this chapter is *not* to advance what I believe to be the correct answer to this innovator's challenge. Rather, it suggests a methodology and a way of thinking about the problem of managing disruptive technological change that should prove useful in many other contexts.

Chapter 10 thus takes us deeply into the innovator's dilemma that "good" companies often begin their descent into failure by aggressively investing in the products and services that their most profitable customers want. No automotive company is currently threatened by electric cars,

Established Technology	Disruptive Technology
Silver halide photographic film	Digital photography
Wireline telephony	Mobile telephony
Circuit-switched telecommunications networks	Packet-switched communications networks
Notebook computers	Hand-held digital appliances
Desktop personal computers	Sony Playstation II, Internet appliances
Full-service stock brokerage	On-line stock brokerage
New York & NASDAQ stock exchanges	Electronic Communications Networks (ECNs)
Full-fee underwriting of new equity and debt issues	Dutch auctions of new equity and debt issues, conducted on the Internet
Credit decisions based upon the personal judgment of bank lending officers	Automated lending decisions based upon credit scoring systems
Bricks & mortar retailing	On-line retailing
Industrial materials distributors	Internet-based sites such as Chemdex and E-steel
Printed greeting cards	Free greeting cards, downloadable over the Internet
Electric utility companies	Distributed power generation (gas turbines, micro-turbines, fuel cells)
Graduate schools of management	Corporate universities and in-house management training programs
Classroom and campus-based instruction	Distance education, typically enabled by the Internet
Standard textbooks	Custom-assembled, modular digital textbooks
Offset printing	Digital printing
Manned fighter and bomber aircraft	Unmanned aircraft
Microsoft Windows operating systems and applications software written in C++.	Internet Protocols (IP), and Java software protocols
Medical doctors	Nurse practitioners
General hospitals	Outpatient clinics and in-home patient care
Open surgery	Arthroscopic and endoscopic surgery
Cardiac bypass surgery	Angioplasty
Magnetic resonance imaging (MRI) and Computer Tomography (CT) Scanning	Ultrasound—initially floor-standing machines, ultimately portable machines

and none contemplates a wholesale leap into that arena. The automobile industry is healthy. Gasoline engines have never been more reliable. Never before has such high performance and quality been available at such low prices. Indeed, aside from governmental mandates, there is no reason why we should expect the established car makers to pursue electric vehicles.

But the electric car *is* a disruptive technology and potential future threat. The innovator's task is to ensure that this innovation—the disruptive technology that doesn't make sense—is taken seriously within the company without putting at risk the needs of present customers who provide profit and growth. As chapter 10 concretely lays out, the problem can be resolved only when new markets are considered and carefully developed around new definitions of value—and when responsibility for building the business is placed within a focused organization whose size and interest are carefully aligned with the unique needs of the market's customers.

WHERE DISRUPTIONS ARE HAPPENING TODAY

One of the most gratifying aspects of my life since the first edition of *The Innovator's Dilemma* was published has been the number of people who have called, representing industries that I had never thought about, who have suggested that forces similar to those historical examples I described in these pages are disrupting their industries as well. Some of these are described in the table on the previous page. Not surprisingly, the Internet looms as an infrastructural technology that is enabling the disruption of many industries.

Each of the innovations in the right column—in the form of a new technology or a new business model—is now in the process of disrupting the established order described in the left column. Will the companies that currently lead their industries using the technologies in the left column survive these attacks? My hope is that the future might be different than the past. I believe that the future *can* be different, if managers will recognize these disruptions for what they are, and address them in a way that accounts for or harnesses the fundamental principles described in the pages that follow.

NOTES

1. John McDonald, "Sears Makes It Look Easy," *Fortune*, May, 1964, 120–121.
2. Zina Moukheiber, "Our Competitive Advantage," *Forbes*, April 12, 1993, 59.

3. Steve Weiner, "It's Not Over Until It's Over," *Forbes*, May 28, 1990, 58.
4. *Business Week*, March 24, 1986, 98.
5. Thomas J. Peters and Robert H. Waterman, *In Search of Excellence* (New York: Harper & Row, 1982).
6. *Business Week*, May 9, 1994, 26.
7. Jeffrey Pfeffer and Gerald R. Salancik, *The External Control of Organizations: A Resource Dependence Perspective* (New York: Harper & Row, 1978).

Part **One**

WHY GREAT COMPANIES CAN FAIL

CHAPTER **ONE**

How Can Great Firms Fail? Insights from the Hard Disk Drive Industry

When I began my search for an answer to the puzzle of why the best firms can fail, a friend offered some sage advice. "Those who study genetics avoid studying humans," he noted. "Because new generations come along only every thirty years or so, it takes a long time to understand the cause and effect of any changes. Instead, they study fruit flies, because they are conceived, born, mature, and die all within a single day. If you want to understand why something happens in business, study the disk drive industry. Those companies are the closest things to fruit flies that the business world will ever see."

Indeed, nowhere in the history of business has there been an industry like disk drives, where changes in technology, market structure, global scope, and vertical integration have been so pervasive, rapid, and unrelenting. While this pace and complexity might be a nightmare for managers, my friend was right about its being fertile ground for research. Few industries offer researchers the same opportunities for developing theories about how different types of change cause certain types of firms to succeed or fail or for testing those theories as the industry repeats its cycles of change.

This chapter summarizes the history of the disk drive industry in all its complexity. Some readers will be interested in it for the sake of history itself.[1] But the value of understanding this history is that out of its complexity emerge a few stunningly simple and consistent factors that have repeatedly determined the success and failure of the industry's best firms. Simply put, when the best firms succeeded, they did so because they listened responsively to their customers and invested aggressively in the technology, products, and manufacturing capabilities that satisfied their customers' next-generation needs. But, paradoxically, when the best firms subsequently failed, it was for the same reasons—they listened responsively to their customers and invested aggressively in the technology, products, and manufacturing capabilities that satisfied their customers' next-generation needs. This is one of the innovator's dilemmas: Blindly following the maxim that good managers should keep close to their customers can sometimes be a fatal mistake.

The history of the disk drive industry provides a framework for understanding when "keeping close to your customers" is good advice—and when it is not. The robustness of this framework could only be explored by researching the industry's history in careful detail. Some of that detail is recounted here, and elsewhere in this book, in the hope that readers who are immersed in the detail of their own industries will be better able to recognize how similar patterns have affected their own fortunes and those of their competitors.

HOW DISK DRIVES WORK

Disk drives write and read information that computers use. They comprise read-write heads mounted at the end of an arm that swings over the surface of a rotating disk in much the same way that a phonograph needle and arm reach over a record; aluminum or glass disks coated with magnetic material; at least two electric motors, a spin motor that drives the rotation of the disks and an actuator motor that moves the head to the desired position over the disk; and a variety of electronic circuits that control the drive's operation and its interface with the computer. See Figure 1.1 for an illustration of a typical disk drive.

The read-write head is a tiny electromagnet whose polarity changes whenever the direction of the electrical current running through it changes. Because opposite magnetic poles attract, when the polarity of the head becomes positive, the polarity of the area on the disk beneath the head switches to negative, and vice versa. By rapidly changing the direction of current flowing through the head's electromagnet as the disk spins beneath

Figure 1.1 Primary Components of a Typical Disk Drive

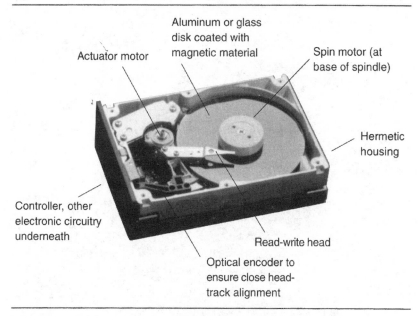

the head, a sequence of positively and negatively oriented magnetic domains are created in concentric tracks on the disk's surface. Disk drives can use the positive and negative domains on the disk as a binary numeric system—1 and 0—to "write" information onto disks. Drives read information from disks in essentially the opposite process: Changes in the magnetic flux fields on the disk surface induce changes in the micro current flowing through the head.

EMERGENCE OF THE EARLIEST DISK DRIVES

A team of researchers at IBM's San Jose research laboratories developed the first disk drive between 1952 and 1956. Named RAMAC (for Random Access Method for Accounting and Control), this drive was the size of a large refrigerator, incorporated fifty twenty-four-inch disks, and could store 5 megabytes (MB) of information (see Figure 1.2). Most of the fundamental architectural concepts and component technologies that defined today's dominant disk drive design were also developed at IBM. These include its removable packs of rigid disks (introduced in 1961);

Figure 1.2 The First Disk Drive, Developed by IBM

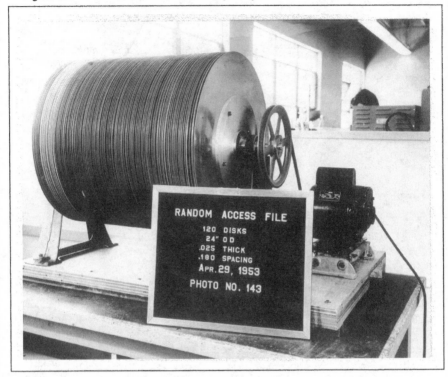

Source: Courtesy of International Business Machines Corporation.

the floppy disk drive (1971); and the Winchester architecture (1973). All had a powerful, defining influence on the way engineers in the rest of the industry defined what disk drives were and what they could do.

As IBM produced drives to meet its own needs, an independent disk drive industry emerged serving two distinct markets. A few firms developed the plug-compatible market (PCM) in the 1960s, selling souped-up copies of IBM drives directly to IBM customers at discount prices. Although most of IBM's competitors in computers (for example, Control Data, Burroughs, and Univac) were integrated vertically into the manufacture of their own disk drives, the emergence in the 1970s of smaller, nonintegrated computer makers such as Nixdorf, Wang, and Prime spawned an original equipment market (OEM) for disk drives as well. By 1976 about $1 billion worth of disk drives were produced, of which captive production accounted for 50 percent and PCM and OEM for about 25 percent each.

The next dozen years unfolded a remarkable story of rapid growth, market turbulence, and technology-driven performance improvements. The value of drives produced rose to about $18 billion by 1995. By the mid-1980s the PCM market had become insignificant, while OEM output grew to represent about three-fourths of world production. Of the seventeen firms populating the industry in 1976—all of which were relatively large, diversified corporations such as Diablo, Ampex, Memorex, EMM, and Control Data—all except IBM's disk drive operation had failed or had been acquired by 1995. During this period an additional 129 firms entered the industry, and 109 of those also failed. Aside from IBM, Fujitsu, Hitachi, and NEC, all of the producers remaining by 1996 had entered the industry as start-ups after 1976.

Some have attributed the high mortality rate among the integrated firms that created the industry to its nearly unfathomable pace of technological change. Indeed, the pace of change has been breathtaking. The number of megabits (Mb) of information that the industry's engineers have been able to pack into a square inch of disk surface has increased by 35 percent per year, on average, from 50 Kb in 1967 to 1.7 Mb in 1973, 12 Mb in 1981, and 1100 Mb by 1995. The physical size of the drives was reduced at a similar pace: The smallest available 20 MB drive shrank from 800 cubic inches (in.³) in 1978 to 1.4 in.³ by 1993—a 35 percent annual rate of reduction.

Figure 1.3 shows that the slope of the industry's experience curve (which correlates the cumulative number of terabytes (one thousand gigabytes) of disk storage capacity shipped in the industry's history to the constant-dollar price per megabyte of memory) was 53 percent—meaning that with each doubling of cumulative terabytes shipped, cost per megabyte fell to 53 percent of its former level. This is a much steeper rate of price decline than the 70 percent slope observed in the markets for most other microelectronics products. The price per megabyte has declined at about 5 percent per *quarter* for more than twenty years.

THE IMPACT OF TECHNOLOGICAL CHANGE

My investigation into why leading firms found it so difficult to stay atop the disk drive industry led me to develop the "technology mudslide hypothesis": Coping with the relentless onslaught of technology change

Figure 1.3 Disk Drive Price Experience Curve

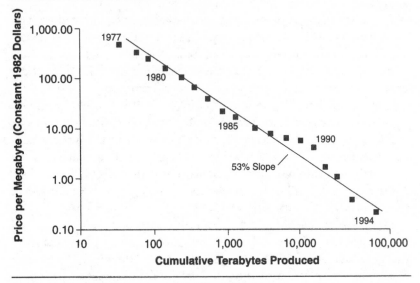

Source: Data are from various issues of *Disk/Trend Report*.

was akin to trying to climb a mudslide raging down a hill. You have to scramble with everything you've got to stay on top of it, and if you ever once stop to catch your breath, you get buried.

To test this hypothesis, I assembled and analyzed a database consisting of the technical and performance specifications of every model of disk drive introduced by every company in the world disk drive industry for each of the years between 1975 and 1994.[2] This database enabled me to identify the firms that led in introducing each new technology; to trace how new technologies were diffused through the industry over time; to see which firms led and which lagged; and to measure the impact each technological innovation had on capacity, speed, and other parameters of disk drive performance. By carefully reconstructing the history of each technological change in the industry, the changes that catapulted entrants to success or that precipitated the failure of established leaders could be identified.

This study led me to a very different view of technology change than the work of prior scholars on this question had led me to expect. Essentially, it revealed that neither the pace nor the difficulty of technological change lay at the root of the leading firms' failures. The technology mudslide hypothesis was wrong.

The manufacturers of most products have established a trajectory of performance improvement over time.[3] Intel, for example, pushed the speed of its microprocessors ahead by about 20 percent per year, from its 8 megahertz (MHz) 8088 processor in 1979 to its 133 MHz Pentium chip in 1994. Eli Lilly and Company improved the purity of its insulin from 50,000 impure parts per million (ppm) in 1925 to 10 ppm in 1980, a 14 percent annual rate of improvement. When a measurable trajectory of improvement has been established, determining whether a new technology is likely to improve a product's performance relative to earlier products is an unambiguous question.

But in other cases, the impact of technological change is quite different. For instance, is a notebook computer better than a mainframe? This is an ambiguous question because the notebook computer established a completely new performance trajectory, with a definition of performance that differs substantially from the way mainframe performance is measured. Notebooks, as a consequence, are generally sold for very different uses.

This study of technological change over the history of the disk drive industry revealed two types of technology change, each with very different effects on the industry's leaders. Technologies of the first sort *sustained* the industry's rate of improvement in product performance (total capacity and recording density were the two most common measures) and ranged in difficulty from incremental to radical. The industry's dominant firms always led in developing and adopting these technologies. By contrast, innovations of the second sort *disrupted* or redefined performance trajectories—and consistently resulted in the failure of the industry's leading firms.[4]

The remainder of this chapter illustrates the distinction between sustaining and disruptive technologies by describing prominent examples of each and summarizing the role these played in the industry's development. This discussion focuses on differences in how established firms came to lead or lag in developing and adopting new technologies, compared with entrant firms. To arrive at these examples, each new technology in the industry was examined. In analyzing which firms led and lagged at each of these points of change, I defined *established firms* to be those that had been established in the industry prior to the advent of the technology in question, practicing the prior technology. I defined *entrant firms* as those that were new to the industry at that point of technology change. Hence, a given firm would be considered an entrant at one specific point in the industry's history, for example, at the emergence of the 8-inch drive. Yet the same firm would be considered an established firm when technologies that emerged subsequent to the firm's entry were studied.

SUSTAINING TECHNOLOGICAL CHANGES

In the history of the disk drive industry, most technology changes have sustained or reinforced established trajectories of product performance improvement. Figure 1.4, which compares the average recording density of drives that employed successive generations of head and disk technologies, maps an example of this. The first curve plots the density of drives that used conventional particulate oxide disk technology and ferrite head technology; the second charts the average density of drives that used new-technology thin-film heads and disks; the third marks the improvements in density achievable with the latest head technology, magneto-resistive heads.[5]

The way such new technologies as these emerge to surpass the perfor-

Figure 1.4 Impact of New Read-Write Head Technologies in Sustaining the Trajectory of Improvement in Recording Density

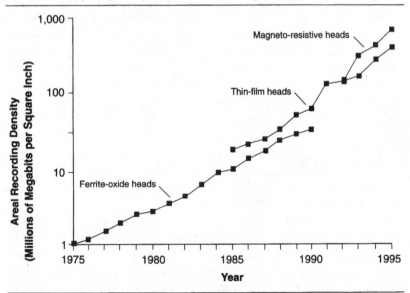

Source: Data are from various issues of *Disk/Trend Report.*

mance of the old resembles a series of intersecting technology S-curves.[6] Movement along a given S-curve is generally the result of incremental improvements within an existing technological approach, whereas jumping onto the next technology curve implies adopting a radically new technology. In the cases measured in Figure 1.4, incremental advances, such as grinding the ferrite heads to finer, more precise dimensions and using smaller and more finely dispersed oxide particles on the disk's surface, led to the improvements in density from 1 to 20 megabits per square inch (Mbpsi) between 1976 and 1989. As S-curve theory would predict, the improvement in recording density obtainable with ferrite/oxide technology began to level off toward the end of the period, suggesting a maturing technology. The thin-film head and disk technologies' effect on the industry sustained performance improvement at its historical rate. Thin-film heads were barely established in the early 1990s, when even more advanced magneto-resistive head technology emerged. The impact of magneto-resistive technology sustained, or even accelerated, the rate of performance improvement.

Figure 1.5 describes a sustaining technological change of a very different character: an innovation in product architecture, in which the 14-inch Winchester drive is substituted for removable disk packs, which had been the dominant design between 1962 and 1978. Just as in the thin-film for ferrite/oxide substitution, the impact of Winchester technology sustained the historically established rate of performance improvement. Similar graphs could be constructed for most other technological innovations in the industry, such as embedded servo systems, RLL and PRML recording codes, higher RPM motors, and embedded interfaces. Some of these were straightforward technology improvements; others were radical departures. But all had a similar impact on the industry: They helped manufacturers to sustain the rate of historical performance improvement that their customers had come to expect.[7]

In literally every case of sustaining technology change in the disk drive industry, established firms led in development and commercialization. The emergence of new disk and head technologies illustrates this.

In the 1970s, some manufacturers sensed that they were reaching the limit on the number of bits of information they could pack onto oxide disks. In response, disk drive manufacturers began studying ways of applying super-thin films of magnetic metal on aluminum to sustain the historical rate of improvements in recording density. The use of thin-film coatings was then highly developed in the integrated circuit industry, but

Figure 1.5 Sustaining Impact of the Winchester Architecture on the Recording Density of 14-inch Disk Drives

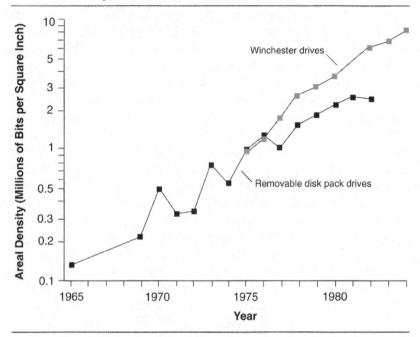

Source: Data are from various issues of *Disk/Trend Report.*

its application to magnetic disks still presented substantial challenges. Experts estimate that the pioneers of thin-film disk technology—IBM, Control Data, Digital Equipment, Storage Technology, and Ampex—each took more than eight years and spent more than $50 million in that effort. Between 1984 and 1986, about two-thirds of the producers active in 1984 introduced drives with thin-film disks. The overwhelming majority of these were established industry incumbents. Only a few entrant firms attempted to use thin-film disks in their initial products, and most of those folded shortly after entry.

The same pattern was apparent in the emergence of thin-film heads. Manufacturers of ferrite heads saw as early as 1965 the approaching limit to improvements in this technology; by 1981 many believed that the limits of precision would soon be reached. Researchers turned to thin-film technology, produced by sputtering thin films of metal on the recording head and then using photolithography to etch much finer electromagnets than could be attained with ferrite technology. Again, this proved extraordinarily difficult. Burroughs in 1976, IBM in 1979, and other established firms first successfully incorporated thin-film heads in disk drives. In the period between 1982 and 1986, during which some sixty firms entered the rigid disk drive industry, only four (all commercial failures) attempted to do so using thin-film heads in their initial products as a source of performance advantage. All other entrant firms—even aggressively performance-oriented firms such as Maxtor and Conner Peripherals—found it preferable to learn their way using conventional ferrite heads first, before tackling thin-film technology.

As was the case with thin-film disks, the introduction of thin-film heads entailed the sort of sustained investment that only established firms could handle. IBM and its rivals each spent more than $100 million developing thin-film heads. The pattern was repeated in the next-generation magneto-resistive head technology: The industry's largest firms—IBM, Seagate, and Quantum—led the race.

The established firms were the leading innovators not just in developing risky, complex, and expensive component technologies such as thin-film heads and disks, but in *literally every other one of the sustaining innovations in the industry's history.* Even in relatively simple innovations, such as RLL recording codes (which took the industry from double- to triple-density disks), established firms were the successful pioneers, and entrant firms were the technology followers. This was also true for those architectural innovations—for example, 14-inch and 2.5-inch Winchester drives—whose impact was to sustain established improvement trajectories. Established firms beat out the entrants.

Figure 1.6 summarizes this pattern of technology leadership among established and entrant firms offering products based on new sustaining technologies during the years when those technologies were emerging. The pattern is stunningly consistent. Whether the technology was radical or incremental, expensive or cheap, software or hardware, component or architecture, competence-enhancing or competence-destroying, the pattern was the same. When faced with sustaining technology change that gave existing customers something more and better in what they wanted, the leading practitioners of the prior technology led the industry in the development and adoption of the new. Clearly, the leaders in this industry did not fail because they became passive, arrogant, or risk-averse or because they couldn't keep up with the stunning rate of technological change. My technology mudslide hypothesis wasn't correct.

Figure 1.6   Leadership of Established Firms in Sustaining Technologies

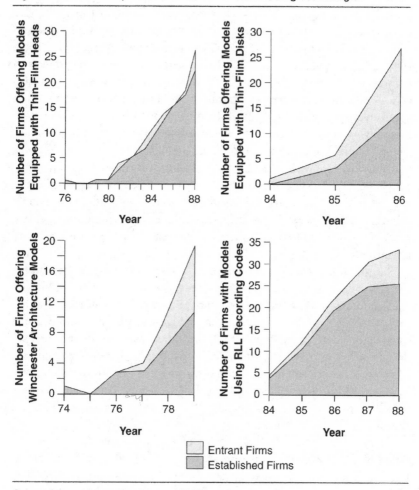

Entrant Firms
Established Firms

Source: Data are from various issues of *Disk/Trend Report.*

FAILURE IN THE FACE OF DISRUPTIVE TECHNOLOGICAL CHANGES

Most technological change in the disk drive industry has consisted of sustaining innovations of the sort described above. In contrast, there have been only a few of the other sort of technological change, called disruptive technologies. These were the changes that toppled the industry's leaders.

The most important disruptive technologies were the architectural innovations that shrunk the size of the drives—from 14-inch diameter disks
to diameters of 8, 5.25, and 3.5-inches and then from 2.5 to 1.8 inches.
Table 1.1 illustrates the ways these innovations were disruptive. Based
on 1981 data, it compares the attributes of a typical 5.25-inch drive, a
new architecture that had been in the market for less than a year, with
those of a typical 8-inch drive, which at that time was the standard drive
used by minicomputer manufacturers. Along the dimensions of performance important to established minicomputer manufacturers—capacity,
cost per megabyte, and access time—the 8-inch product was vastly superior. The 5.25-inch architecture did not address the perceived needs of
minicomputer manufacturers at that time. On the other hand, the 5.25-
inch drive had features that appealed to the desktop personal computer
market segment just emerging in the period between 1980 and 1982. It
was small and lightweight, and, priced at around $2,000, it could be
incorporated into desktop machines economically.

Generally disruptive innovations were technologically straightforward,
consisting of off-the-shelf components put together in a product architecture that was often simpler than prior approaches.[8] They offered less of
what customers in established markets wanted and so could rarely be
initially employed there. They offered a different package of attributes
valued only in emerging markets remote from, and unimportant to, the
mainstream.

The trajectory map in Figure 1.7 shows how this series of simple but
disruptive technologies proved to be the undoing of some very aggressive,

Table 1.1 A Disruptive Technology Change: The 5.25-inch
Winchester Disk Drive (1981)

Attribute	8-Inch Drives (Minicomputer Market)	5.25-Inch Drives (Desktop Computer Market)
Capacity (megabytes)	60	10
Physical volume (cubic inches)	566	150
Weight (pounds)	21	6
Access time (milliseconds)	30	160
Cost per megabyte	$50	$200
Unit cost	$3000	$2000

Source: Data are from various issues of *Disk/Trend Report.*

Figure 1.7 Intersecting Trajectories of Capacity Demanded versus Capacity Supplied in Rigid Disk Drives

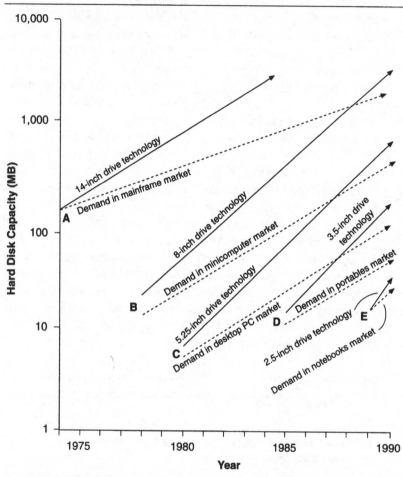

Source: Clayton M. Christensen, "The Rigid Disk Drive Industry: A History of Commercial and Technological Turbulence," *Business History Review* 67, no. 4 (Winter 1993): 559. Reprinted by permission.

astutely managed disk drive companies. Until the mid-1970s, 14-inch drives with removable packs of disks accounted for nearly all disk drive sales. The 14-inch Winchester architecture then emerged to sustain the trajectory of recording density improvement. Nearly all of these drives (removable disks and Winchesters) were sold to mainframe computer manufacturers, and the same companies that led the market in disk pack drives led the industry's transition to the Winchester technology.

The trajectory map shows that the hard disk capacity provided in the median priced, typically configured mainframe computer system in 1974 was about 130 MB per computer. This increased at a 15 percent annual rate over the next fifteen years—a trajectory representing the disk capacity demanded by the typical users of new mainframe computers. At the same time, the capacity of the average 14-inch drive introduced for sale each year increased at a faster, 22 percent rate, reaching beyond the mainframe market to the large scientific and supercomputer markets.[9]

Between 1978 and 1980, several entrant firms—Shugart Associates, Micropolis, Priam, and Quantum—developed smaller 8-inch drives with 10, 20, 30, and 40 MB capacity. These drives were of no interest to mainframe computer manufacturers, which at that time were demanding drives with 300 to 400 MB capacity. These 8-inch entrants therefore sold their disruptive drives into a new application—minicomputers.[10] The customers—Wang, DEC, Data General, Prime, and Hewlett-Packard—did not manufacture mainframes, and their customers often used software substantially different from that used in mainframes. These firms hitherto had been unable to offer disk drives in their small, desk-side minicomputers because 14-inch models were too big and expensive. Although initially the cost per megabyte of capacity of 8-inch drives was higher than that of 14-inch drives, these new customers were willing to pay a premium for other attributes that were important to them—especially smaller size. Smallness had little value to mainframe users.

Once the use of 8-inch drives became established in minicomputers, the hard disk capacity shipped with the median-priced minicomputer grew about 25 percent per year: a trajectory determined by the ways in which minicomputer owners learned to use their machines. At the same time, however, the 8-inch drive makers found that, by aggressively adopting sustaining innovations, they could increase the capacity of their products at a rate of more than 40 percent per year—nearly double the rate of increase demanded by their original "home" minicomputer market. In consequence, by the mid-1980s, 8-inch drive makers were able to provide the capacities required for lower-end mainframe computers. Unit volumes had grown significantly so that the cost per megabyte of 8-inch drives had declined below that of 14-inch drives, and other advantages became apparent: For example, the same percentage mechanical vibration in an 8-inch drive, as opposed to a 14-inch drive, caused much less variance in the absolute position of the head over the disk. Within a three-to-four-year period, therefore, 8-inch drives began to invade the market above them, substituting for 14-inch drives in the lower-end mainframe computer market.

As the 8-inch products penetrated the mainframe market, the established manufacturers of 14-inch drives began to fail. Two-thirds of them never introduced an 8-inch model. The one-third that introduced 8-inch models did so about two years behind the 8-inch entrant manufacturers. Ultimately, every 14-inch drive maker was driven from the industry.[11]

The 14-inch drive makers were not toppled by the 8-inch entrants because of technology. The 8-inch products generally incorporated standard off-the-shelf components, and when those 14-inch drive makers that did introduce 8-inch models got around to doing so, their products were very performance-competitive in capacity, areal density, access time, and price per megabyte. The 8-inch models introduced by the established firms in 1981 were nearly identical in performance to the average of those introduced that year by the entrant firms. In addition, the rates of improvement in key attributes (measured between 1979 and 1983) were stunningly similar between established and entrant firms.[12]

Held Captive by Their Customers

Why were the leading drive makers unable to launch 8-inch drives until it was too late? Clearly, they were technologically capable of producing these drives. Their failure resulted from delay in making the strategic commitment to enter the emerging market in which the 8-inch drives initially could be sold. Interviews with marketing and engineering executives close to these companies suggest that the established 14-inch drive manufacturers were held captive by customers. Mainframe computer manufacturers did not need an 8-inch drive. In fact, they explicitly did not want it: they wanted drives with increased capacity at a lower cost per megabyte. The 14-inch drive manufacturers were listening and responding to their established customers. And their customers—in a way that was not apparent to either the disk drive manufacturers or their computer-making customers—were pulling them along a trajectory of 22 percent capacity growth in a 14-inch platform that would ultimately prove fatal.[13]

Figure 1.7 maps the disparate trajectories of performance improvement demanded in the computer product segments that emerged later, compared to the capacity that changes in component technology and refinements in system design made available within each successive architecture. The solid lines emanating from points A, B, C, D, and E measure the disk drive capacity provided with the median-priced computer in each category, while the dotted lines from the same points measure the average capacity of all disk drives introduced for sale in each architecture, for each year. These transitions are briefly described below.

The Advent of the 5.25-inch Drive

In 1980, Seagate Technology introduced 5.25-inch disk drives. Their capacities of 5 and 10 MB were of no interest to minicomputer manufacturers, who were demanding drives of 40 and 60 MB from their suppliers. Seagate and other firms that entered with 5.25-inch drives in the period 1980 to 1983 (for example, Miniscribe, Computer Memories, and International Memories) had to pioneer new applications for their products and turned primarily to desktop personal computer makers. By 1990, the use of hard drives in desktop computers was an obvious application for magnetic recording. It was not at all clear in 1980, however, when the market was just emerging, that many people could ever afford or use a hard drive on the desktop. The early 5.25-inch drive makers found this application (one might even say that they *enabled* it) by trial and error, selling drives to whomever would buy them.

Once the use of hard drives was established in desktop PCs, the disk capacity shipped with the median-priced machine (that is, the capacity demanded by the general PC user) increased about 25 percent per year. Again, the technology improved at nearly twice the rate demanded in the new market: The capacity of new 5.25-inch drives increased about 50 percent per year between 1980 and 1990. As in the 8-inch for 14-inch substitution, the first firms to produce 5.25-inch drives were entrants; on average, established firms lagged behind entrants by two years. By 1985, only half of the firms producing 8-inch drives had introduced 5.25-inch models. The other half never did.

Growth in the use of 5.25-inch drives occurred in two waves. The first followed creation of a new application for rigid disk drives: desktop computing, in which product attributes such as physical size, relatively unimportant in established applications, were highly valued. The second wave followed substitution of 5.25-inch disks for larger drives in established minicomputer and mainframe computer markets, as the rapidly increasing capacity of 5.25-inch drives intersected the more slowly growing trajectories of capacity demanded in these markets. Of the four leading 8-inch drive makers—Shugart Associates, Micropolis, Priam, and Quantum—only Micropolis survived to become a significant manufacturer of 5.25-inch drives, and that was accomplished only with Herculean managerial effort, as described in chapter 5.

The Pattern Is Repeated: The Emergence of the 3.5-inch Drive

The 3.5-inch drive was first developed in 1984 by Rodime, a Scottish entrant. Sales of this architecture were not significant, however, until Conner Peripherals, a spinoff of 5.25-inch drive makers Seagate and Miniscribe, started shipping product in 1987. Conner had developed a small, lightweight drive architecture that was much more rugged than its 5.25-inch ancestors. It handled electronically functions that had previously been managed with mechanical parts, and it used microcode to replace functions that had previously been addressed electronically. Nearly all of Conner's first year revenues of $113 million[14] came from Compaq Computer, which had aided Conner's start-up with a $30 million investment. The Conner drives were used primarily in a new application—portable and laptop machines, in addition to "small footprint" desktop models—where customers were willing to accept lower capacities and higher costs per megabyte to get lighter weight, greater ruggedness, and lower power consumption.

Seagate engineers were not oblivious to the coming of the 3.5-inch architecture. Indeed, in early 1985, less than one year after Rodime introduced the first 3.5-inch drive and two years *before* Conner Peripherals started shipping its product, Seagate personnel showed working 3.5-inch prototype drives to customers for evaluation. The initiative for the new drives came from Seagate's engineering organization. Opposition to the program came primarily from the marketing organization and Seagate's executive team; they argued that the market wanted higher capacity drives at a lower cost per megabyte and that 3.5-inch drives could never be built at a lower cost per megabyte than 5.25-inch drives.

Seagate's marketers tested the 3.5-inch prototypes with customers in the desktop computing market it already served—manufacturers like IBM, and value-added resellers of full-sized desktop computer systems. Not surprisingly, they indicated little interest in the smaller drive. They were looking for capacities of 40 and 60 megabytes for their next-generation machines, while the 3.5-inch architecture could provide only 20 MB—and at higher costs.[15]

In response to lukewarm reviews from customers, Seagate's program manager lowered his 3.5-inch sales estimates, and the firm's executives canceled the program. Their reasoning? The markets for 5.25-inch products were larger, and the sales generated by spending the engineering effort on new 5.25-inch products would create greater revenues for the company than would efforts targeted at new 3.5-inch products.

In retrospect, it appears that Seagate executives read the market—at least their own market—very accurately. With established applications and product architectures of their own, such as the IBM XT and AT, these customers saw no value in the improved ruggedness or the reduced size, weight, and power consumption of 3.5-inch products.

Seagate finally began shipping 3.5-inch drives in early 1988—the same year in which the performance trajectory of 3.5-inch drives (shown in Figure 1.7) intersected the trajectory of capacity demanded in desktop computers. By that time, the industry had shipped, cumulatively, nearly $750 million in 3.5-inch products. Interestingly, according to industry observers, as of 1991 almost none of Seagate's 3.5-inch products had been sold to manufacturers of portable/laptop/notebook computers. In other words, Seagate's primary customers were still desktop computer manufacturers, and many of its 3.5-inch drives were shipped with frames for mounting them in computers designed for 5.25-inch drives.

The fear of cannibalizing sales of existing products is often cited as a reason why established firms delay the introduction of new technologies. As the Seagate-Conner experience illustrates, however, if new technologies enable new market applications to emerge, the introduction of new technology may not be inherently cannibalistic. But when established firms wait until a new technology has become commercially mature in its new applications and launch their own version of the technology only in response to an attack on their home markets, the fear of cannibalization can become a self-fulfilling prophecy.

Although we have been looking at Seagate's response to the development of the 3.5-inch drive architecture, its behavior was not atypical; by 1988, only 35 percent of the drive manufacturers that had established themselves making 5.25-inch products for the desktop PC market had introduced 3.5-inch drives. Similar to earlier product architecture transitions, the barrier to development of a competitive 3.5-inch product does not appear to have been engineering-based. As in the 14- to 8-inch transition, the new-architecture drives introduced by the incumbent, established firms during the transitions from 8 to 5.25 inches and from 5.25 to 3.5 inches were fully performance-competitive with those of entrant drives. Rather, the 5.25-inch drive manufacturers seem to have been misled by their customers, notably IBM and its direct competitors and resellers, who themselves seemed as oblivious as Seagate to the potential benefits and possibilities of portable computing and the new disk drive architecture that might facilitate it.

Prairietek, Conner, and the 2.5-inch Drive

In 1989 an industry entrant in Longmont, Colorado, Prairietek, upstaged the industry by announcing a 2.5-inch drive, capturing nearly all $30 million of this nascent market. But Conner Peripherals announced its own 2.5-inch product in early 1990 and by the end of that year had claimed 95 percent of the 2.5-inch drive market. Prairietek declared bankruptcy in late 1991, by which time each of the other 3.5-inch drivemakers— Quantum, Seagate, Western Digital, and Maxtor—had introduced 2.5-inch drives of their own.

What had changed? Had the incumbent leading firms finally learned the lessons of history? Not really. Although Figure 1.7 shows the 2.5-inch drive had significantly less capacity than the 3.5-inch drives, the portable computing markets into which the smaller drives were sold valued *other* attributes: weight, ruggedness, low power consumption, small physical size, and so on. Along *these* dimensions, the 2.5-inch drive offered improved performance over that of the 3.5-inch product: It was a *sustaining* technology. In fact, the computer makers who bought Conner's 3.5-inch drive—laptop computer manufacturers such as Toshiba, Zenith, and Sharp—were the leading makers of notebook computers, and these firms needed the smaller 2.5-inch drive architecture. Hence, Conner and its competitors in the 3.5-inch market followed their customers seamlessly across the transition to 2.5-inch drives.

In 1992, however, the 1.8-inch drive emerged, with a distinctly disruptive character. Although its story will be recounted in detail later, it suffices to state here that by 1995, it was *entrant* firms that controlled 98 percent of the $130 million 1.8-inch drive market. Moreover, the largest initial market for 1.8-inch drives wasn't in computing at all. It was in portable heart monitoring devices!

Figure 1.8 summarizes this pattern of entrant firms' leadership in disruptive technology. It shows, for example, that two years after the 8-inch drive was introduced, two-thirds of the firms producing it (four of six), were entrants. And, two years after the first 5.25-inch drive was intro-

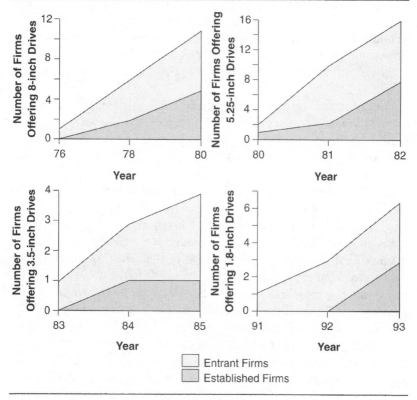

Figure 1.8 Leadership of Entrant Firms in Disruptive Technology

Entrant Firms
Established Firms

Source: Data are from various issues of *Disk/Trend Report.*

duced, 80 percent of the firms producing these disruptive drives were entrants.

SUMMARY

There are several patterns in the history of innovation in the disk drive industry. The first is that the disruptive innovations were technologically straightforward. They generally packaged known technologies in a unique architecture and enabled the use of these products in applications where magnetic data storage and retrieval previously had not been technologically or economically feasible.

The second pattern is that the purpose of advanced technology development in the industry was always to *sustain* established trajectories of performance improvement: to reach the higher-performance, higher-margin domain of the upper right of the trajectory map. Many of these technologies were radically new and difficult, but they were not disruptive. The customers of the leading disk drive suppliers led them toward these achievements. Sustaining technologies, as a result, did not precipitate failure.

The third pattern shows that, despite the established firms' technological prowess in leading sustaining innovations, from the simplest to the most radical, the firms that led the industry in every instance of developing and adopting disruptive technologies were entrants to the industry, not its incumbent leaders.

This book began by posing a puzzle: Why was it that firms that could be esteemed as aggressive, innovative, customer-sensitive organizations could ignore or attend belatedly to technological innovations with enormous strategic importance? In the context of the preceding analysis of the disk drive industry, this question can be sharpened considerably. The established firms were, in fact, aggressive, innovative, and customer-sensitive in their approaches to sustaining innovations of every sort. But the problem established firms seem unable to confront successfully is that of *downward* vision and mobility, in terms of the trajectory map. Finding new applications and markets for these new products seems to be a capability that each of these firms exhibited once, upon entry, and then apparently lost. It was as if the leading firms were held captive by their customers, enabling attacking entrant firms to topple the incumbent industry leaders each time a disruptive technology emerged.[16] Why this happened, and is still happening, is the subject of the next chapter.

APPENDIX 1.1:
A NOTE ON THE DATA AND METHOD
USED TO GENERATE FIGURE 1.7

The trajectories mapped in Figure 1.7 were calculated as follows. Data on the capacity provided with computers was obtained from *Data Sources*, an annual publication listing the technical specifications of all computer models available from every computer manufacturer. For instances in which particular models were available with different features and configurations, the manufacturer provided *Data Sources* with a "typical" system configuration with defined random access memory (RAM) capacity, performance specifications of peripheral equipment (including disk drives), list prices, and year of introduction. For instances in which a given computer model was offered for sale over a sequence of years, the hard disk capacity provided in the typical configuration typically increased. *Data Sources* used the categories mainframe, mini/midrange, desktop personal, portable and laptop, and notebook. As of 1993, 1.8-inch drives were not being used in hand-held computers, so no data on that potential market existed.

For Figure 1.7, for each year and each class of computers, all models available for sale were ranked by price and the hard disk capacity provided with the median-priced model identified. The best-fit lines through the resultant time series were plotted as the solid lines in Figure 1.7 for expository simplification to indicate the trend in typical machines. In reality, of course, there is a wide band around these lines. The *frontier* of performance—the highest capacity offered with the most expensive computers—was substantially higher than the typical values shown.

The dotted lines in Figure 1.7 represent the best-fit line through the unweighted average capacity of all disk drives introduced for sale in each given architecture for each year. This data was taken from *Disk/Trend Report*. Again, for expository simplification, only this average line is shown. There was a wide band of capacities introduced for sale in each year, so that the frontier or highest capacity drive introduced in each year was substantially above the average shown. Stated in another way, a distinction must be made between the full range of products available for purchase and those in typical systems. The upper and lower bands around the median and average figures shown in Figure 1.7 are generally parallel to the lines shown.

Because higher capacity drives were available in the market than were offered with the median-priced systems, the solid-line trajectories in Figure 1.7, as I state in the text, represent the capacities "demanded" in each market. In other words, the capacity per machine was not constrained by technological availability. Rather, it represents the selection of hard disk capacity by computer users, given the prevailing cost.

NOTES

1. A more complete history of the disk drive industry can be found in Clayton M. Christensen, "The Rigid Disk Drive Industry: A History of Commercial and Technological Turbulence," *Business History Review* (67), Winter, 1993, 531–588. This history focuses only on the manufacturers of rigid disk drives or hard drives—products on which data are stored on rigid metal platters. Companies manufacturing floppy disk drives (removable diskettes of flexible mylar coated with iron oxide on which data are stored) historically were different firms from those making hard disk drives.

2. Much of the data for this analysis came from *Disk/Trend Report,* a highly respected annual market research publication, augmented with more detailed product-specification sheets obtained from the disk drive manufacturers themselves. I am grateful to the editors and staff at Disk/Trend, Inc., for their patient and generous assistance in this project.

3. The concept of trajectories of technological progress was examined by Giovanni Dosi in "Technological Paradigms and Technological Trajectories," *Research Policy* (11), 1982, 147–162.

4. The ways in which the findings of this study differ from those of some earlier scholars of technology change while building upon those of others are discussed in greater detail in chapter 2.

5. The first technology for making heads built an electromagnet by wrapping a fine thread of copper wire around a core of iron oxide (ferrite); hence the term *ferrite head.* Incremental improvements to this approach involved learning to grind the ferrite to finer and finer dimensions, using better lapping techniques, and strengthening the ferrite by doping it with barium. *Thin-film heads* were made photolithographically, using technology similar to that used in making integrated circuits on silicon wafers to etch the electromagnet on the surface of the head. This was difficult because it involved much thicker layers of material than were common in IC manufacturing. The third technology, adopted starting in the mid-1990s, was called *magneto-resistive heads.* These were also made with thin-film photolithography, but used the principle that changes in the magnetic flux field on the disk surface changed the electrical resistivity of the circuitry in the head. By measuring changes in resistivity rather than changes in the direction of current flow, magneto-resistive heads were much more sensitive, and hence permitted denser data recording, than prior technology. In the evolution of disk technology, the earliest disks were made by coating fine needle-shaped particles of iron oxide—literally rust—over the surface of a flat, polished aluminum platter. Hence, these disks were called *oxide* disks. Incremental improvements to this technology involved making finer and finer iron oxide particles, and dispersing them more uniformly, with fewer uncoated voids on the aluminum platter's surface. This was supplanted by a sputtering technology, also borrowed from semiconductor processing, that coated the aluminum platter with a thin film of metal a few angstroms thick. The thinness of this layer; its continuous, rather than particulate nature; and the process's flexibility in depositing magnetic materials with higher coercivity, enabled denser recording on thin-film disks than was feasible on oxide disks.

6. Richard J. Foster, *Innovation: The Attacker's Advantage* (New York: Summit Books, 1986).

7. The examples of technology change presented in Figures 1.1 and 1.2 introduce

some ambiguity to the unqualified term *discontinuity*, as used by Giovanni Dosi (see "Technological Paradigms and Technological Trajectories," *Research Policy* [11] 1982), Michael L. Tushman and Philip Anderson (see "Technological Discontinuities and Organizational Environments," *Administrative Science Quarterly* [31], 1986), and others. The innovations in head and disk technology described in Figure 1.4 represent *positive* discontinuities in an established technological trajectory, while the trajectory-disrupting technologies charted in Figure 1.7 represent *negative* discontinuities. As will be shown below, established firms seemed quite capable of leading the industry over positive discontinuities, but generally lost their industry lead when faced with negative discontinuities.

8. This tendency consistently appears across a range of industries. Richard S. Rosenbloom and Clayton M. Christensen (in "Technological Discontinuities, Organizational Capabilities, and Strategic Commitments," *Industrial and Corporate Change* [3], 1994, 655–685) suggest a much broader set of industries in which leading firms may have been toppled by technologically straightforward disruptive innovations than is covered in this book.

9. A summary of the data and procedures used to generate Figure 1.7 is included in Appendix 1.1.

10. The minicomputer market was not new in 1978, but it was a new application for Winchester-technology disk drives.

11. This statement applies only to independent drive makers competing in the OEM market. Some of the vertically integrated computer makers, such as IBM, have survived across these generations with the benefit of a captive internal market. Even IBM, however, addressed the sequence of different emerging markets for disk drives by creating autonomous "start-up" disk drive organizations to address each one. Its San Jose organization focused on high-end (primarily mainframe) applications. A separate division in Rochester, MN, focused on mid-range computers and workstations. IBM created a different organization in Fujisawa, Japan, to produce drives for the desktop personal computer market.

12. This result is very different from that observed by Rebecca M. Henderson (see *The Failure of Established Firms in the Face of Technological Change: A Study of the Semiconductor Photolithographic Alignment Industry*, dissertation, Harvard University, 1988), who found the new-architecture aligners produced by the established manufacturers to be inferior in performance to those produced by entrant firms. One possible reason for these different results is that the successful entrants in the photolithographic aligner industry studied by Henderson brought to the new product a well-developed body of technological knowledge and experience developed and refined in other markets. In the case studied here, none of the entrants brought such well-

developed knowledge with them. Most, in fact, were *de novo* start-ups composed of managers and engineers who had defected from established drive manufacturing firms.

13. This finding is similar to the phenomenon observed by Joseph L. Bower, who saw that explicit customer demands have tremendous power as a source of impetus in the resource allocation process: "When the discrepancy (the problem to be solved by a proposed investment) was defined in terms of cost and quality, the projects languished. In all four cases, the definition process moved toward completion when capacity to meet sales was perceived to be inadequate. . . . In short, pressure from the market reduces both the probability and the cost of being wrong." Although Bower specifically refers to manufacturing capacity, the same fundamental phenomenon—the power of the known needs of known customers in marshaling and directing the investments of a firm—affects response to disruptive technology. See Joseph L. Bower, *Managing the Resource Allocation Process* (Homewood, IL: Richard D. Irwin, 1970) 254.

14. In booking $113 million in revenues, Conner Peripherals set a record for booking more revenues in its first year of operation than any manufacturing company in United States history.

15. This finding is consistent with what Robert Burgelman has observed. He noted that one of the greatest difficulties encountered by corporate entrepreneurs has been finding the right "beta test sites" where products could be interactively developed and refined with customers. Generally, a new venture's entrée to the customer was provided by the salesperson representing the firm's established product lines. This helped the firm develop new products for established markets but not to identify new applications for new technology. See Robert A. Burgelman and Leonard Sayles, *Inside Corporate Innovation* (New York: The Free Press, 1986) 76–80.

16. I believe this insight—that attacking firms have an advantage in disruptive innovations but not in sustaining ones—clarifies, but is not in conflict with, Foster's assertions about the attacker's advantage. The historical examples Foster uses to substantiate his theory generally seem to have been disruptive innovations. See Richard J. Foster, *Innovation: The Attacker's Advantage* (New York: Summit Books, 1986).

CHAPTER TWO

Value Networks and the Impetus to Innovate

From the earliest studies of the problems of innovation, scholars, consultants, and managers have tried to explain why leading firms frequently stumble when confronting technology change. Most explanations either zero in on managerial, organizational, and cultural responses to technological change or focus on the ability of established firms to deal with radically new technology; doing the latter requires a very different set of skills from those that an established firm historically has developed. Both approaches, useful in explaining why some companies stumble in the face of technological change, are summarized below. The primary purpose of this chapter, however, is to propose a third theory of why good companies can fail, based upon the concept of a *value network*. The value network concept seems to have much greater power than the other two theories in explaining what we observed in the disk drive industry.

ORGANIZATIONAL AND MANAGERIAL EXPLANATIONS OF FAILURE

One explanation for why good companies fail points to organizational impediments as the source of the problem. While many analyses of this type stop with such simple rationales as bureaucracy, complacency, or "risk-averse" culture, some remarkably insightful studies exist in this tradition. Henderson and Clark,[1] for example, conclude that companies' organizational structures typically facilitate component-level innovations, because most product development organizations consist of subgroups that correspond to a product's components. Such systems work very well as long as the product's fundamental architecture does not require change. But, say the authors, when architectural technology change is required, this type of structure impedes innovations that require people and groups to communicate and work together in new ways.

This notion has considerable face validity. In one incident recounted in Tracy Kidder's Pulitzer Prize–winning narrative, *The Soul of a New Machine,* Data General engineers developing a next-generation minicomputer intended to leapfrog the product position of Digital Equipment Corporation were allowed by a friend of one team member into his facility in the middle of the night to examine Digital's latest computer, which his company had just bought. When Tom West, Data General's project leader and a former long-time Digital employee, removed the cover of the DEC minicomputer and examined its structure, he saw "Digital's organization chart in the design of the product."[2]

Because an organization's structure and how its groups work together may have been established to facilitate the design of its dominant product, the direction of causality may ultimately reverse itself: The organization's structure and the way its groups learn to work together can then affect the way it can and cannot design new products.

CAPABILITIES AND RADICAL TECHNOLOGY AS AN EXPLANATION

In assessing blame for the failure of good companies, the distinction is sometimes made between innovations requiring very different technological capabilities, that is, so-called radical change, and those that build upon well-practiced technological capabilities, often called incremental innovations.[3] The notion is that the magnitude of the technological change relative to the companies' capabilities will determine which firms triumph after a technology invades an industry. Scholars who support this view find that established firms tend to be good at improving what they have long been good at doing, and that entrant firms seem better suited for exploiting radically new technologies, often because they import the technology into one industry from another, where they had already developed and practiced it.

Clark, for example, has reasoned that companies build the technological capabilities in a product such as an automobile hierarchically and experientially.[4] An organization's historical choices about which technological problems it would solve and which it would avoid determine the sorts of skills and knowledge it accumulates. When optimal resolution of a product or process performance problem demands a very different set of knowledge than a firm has accumulated, it may very well stumble. The research of Tushman, Anderson, and their associates supports Clark's hypothesis.[5] They found that firms failed when a technological change destroyed the value of competencies previously cultivated and succeeded when new technologies enhanced them.

The factors identified by these scholars undoubtedly affect the fortunes of firms confronted with new technologies. Yet the disk drive industry displays a series of anomalies accounted for by neither set of theories. Industry leaders first introduced sustaining technologies of *every* sort, including architectural and component innovations that rendered prior competencies irrelevant and made massive investments in skills and assets obsolete. Nevertheless, these same firms stumbled over technologically straightforward but disruptive changes such as the 8-inch drive.

The history of the disk drive industry, indeed, gives a very different meaning to what constitutes a radical innovation among leading, established firms. As we saw, the nature of the technology involved (components versus architecture and incremental versus radical), the magnitude of the risk, and the time horizon over which the risks needed to be taken had little relationship to the patterns of leadership and followership observed. Rather, if their customers needed an innovation, the leading firms somehow mustered the resources and wherewithal to develop and adopt it. Conversely, if their customers did not want or need an innovation, these firms found it impossible to commercialize even technologically simple innovations.

VALUE NETWORKS AND NEW PERSPECTIVE ON THE DRIVERS OF FAILURE

What, then, *does* account for the success and failure of entrant and established firms? The following discussion synthesizes from the history of the disk drive industry a new perspective on the relation between success or failure and changes in technology and market structure. The concept of the *value network*—the context within which a firm identifies and responds to customers' needs, solves problems, procures input, reacts to competitors, and strives for profit—is central to this synthesis.[6] Within a value network, each firm's competitive strategy, and particularly its past choices of markets, determines its perceptions of the economic value of a new technology. These perceptions, in turn, shape the rewards different firms expect to obtain through pursuit of sustaining and disruptive innovations.[7] In established firms, expected rewards, in their turn, drive the allocation of resources toward sustaining innovations and away from disruptive ones. This pattern of resource allocation accounts for established firms' consistent leadership in the former and their dismal performance in the latter.

Value Networks Mirror Product Architecture

Companies are embedded in value networks because their products generally are embedded, or nested hierarchically, as components within other products and eventually within end systems of use.[8] Consider a 1980s-vintage management information system (MIS) for a large organization, as illustrated in Figure 2.1. The architecture of the MIS ties together various components—a mainframe computer; peripherals such as line printers and tape and disk drives; software; a large, air-conditioned room with cables running under a raised floor; and so on. At the next level, the mainframe computer is itself an architected system, comprising such components as a central processing unit, multi-chip packages and circuit boards, RAM circuits, terminals, controllers, and disk drives. Telescoping down still further, the disk drive is a system whose components include a motor, actuator, spindle, disks, heads, and controller. In turn, the disk itself can be analyzed as a system composed of an aluminum platter, magnetic material, adhesives, abrasives, lubricants, and coatings.

Although the goods and services constituting such a system of use may all be produced within a single, extensively integrated corporation such as AT&T or IBM, most are tradable, especially in more mature markets. This means that, while Figure 2.1 is drawn to describe the nested *physical* architecture of a product system, it also implies the existence of a *nested network of producers and markets* through which the components at each level are made and sold to integrators at the next higher level in the system. Firms that design and assemble disk drives, for example, such as Quantum and Maxtor, procure read-write heads from firms specializing

Figure 2.1 A Nested, or Telescoping, System of Product Architectures

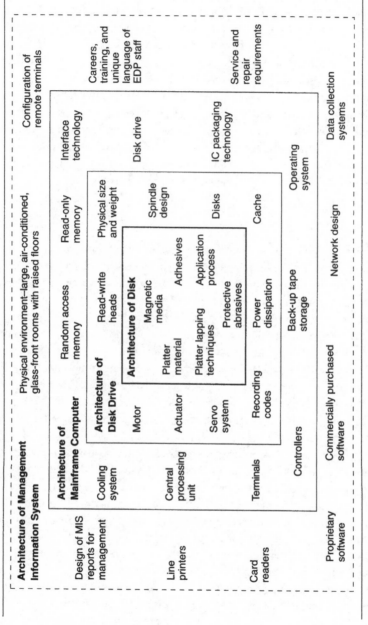

Source: Reprinted from *Research Policy* 24, Clayton M. Christensen and Richard S. Rosenbloom, "Explaining the Attacker's Advantage: Technological Paradigms, Organizational Dynamics, and the Value Network," 233–257, 1995 with kind permission of Elsevier Science—NL, Sara Burgerhartstraat 25, 1055 KV Amsterdam, The Netherlands.

in the manufacture of those heads, and they buy disks from other firms and spin motors, actuator motors, and integrated circuitry from still others. At the next higher level, firms that design and assemble computers may buy their integrated circuits, terminals, disk drives, IC packaging, and power supplies from various firms that manufacture those particular products. This nested commercial system is a *value network*.

Figure 2.2 illustrates three value networks for computing applications: Reading top to bottom they are the value network for a corporate MIS system-of-use, for portable personal computing products, and for computer-automated design (CAD). Drawn only to convey the concept of how networks are bounded and may differ from each other, these depictions are not meant to represent complete structures.

Metrics of Value

The way value is measured differs across networks.[9] In fact, the unique rank-ordering of the importance of various product performance attributes defines, in part, the boundaries of a value network. Examples in Figure 2.2, listed to the right of the center column of component boxes, show how each value network exhibits a very different rank-ordering of important product attributes, even for the same product. In the top-most value network, disk drive performance is measured in terms of capacity, speed, and reliability, whereas in the portable computing value network, the important performance attributes are ruggedness, low power consumption, and small size. Consequently, parallel value networks, each built around a different definition of what makes a product valuable, may exist within the same broadly defined industry.

Although many components in different systems-of-use may carry the same labels (for example, each network in Figure 2.2 involves read-write heads, disk drives, RAM circuits, printers, software, and so on), the nature of components used may be quite different. Generally, a set of competing firms, each with its own value chain,[10] is associated with each box in a network diagram, and the firms supplying the products and services used in each network often differ (as illustrated in Figure 2.2 by the firms listed to the left of the center column of component boxes).

As firms gain experience within a given network, they are likely to develop capabilities, organizational structures, and cultures tailored to their value network's distinctive requirements. Manufacturing volumes, the slope of ramps to volume production, product development cycle

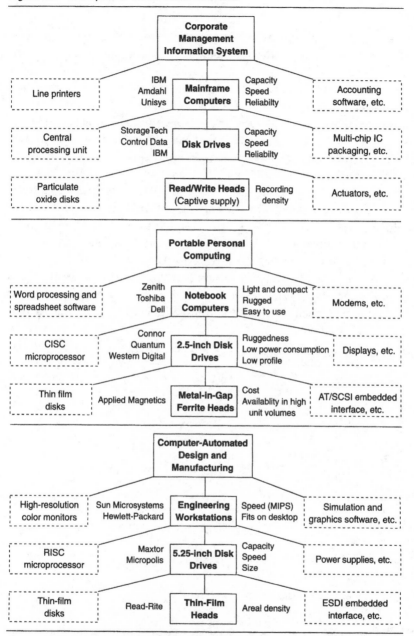

Figure 2.2 Examples of Three Value Networks

Source: Reprinted from *Research Policy* 24, Clayton M. Christensen and Richard S. Rosenbloom, "Explaining the Attacker's Advantage: Technological Paradigms, Organizational Dynamics, and the Value Network," 233–257, 1995 with kind permission of Elsevier Science—NL, Sara Burgerhartstraat 25, 1055 KV Amsterdam, The Netherlands.

times, and organizational consensus identifying the customer and the customer's needs may differ substantially from one value network to the next.

Given the data on the prices, attributes, and performance characteristics of thousands of disk drive models sold between 1976 and 1989, we can use a technique called *hedonic regression analysis* to identify how markets valued individual attributes and how those attribute values changed over time. Essentially, hedonic regression analysis expresses the total price of a product as the sum of individual so-called shadow prices (some positive, others negative) that the market places on each of the product's characteristics. Figure 2.3 shows some results of this analysis to illustrate how different value networks can place very different values on a given performance attribute. Customers in the mainframe computer value network in 1988 were willing on average to pay $1.65 for an incremental megabyte of capacity; but moving across the minicomputer, desktop, and portable computing value networks, the shadow price of an incremental megabyte of capacity declines to $1.50, $1.45, and $1.17, respectively.

Figure 2.3 Difference in the Valuation of Attributes Across Different Value Networks

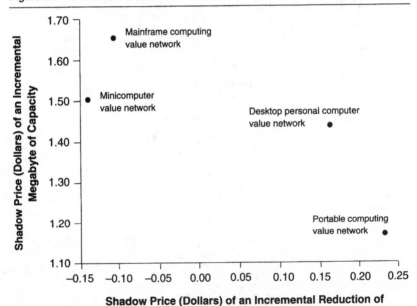

Conversely, portable and desktop computing customers were willing to pay a high price in 1988 for a cubic inch of size reduction, while customers in the other networks placed no value on that attribute at all.[11]

Cost Structures and Value Networks

The definition of a value network goes beyond the attributes of the physical product. For example, competing within the mainframe computer network shown in Figure 2.2 entails a particular cost structure. Research, engineering, and development costs are substantial. Manufacturing overheads are high relative to direct costs because of low unit volumes and customized product configurations. Selling directly to end users involves significant sales force costs, and the field service network to support the complicated machines represents a substantial ongoing expense. All these costs must be incurred in order to provide the types of products and services customers in this value network require. For these reasons, makers of mainframe computers, and makers of the 14-inch disk drives sold to them, historically needed gross profit margins of between 50 percent and 60 percent to cover the overhead cost structure inherent to the value network in which they competed.

Competing in the portable computer value network, however, entails a very different cost structure. These computer makers incur little expense researching component technologies, preferring to build their machines with proven component technologies procured from vendors. Manufacturing involves assembling millions of standard products in low-labor-cost regions. Most sales are made through national retail chains or by mail order. As a result, companies in this value network can be profitable with gross margins of 15 percent to 20 percent. Hence, just as a value network is characterized by a specific rank-ordering of product attributes valued by customers, it is also characterized by a specific cost structure required to provide the valued products and services.

Each value network's unique cost structure is illustrated in Figure 2.4. Gross margins typically obtained by manufacturers of 14-inch disk drives, about 60 percent, are similar to those required by mainframe computer makers: 56 percent. Likewise, the margins 8-inch drive makers earned were similar to those earned by minicomputer companies (about 40 percent), and the margins typical of the desktop value network, 25 percent, also typified both the computer makers and their disk drive suppliers.

The cost structures characteristic of each value network can have a

Figure 2.4 Characteristic Cost Structures of Different Value Networks

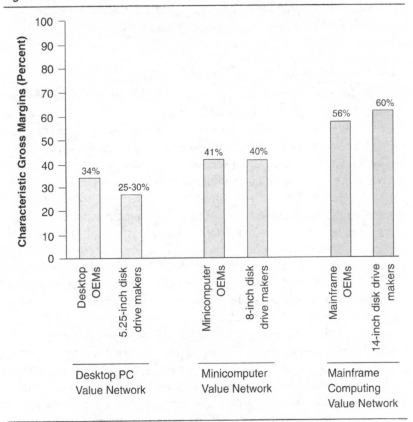

Source: Data are from company annual reports and personal interviews with executives from several representative companies in each network.

powerful effect on the sorts of innovations firms deem profitable. Essentially, innovations that are valued within a firm's value network, or in a network where characteristic gross margins are higher, will be perceived as profitable. Those technologies whose attributes make them valuable only in networks with *lower* gross margins, on the other hand, will not be viewed as profitable, and are unlikely to attract resources or managerial interest. (We will explore the impact of each value network's characteristic cost structures upon the established firms' mobility and fortunes more fully in chapter 4.)

In sum, the attractiveness of a technological opportunity and the degree of difficulty a producer will encounter in exploiting it are determined by, among other factors, the firm's position in the relevant value network. As we shall see, the manifest strength of established firms in sustaining innovation and their weakness in disruptive innovation—and the opposite manifest strengths and weaknesses of entrant firms—are consequences not of differences in technological or organizational capabilities between incumbent and entrant firms, but of their positions in the industry's different value networks.

TECHNOLOGY S-CURVES AND VALUE NETWORKS

The technology S-curve forms the centerpiece of thinking about technology strategy. It suggests that the magnitude of a product's performance improvement in a given time period or due to a given amount of engineering effort is likely to differ as technologies mature. The theory posits that in the early stages of a technology, the rate of progress in performance will be relatively slow. As the technology becomes better understood, controlled, and diffused, the rate of technological improvement will accelerate.[12] But in its mature stages, the technology will asymptotically approach a natural or physical limit such that ever greater periods of time or inputs of engineering effort will be required to achieve improvements. Figure 2.5 illustrates the resulting pattern.

Many scholars have asserted that the essence of strategic technology management is to identify when the point of inflection on the present technology's S-curve has been passed, and to identify and develop whatever successor technology rising from below will eventually supplant the present approach. Hence, as depicted by the dotted curve in Figure 2.5, the challenge is to successfully switch technologies at the point where S-curves of old and new intersect. The inability to anticipate new technologies threatening from below and to switch to them in a timely way has often been cited as the cause of failure of established firms and as the source of advantage for entrant or attacking firms.[13]

How do the concepts of S-curves and of value networks relate to each other?[14] The typical framework of intersecting S-curves illustrated in Figure 2.5 is a conceptualization of *sustaining* technological changes within a single value network, where the vertical axis charts a single measure of product performance (or a rank-ordering of attributes). Note its similarity to Figure 1.4, which measured the sustaining impact of new recording head technologies on the recording density of disk drives. Incremental

Figure 2.5 The Conventional Technology S-Curve

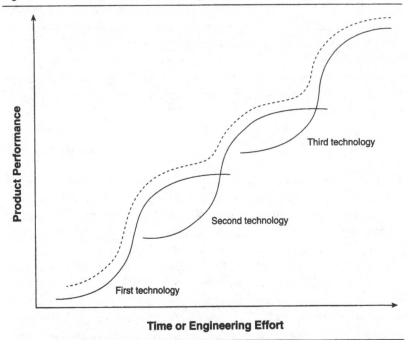

Time or Engineering Effort

Source: Clayton M. Christensen, "Exploring the Limits of the Technology S-Curve. Part I: Component Technologies," *Production and Operations Management* 1, no. 4 (Fall 1992): 340. Reprinted by permission.

improvements within each technology drove improvements along each of the individual curves, while movement to new head technologies involved a more radical leap. Recall that there was not a *single* example in the history of technological innovation in the disk drive industry of an entrant firm leading the industry or securing a viable market position with a sustaining innovation. In every instance, the firms that anticipated the eventual flattening of the current technology and that led in identifying, developing, and implementing the new technology that sustained the over-all pace of progress were the leading practitioners of the prior technology. These firms often incurred enormous financial risks, committing to new technologies a decade or more in advance and wiping out substantial bases of assets and skills. Yet despite these challenges, managers of the industry's established firms navigated the dotted line course shown in Figure 2.5 with remarkable, consistent agility.

A disruptive innovation, however, cannot be plotted in a figure such as 2.5, because the vertical axis for a disruptive innovation, by definition, must measure *different* attributes of performance than those relevant in established value networks. Because a disruptive technology gets its commercial start in emerging value networks before invading established networks, an S-curve framework such as that in Figure 2.6 is needed to describe it. Disruptive technologies emerge and progress on their own, uniquely defined trajectories, in a home value network. If and when they progress to the point that they can satisfy the level and nature of performance demanded in another value network, the disruptive technology can then invade it, knocking out the established technology and its established practitioners, with stunning speed.

Figures 2.5 and 2.6 illustrate clearly the innovator's dilemma that precipitates the failure of leading firms. In disk drives (and in the other industries covered later in this book), prescriptions such as increased investments in R&D; longer investment and planning horizons; technology scanning, forecasting, and mapping; as well as research consortia and joint ventures are all relevant to the challenges posed by the *sustaining* innovations

Figure 2.6   Disruptive Technology S-Curve

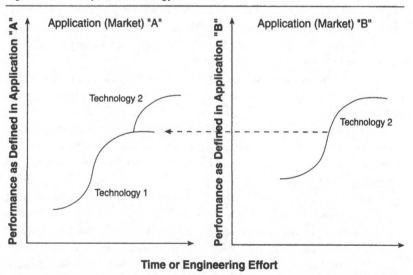

Time or Engineering Effort

Source: Clayton M. Christensen, "Exploring the Limits of the Technology S-Curve. Part I: Component Technologies," *Production and Operations Management* 1, no. 4 (Fall 1992): 361. Reprinted by permission.

whose ideal pattern is depicted in Figure 2.5. Indeed, the evidence suggests that many of the best established firms have applied these remedies and that they can work when managed well in treating sustaining technologies. But none of these solutions addresses the situation in Figure 2.6, because it represents a threat of a fundamentally different nature.

MANAGERIAL DECISION MAKING AND DISRUPTIVE TECHNOLOGICAL CHANGE

Competition within the value networks in which companies are embedded defines in many ways how the firms can earn their money. The network defines the customers' problems to be addressed by the firm's products and services and how much can be paid for solving them. Competition and customer demands in the value network in many ways shape the firms' cost structure, the firm size required to remain competitive, and the necessary rate of growth. Thus, managerial decisions that make sense for companies outside a value network may make no sense at all for those within it, and vice versa.

We saw, in chapter 1, a stunningly consistent pattern of successful implementation of sustaining innovations by established firms and their failure to deal with disruptive ones. The pattern was consistent because the managerial decisions that led to those outcomes made sense. Good managers do what makes sense, and what makes sense is primarily shaped by their value network.

This decision-making pattern, outlined in the six steps below, emerged from my interviews with more than eighty managers who played key roles in the disk drive industry's leading firms, both incumbents and entrants, at times when disruptive technologies had emerged. In these interviews I tried to reconstruct, as accurately and from as many points of view as possible, the forces that influenced these firms' decision-making processes regarding the development and commercialization of technologies either relevant or irrelevant to the value networks in which the firms were at the time embedded. My findings consistently showed that established firms confronted with disruptive technology change did not have trouble developing the requisite *technology*: Prototypes of the new drives had often been developed before management was asked to make a decision. Rather, disruptive projects stalled when it came to allocating scarce resources among competing product and technology development proposals (allocating resources between the two value networks shown at right and left in Figure 2.6, for example). Sustaining projects addressing the needs of the firms' most powerful customers (the new waves of technology within the value network depicted in Figure 2.5) *almost always* preempted resources from disruptive technologies with small markets and poorly defined customer needs.

This characteristic pattern of decisions is summarized in the following pages. Because the experience was so archetypal, the struggle of Seagate Technology, the industry's dominant maker of 5.25-inch drives, to successfully commercialize the disruptive 3.5-inch drive is recounted in detail to illustrate each of the steps in the pattern.[15]

Step 1: Disruptive Technologies Were First Developed within Established Firms

Although entrants led in *commercializing* disruptive technologies, their development was often the work of engineers at established firms, using bootlegged resources. Rarely initiated by senior management, these architecturally innovative designs almost always employed off-the-shelf components. Thus, engineers at Seagate Technology, the leading 5.25-inch drive maker, were, in 1985, the second in the industry to develop working prototypes of 3.5-inch models. They made some eighty prototype models before the issue of formal project approval was raised with senior management. The same thing happened earlier at Control Data and Memorex, the dominant 14-inch drive makers, where engineers had designed working 8-inch drives internally, nearly two years before the product appeared in the market.

Step 2: Marketing Personnel Then Sought Reactions from Their Lead Customers

The engineers then showed their prototypes to marketing personnel, asking whether a market for the smaller, less expensive (and lower performance) drives existed. The marketing organization, using its habitual procedure for testing the market appeal of new drives, showed the prototypes to lead customers of the existing product line, asking them for an evaluation.[16] Thus, Seagate marketers tested the new 3.5-inch drives with IBM's PC Division and other makers of XT- and AT-class desktop personal computers—even though the drives had significantly less capacity than the mainstream desktop market demanded.

Not surprisingly, therefore, IBM showed no interest in Seagate's disruptive 3.5-inch drives. IBM's engineers and marketers were looking for 40 and 60 MB drives, and they already had a slot for 5.25-inch drives designed into their computer; they needed new drives that would take them further along their established performance trajectory. Finding little customer interest, Seagate's marketers drew up pessimistic sales forecasts. In addition, because the products were simpler, with lower performance, forecast profit margins were lower than those for higher performance products, and Seagate's financial analysts, therefore, joined their marketing colleagues in opposing the disruptive program. Working from such input, senior managers shelved the 3.5-inch drive—just as it was becoming firmly established in the laptop market.

This was a complex decision, made in a context of competing proposals to expend the same resources to develop new products that marketers felt were critical to remaining competitive with current customers and achieving aggressive growth and profit targets. "We needed a new model," recalled a former Seagate manager, "which could become the next ST412 [a very successful product generating $300 million sales annually in the desktop market that was near the end of its life cycle]. Our forecasts for the 3.5-inch drive were under $50 million because the laptop market was just emerging, and the 3.5-inch product just didn't fit the bill."

Seagate managers made an explicit decision not to pursue the disruptive technology. In other cases, managers did approve resources for pursuing a disruptive product—but, in the day-to-day decisions about how time and money would actually be allocated, engineers and marketers, acting in the best interests of the company, consciously and unconsciously starved the disruptive project of resources necessary for a timely launch.

When engineers at Control Data, the leading 14-inch drive maker, were officially chartered to develop CDC's initial 8-inch drives, its customers were looking for an average of 300 MB per computer, whereas CDC's earliest 8-inch drives offered less than 60 MB. The 8-inch project was given low priority, and engineers assigned to its development kept getting pulled off to work on problems with 14-inch drives being designed for more important customers. Similar problems plagued the belated launches of Quantum's and Micropolis's 5.25-inch products.

Step 3: Established Firms Step Up the Pace of Sustaining Technological Development

In response to the needs of current customers, the marketing managers threw impetus behind alternative sustaining projects, such as incorporating better heads or developing new recording codes. These gave customers what they wanted and could be targeted at large markets to generate the necessary sales and profits for maintaining growth. Although often involving greater development expense, such sustaining investments appeared *far* less risky than investments in the disruptive technology: The customers existed, and their needs were known.

Seagate's decision to shelve the 3.5-inch drive in 1985 to 1986, for example, seems starkly rational. Its view downmarket (in terms of the disk drive trajectory map) was toward a small total market forecast for 1987 for 3.5-inch drives. Gross margins in that market were uncertain, but manufacturing executives predicted that costs per megabyte for 3.5-inch drives would be much higher than for 5.25-inch drives. Seagate's view upmarket was quite different. Volumes in 5.25-inch drives with capacities of 60 to 100 MB were forecast to be $500 million by 1987. Companies serving the 60 to 100 MB market were earning gross margins of between 35 and 40 percent, whereas Seagate's margins in its high-volume 20 MB drives were between 25 and 30 percent. It simply did not make sense for Seagate to put its resources behind the 3.5-inch drive when competing proposals to move upmarket by developing its ST251 line of drives were also being actively evaluated.

After Seagate executives shelved the 3.5-inch project, the firm began introducing new 5.25-inch models at a dramatically accelerated rate. In 1985, 1986, and 1987, the numbers of new models annually introduced as a percentage of the total number of its models on the market in the prior year were 57, 78, and 115 percent, respectively. And during the same period, Seagate incorporated complex and sophisticated new component technologies such as thin-film disks, voice-coil actuators,[17] RLL codes, and embedded SCSI interfaces. Clearly, the motivation in doing this was to win the competitive wars against other established firms, which were making similar improvements, rather than to prepare for an attack by entrants from below.[18]

Step 4: New Companies Were Formed, and Markets for the Disruptive Technologies Were Found by Trial and Error

New companies, usually including frustrated engineers from established firms, were formed to exploit the disruptive product architecture. The founders of the leading 3.5-inch drive maker, Conner Peripherals, were disaffected employees from Seagate and Miniscribe, the two largest 5.25-inch manufacturers. The founders of 8-inch drive maker Micropolis came from Pertec, a 14-inch drive manufacturer, and the founders of Shugart and Quantum defected from Memorex.[19]

The start-ups, however, were as unsuccessful as their former employers in attracting established computer makers to the disruptive architecture. Consequently, they had to find *new* customers. The applications that emerged in this very uncertain, probing process were the minicomputer, the desktop personal computer, and the laptop computer. In retrospect, these were obvious markets for hard drives, but at the time, their ultimate size and significance were highly uncertain. Micropolis was founded before the emergence of the desk-side minicomputer and word processor markets in which its products came to be used. Seagate began when personal computers were simple toys for hobbyists, two years before IBM introduced its PC. And Conner Peripherals got its start before Compaq knew the potential size of the portable computer market. The founders of these firms sold their products without a clear marketing strategy— essentially selling to whoever would buy. Out of what was largely a trial-and-error approach to the market, the ultimately dominant applications for their products emerged.

Step 5: The Entrants Moved Upmarket

Once the start-ups had discovered an operating base in new markets, they realized that, by adopting sustaining improvements in new component technologies,[20] they could increase the capacity of their drives at a faster rate than their new market required. They blazed trajectories of 50 percent annual improvement, fixing their sights on the large, established computer markets immediately above them on the performance scale.

The established firms' views downmarket and the entrant firms' views upmarket were asymmetrical. In contrast to the unattractive margins and market size that established firms saw when eyeing the new, emerging markets for simpler drives, the entrants saw the potential volumes and margins in the upscale, high-performance markets above them as highly attractive. Customers in these established markets eventually embraced the new architectures they had rejected earlier, because once their needs for capacity and speed were met, the new drives' smaller size and architectural simplicity made them cheaper, faster, and more reliable than the older architectures. Thus, Seagate, which started in the desktop personal computer market, subsequently invaded and came to dominate the minicomputer, engineering workstation, and mainframe computer markets for disk drives. Seagate, in turn, was driven from the desktop personal computer market for disk drives by Conner and Quantum, the pioneering manufacturers of 3.5-inch drives.

Step 6: *Established Firms Belatedly Jumped on the Bandwagon to Defend Their Customer Base*

When the smaller models began to invade established market segments, the drive makers that had initially controlled those markets took their prototypes off the shelf (where they had been put in Step 3) and introduced them in order to defend their customer base in their own market. By this time, of course, the new architecture had shed its disruptive character and become fully performance-competitive with the larger drives in the established markets. Although some established manufacturers were able to defend their market positions through belated introduction of the new architecture, many found that the entrant firms had developed insurmountable advantages in manufacturing cost and design experience, and they eventually withdrew from the market. The firms attacking from value networks below brought with them cost structures set to achieve profitability at lower gross margins. The attackers therefore were able to price their products profitably, while the defending, established firms experienced a severe price war.

For established manufacturers that did succeed in introducing the new architectures, survival was the only reward. None ever won a significant share of the new market; the new drives simply cannibalized sales of older products to existing customers. Thus, as of 1991, almost none of Seagate's 3.5-inch drives had been sold to portable/laptop manufacturers: Its 3.5-inch customers still were desktop computer manufacturers, and many of its 3.5-inch drives continued to be shipped with frames permitting them to be mounted in XT- and AT-class computers designed to accommodate 5.25-inch drives.

Control Data, the 14-inch leader, never captured even a 1 percent share of the minicomputer market. It introduced its 8-inch drives nearly three years after the pioneering start-ups did, and nearly all of its drives were sold to its existing mainframe customers. Miniscribe, Quantum, and Micropolis all had the same cannibalistic experience when they belatedly introduced disruptive technology drives. They failed to capture a significant share of the new market, and at best succeeded in defending a portion of their prior business.

The popular slogan "stay close to your customers" appears not always to be robust advice.[21] One instead might expect customers to lead their suppliers toward sustaining innovations and to provide no leadership—or even to explicitly *mis*lead—in instances of disruptive technology change.[22]

FLASH MEMORY AND THE VALUE NETWORK

The predictive power of the value network framework is currently being tested with the emergence of *flash memory:* a solid-state semiconductor memory technology that stores data on silicon memory chips. Flash differs from conventional dynamic random access memory (DRAM) technology in that the chip retains the data even when the power is off. Flash memory is a disruptive technology. Flash chips consume less than 5 percent of the power that a disk drive of equivalent capacity would consume, and because they have no moving parts, they are far more rugged than disk memory. Flash chips have disadvantages, of course. Depending on the amount of memory, the cost per megabyte of flash can be between five and fifty times greater than disk memory. And flash chips are not as robust for writing: They can only be overwritten a few hundred thousand times before wearing out, rather than a few million times for disk drives.

The initial applications for flash memory were in value networks quite distant from computing; they were in devices such as cellular phones, heart monitoring devices, modems, and industrial robots in which individually packaged flash chips were embedded. Disk drives were too big, too fragile, and used too much power to be used in these markets. By 1994, these applications for individually packaged flash chips—"socket flash" in industry parlance—accounted for $1.3 billion in industry revenues, having grown from nothing in 1987.

In the early 1990s, the flash makers produced a new product format, called a flash card: credit card–sized devices on which multiple flash chips, linked and governed by controller circuitry, were mounted. The chips on flash cards were controlled by the same control circuitry, SCSI (Small Computer Standard Interface, an acronym first used by Apple), as was used in disk drives, meaning that in concept, a flash card could be used like a disk drive for mass storage. The flash card market grew from $45 million in 1993 to $80 million in 1994, and forecasters were eyeing a $230 million flash card market by 1996.

Will flash cards invade the disk drive makers' core markets and supplant magnetic memory? If they do, what will happen to the disk drive makers?

Will they stay atop their markets, catching this new technological wave? Or will they be driven out?

The Capabilities Viewpoint

Clark's concept of technological hierarchies (see note 4) focuses on the skills and technological understanding that a company accumulates as the result of the product and process technology problems it has addressed in the past. In evaluating the threat to the disk drive makers of flash memory, someone using Clark's framework, or the related findings of Tushman and Anderson (see note 5), would focus on the extent to which disk drive makers have historically developed expertise in integrated circuit design and in the design and control of devices composed of multiple integrated circuits. These frameworks would lead us to expect that drive makers will stumble badly in their attempts to develop flash products if they have limited expertise in these domains and will succeed if their experience and expertise are deep.

On its surface, flash memory involves radically different *electronics* technology than the core competence of disk drive makers (magnetics and mechanics). But such firms as Quantum, Seagate, and Western Digital have developed deep expertise in custom integrated circuit design through embedding increasingly intelligent control circuitry and cache memory in their drives. Consistent with the practice in much of the ASIC (application-specific integrated circuit) industry, their controller chips are fabricated by independent, third-party fabricators that own excess clean room semiconductor processing capacity.

Each of today's leading disk drive manufacturers got its start by designing drives, procuring components from independent suppliers, assembling them either in its own factories or by contract, and then selling them. The flash card business is very similar. Flash card makers design the card and procure the component flash chips; they design and have fabricated an interface circuit, such as SCSI, to govern the drive's interaction with the computing device; they assemble them either in-house or by contract; and they then market them.

In other words, flash memory actually *builds upon* important competencies that many drive makers have developed. The capabilities viewpoint, therefore, would lead us to expect that disk drive makers may *not* stumble badly in bringing flash storage technology to the market. More specifically, the viewpoint predicts that those firms with the deepest experience in IC design—Quantum, Seagate, and Western Digital—will bring flash products to market quite readily. Others, which historically outsourced much of their electronic circuit design, may face more of a struggle.

This has, indeed, been the case to date. Seagate entered the flash market in 1993 via its purchase of a 25 percent equity stake in Sundisk Corporation. Seagate and SunDisk together designed the chips and cards; the chips were fabricated by Matsushita, and the cards were assembled by a Korean manufacturer, Anam. Seagate itself marketed the cards. Quantum entered with a different partner, Silicon Storage Technology, which designed the chips that were then fabricated and assembled by contract.

The Organizational Structure Framework

Flash technology is what Henderson and Clark would call *radical* technology. Its product architecture and fundamental technological concept are novel compared to disk drives. The organizational structure viewpoint would predict that, unless they created organizationally independent groups to design flash products, established firms would stumble badly. Seagate and Quantum did, indeed, rely on independent groups and did develop competitive products.

The Technology S-Curve Framework

The technology S-curve is often used to predict whether an emerging technology is likely to supplant an established one. The operative trigger is the slope of the curve of the established technology. If the curve has passed its point of inflection, so that its second derivative is negative (the technology is improving at a decreasing rate), then a new technology may emerge to supplant the established one. Figure 2.7 shows that the S-curve for magnetic disk recording still has not hit its point of inflection: Not only is the areal density improving, as of 1995, it was improving at an *increasing* rate.

The S-curve framework would lead us to predict, therefore, that whether or not established disk drive companies possess the capability to design flash cards, flash memory will not pose a threat to them until the magnetic memory S-curve has passed its point of inflection and the rate of improvement in density begins to decline.

Insights from the Value Network Framework

The value network framework asserts that none of the foregoing frameworks is a sufficient predictor of success. Specifically, even where estab-

Figure 2.7 Improvements in Areal Density of New Disk Drives (Densities in Millions of Bits per Square Inch)

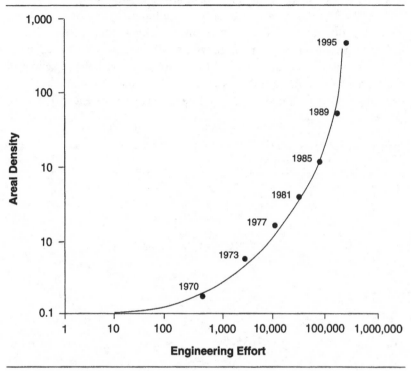

Source: Data are from various issues of *Disk/Trend Report.*

lished firms did not possess the requisite technological skills to develop a new technology, they would marshal the resources to develop or acquire them if their customers demanded it. Furthermore, the value network suggests that technology S-curves are useful predictors only with sustaining technologies. Disruptive technologies generally improve at a parallel pace with established ones—their trajectories do not intersect. The S-curve framework, therefore, asks the *wrong question* when it is used to assess disruptive technology. What matters instead is whether the disruptive technology is improving from below along a trajectory that will ultimately intersect with what the *market* needs.

The value network framework would assert that even though firms such as Seagate and Quantum are able *technologically* to develop competitive flash memory products, whether they invest the resources and managerial energy to build strong market positions in the technology will depend on whether flash memory can be initially valued and deployed within the value networks in which the firms make their money.

As of 1996, flash memory can only be used in value networks different from those of the typical disk drive maker. This is illustrated in Figure 2.8, which plots the average megabytes of capacity of flash cards introduced each year between 1992 and 1995, compared with the capacities of 2.5- and 1.8-inch drives and with the capacity demanded in the notebook computer market. Even though they are rugged and consume little power,

Figure 2.8   Comparison of Disk Drive Memory Capacity to Flash Card Memory Capacity

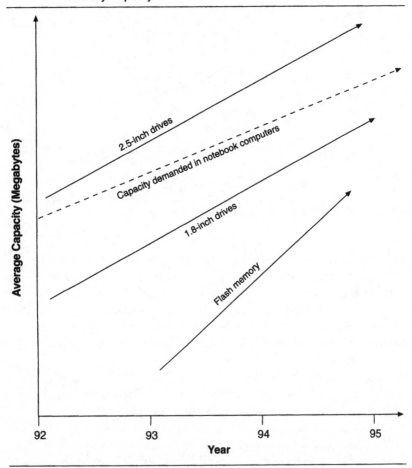

Source: Data are from various issues of *Disk/Trend Report.*

flash cards simply don't yet pack the capacity to become the main mass storage devices in notebook computers. And the price of the flash capacity required to meet what the low end of the portable computing market demands (about 350 MB in 1995) is too high: The cost of that much flash capacity would be fifty times higher than comparable disk storage.[23] The low power consumption and ruggedness of flash certainly have no value and command no price premium on the desktop. There is, in other words, no way to use flash today in the markets where firms such as Quantum and Seagate make their money.

Hence, because flash cards are being used in markets completely different from those Quantum and Seagate typically engage—palmtop computers, electronic clipboards, cash registers, electronic cameras, and so on—the value network framework would predict that firms similar to Quantum and Seagate are *not* likely to build market-leading positions in flash memory. This is not because the technology is too difficult or their organizational structures impede effective development, but because their resources will become absorbed in fighting for and defending larger chunks of business in the mainstream disk drive value networks in which they currently make their money.

Indeed, the marketing director for a leading flash card producer observed, "We're finding that as hard disk drive manufacturers move up to the gigabyte range, they are unable to be cost competitive at the lower capacities. As a result, disk drive makers are pulling out of markets in the 10 to 40 megabyte range and creating a vacuum into which flash can move."[24]

The drive makers' efforts to build flash card businesses have in fact floundered. By 1995, neither Quantum nor Seagate had built market shares of even 1 percent of the flash card market. Both companies subsequently concluded that the opportunity in flash cards was not yet substantial enough, and withdrew their products from the market the same year. Seagate retained its minority stake in SunDisk (renamed SanDisk), however, a strategy which, as we shall see, is an effective way to address disruptive technology.

IMPLICATIONS OF THE VALUE NETWORK FRAMEWORK FOR INNOVATION

Value networks strongly define and delimit what companies within them can and cannot do. This chapter closes with five propositions about the nature of technological change and the problems successful incumbent firms encounter, which the value network perspective highlights.

1. The context, or value network, in which a firm competes has a profound influence on its ability to marshal and focus the necessary resources and capabilities to overcome the technological and organizational hurdles that impede innovation. The boundaries of a value network are determined by a unique definition of product performance—a rank-ordering of the importance of various performance attributes differing markedly from that employed in other systems-of-use in a broadly defined industry. Value networks are also defined by particular cost structures inherent in addressing customers' needs within the network.

2. A key determinant of the probability of an innovative effort's commercial success is the degree to which it addresses the well-understood needs of known actors within the value network. Incumbent firms are likely to lead their industries in innovations of all sorts—architecture and components—that address needs within their value network, regardless of intrinsic technological character or difficulty. These are straightforward innovations; their value and application are clear. Conversely, incumbent firms are likely to lag in the development of technologies—even those in which the technology involved is intrinsically simple—that only address customers' needs in emerging value networks. Disruptive innovations are complex because their value and application are uncertain, according to the criteria used by incumbent firms.

3. Established firms' decisions to ignore technologies that do not address their customers' needs become fatal when two distinct trajectories interact. The first defines the performance demanded over time within a given value network, and the second traces the performance that technologists are able to provide within a given technological paradigm. The trajectory of performance improvement that technology is able to provide may have a distinctly different slope from the trajectory of performance improvement demanded in the system-of-use by downstream customers within any given value network. When the slopes of these two trajectories are similar, we expect the technology to remain relatively contained within its initial value network. But when the slopes differ, new technologies that are initially performance-competitive only within emerging or commercially remote value networks may migrate into other networks, providing a vehicle for innovators in new networks to attack established ones. When such an attack occurs, it is because technological progress has diminished the relevancce of differences in the rank-ordering of performance attributes

across different value networks. For example, the disk drive attributes of size and weight were far more important in the desktop computing value network than they were in the mainframe and minicomputer value networks. When technological progress in 5.25-inch drives enabled manufacturers to satisfy the attribute prioritization in the mainframe and minicomputer networks, which prized total capacity and high speed, *as well as* that in the desktop network, the boundaries between the value networks ceased to be barriers to entry for 5.25-inch drive makers.

4. Entrant firms have an attacker's advantage over established firms in those innovations—generally new product architectures involving little new technology per se—that disrupt or redefine the level, rate, and direction of progress in an established technological trajectory. This is so because such technologies generate no value within the established network. The only way established firms can lead in commercializing such technologies is to enter the value network in which they create value. As Richard Tedlow noted in his history of retailing in America (in which supermarkets and discount retailing play the role of disruptive technologies), "the most formidable barrier the established firms faced is that they did not want to do this."[25]

5. In these instances, although this "attacker's advantage" is *associated* with a disruptive technology change, the essence of the attacker's advantage is in the ease with which entrants, relative to incumbents, can identify and make strategic commitments to attack and develop emerging market applications, or value networks. At its core, therefore, the issue may be the relative flexibility of successful established firms versus entrant firms to change *strategies and cost structures,* not technologies.

These propositions provide new dimensions for analyzing technological innovation. In addition to the required capabilities inherent in new technologies and in the innovating organization, firms faced with disruptive technologies must examine the implications of innovation for their relevant value networks. The key considerations are whether the performance attributes implicit in the innovation will be valued within the networks already served by the innovator; whether other networks must be addressed or new ones created in order to realize value for the innovation; and whether market and technological trajectories may eventually intersect, carrying technologies that do not address customers' needs today to squarely address their needs in the future.

These considerations apply not simply to firms grappling with the most modern technologies, such as the fast-paced, complex advanced electronic, mechanical, and magnetics technologies covered in this chapter. Chapter 3 examines them in the context of a very different industry: earthmoving equipment.

NOTES

1. See Rebecca M. Henderson and Kim B. Clark, "Architectural Innovation: The Reconfiguration of Existing Systems and the Failure of Established Firms" *Administrative Science Quarterly* (35), 1990, 9–30.

2. Tracy Kidder, *The Soul of a New Machine* (New York: Avon Books, Inc., 1981).

3. A few scholars have sought to measure the proportion of technological progress attributable to radical versus incremental advances. In an empirical study of a series of novel processes in petroleum refining, for example, John Enos found that half the economic benefits of new technology came from process improvements introduced after a new technology was commercially established. See J. L. Enos, "Invention and Innovation in the Petroleum Refining Industry," in *The Rate and Direction of Inventive Activity: Economic and Social Factors,* National Bureau of Economic Research Report (Princeton, NJ: Princeton University Press, 1962), 299–321. My study of the disk drive industry has shown the same result. Half the advance in areal density (megabits per square inch of disk surface) can be attributed to new component technologies and half to incremental improvements in existing components and refinements in system design. See Clayton M. Christensen, "Exploring the Limits of the Technology S-Curve," *Production and Operations Management* (1), 1992, 334–366.

4. See Kim B. Clark, "The Interaction of Design Hierarchies and Market Concepts in Technological Evolution," *Research Policy* (14), 1985, 235–251. Clark suggests, for example, that the early selections by automotive engineers of gasoline over steam or electrically powered engines defined the technical agenda for subsequent generations of engineers, who consequently did not pursue refinements in electric or steam propulsion. Clark has thus shown that the design skills and technological knowledge resident in companies today result from the cumulative choices engineers have made of what to tackle versus what to leave alone. Clark posits that technological improvements requiring that companies build upon or extend an existing cumulative body of knowledge favor an industry's established firms. Conversely, when changes require a completely different body of knowledge, established firms will be at a disadvantage compared to firms that had already accumulated a different hierarchically structured body of knowledge, most likely in another industry.

5. See, for example, Michael L. Tushman and Philip Anderson, "Technological Discontinuities and Organizational Environments," *Administrative Science Quarterly* (31), 1986, 439–465; and Philip Anderson and Michael Tushman, "Technological Discontinuities and Dominant Designs," *Administrative Science Quarterly* (35), 1990, 604–633.

6. The concept of *value network* builds on Giovanni Dosi's concept of *technological paradigms*. See Giovanni Dosi, "Technological Paradigms and Technological Trajectories, *Research Policy* (11), 1982, 147–162. Dosi characterizes a technological paradigm as a "pattern of solution of selected technological problems, based on selected principles derived from natural sciences and on selected material technologies" (152). New paradigms represent discontinuities in trajectories of progress as defined within earlier paradigms. They tend to redefine the very meaning of progress, and point technologists toward new classes of problems as the targets of ensuing normal technology development. The question examined by Dosi—how new technologies are selected and retained—is closely related to the question of why firms succeed or fail as beneficiaries of such changes.

7. Value network, as presented here, draws heavily on ideas I developed jointly with Professor Richard S. Rosenbloom and which are summarized in two journal articles: Clayton M. Christensen and Richard S. Rosenbloom, "Explaining the Attacker's Advantage: The Technological Paradigms, Organizational Dynamics, and the Value Network," *Research Policy* (24), 1995, 233–257; and Richard S. Rosenbloom and Clayton M. Christensen, "Technological Discontinuities, Organizational Capabilities, and Strategic Commitments," *Industrial and Corporate Change* (3), 1994, 655–685. I am heavily indebted to Professor Rosenbloom for his contributions to the development of these perspectives.

8. See D. L. Marples, "The Decisions of Engineering Design," *IEEE Transactions on Engineering Management* EM8, 1961, 55–71; and C. Alexander, *Notes on the Synthesis of Form* (Cambridge, MA: Harvard University Press, 1964).

9. On this point, too, correspondence between the concept of the value network and Dosi's concept of technological paradigms is strong. (See note 6.) The scope and boundaries of a value network are defined by the dominant technological paradigm and the corresponding technological trajectory employed at the higher levels of the network. As Dosi suggests, *value* can be defined as a function of the dominant technological paradigm in the ultimate system of use in the value network.

10. Michael Porter, *Competitive Advantage* (New York: The Free Press, 1985).

11. A more complete report of this analysis can be found in chapter 7 of Clayton M. Christensen, *The Innovator's Challenge: Understanding the Influence of Market Environment on Processes of Technology Development in the Rigid*

Disk Drive Industry, thesis, Harvard University Graduate School of Business Administration, 1992.

12. D. Sahal, *Patterns of Technological Innovation* (London: Addison Wesley, 1981).

13. The most widely read proponent of this view is Richard Foster; see, for example, his *Innovation: The Attacker's Advantage* (New York: Summit Books, 1986).

14. The insights summarized here are articulated more completely in C. M. Christensen, "Exploring the Limits of the Technology S-Curve," *Production and Operations Management* (1), 1992, 334–366.

15. A fuller account of similar decisions made in other firms can be found in Clayton M. Christensen, *The Innovator's Challenge: Understanding the Influence of Market Environment on Processes of Technology Development in the Rigid Disk Drive Industry,* thesis, Harvard University Graduate School of Business Administration, 1992.

16. This procedure is consistent with Robert Burgelman's observation that one of the greatest difficulties encountered by corporate entrepreneurs is in finding the right "beta test sites," where products can be interactively developed and refined with customers. Generally, the entrée to the customer was provided by the salesperson who sold the firm's established product lines. This helped the firm develop new products for established markets, but not identify new applications for its new technology. See Robert Burgelman and Leonard Sayles, *Inside Corporate Innovation* (New York: The Free Press, 1986) 76–80. Professor Rebecca Henderson pointed out to me that this tendency always to take new technologies to mainstream customers reflects a rather narrow *marketing* competence—that although many scholars tend to frame the issue as one of technological competence, such inability to find new markets for new technologies may be a firm's most serious handicap in innovation.

17. Voice coil motors were more expensive than the stepper motors that Seagate had previously used. While not new to the market, they were new to Seagate.

18. This is consistent with the findings reported by Arnold Cooper and Dan Schendel in "Strategic Responses to Technological Threats," *Business Horizons* (19), February, 1976, 61–69.

19. Ultimately, nearly all North American disk drive manufacturers can trace their founders' genealogy to IBM's San Jose division, which developed and manufactured its magnetic recording products. See Clayton M. Christensen, "The Rigid Disk Drive Industry: A History of Commercial and Technological Turbulence," *Business History Review* (67), Winter, 1993, 531–588.

20. In general, these component technologies were developed within the largest of the established firms that dominated the established markets above these entrants. This is because new components generally (but not always) have

a sustaining impact on technology trajectories. These high-end, established firms typically were engaged in the hottest pursuit of sustaining innovations.

21. The research of Eric von Hippel, frequently cited as evidence of the value of listening to customers, indicates that customers originate a large majority of new product ideas (see Eric von Hippel, *The Sources of Innovation* [New York: Oxford University Press, 1988]). One fruitful avenue for future research would be to revisit von Hippel's data in light of the framework presented here. The value network framework would predict that the innovations toward which the customers in von Hippel's study led their suppliers would have been sustaining innovations. We would expect disruptive innovations to have come from other sources.

22. Henderson saw similar potential danger for being misled by customers in her study of photolithographic aligner equipment manufacturers. See Rebecca M. Henderson, "Keeping Too Close to Your Customers," Massachusetts Institute of Technology Sloan School of Management working paper, 1993.

23. Many industry observers have noted that there seems to be a floor on the cost of making a disk drive, somewhere around $120 per device, below which even the best manufacturers cannot plunge. This is the basic cost of designing, producing, and assembling the requisite components. Drive makers keep reducing costs per megabyte by continuously increasing the number of megabytes available in that basic $120 box. The effect of this floor on the competition between disk drives and flash cards may be profound. It means that in low-capacity applications, as the price of flash memory falls, flash will become cost-competitive with disk memory. The frontier above which magnetic disk drives have lower costs per megabyte than flash will keep moving upmarket, in a manner perfectly analogous to the upmarket movement of larger disk drive architectures. Experts predicted, in fact, that by 1997, a 40 MB flash card would be priced comparably to a 40 MB disk drive.

24. Lewis H. Young, "Samsung Banks on Tiny Flash Cell," *Electronic Business Buyer* (21), July, 1995, 28.

25. Richard Tedlow, *New and Improved: A History of Mass Marketing in America* (Boston: Harvard Business School Press, 1994).

CHAPTER **THREE**

Disruptive Technological Change in the Mechanical Excavator Industry

Excavators and their steam shovel predecessors are huge pieces of capital equipment sold to excavation contractors. While few observers consider this a fast-moving, technologically dynamic industry, it has points in common with the disk drive industry: Over its history, leading firms have successfully adopted a series of *sustaining* innovations, both incremental and radical, in components and architecture, but almost the entire population of mechanical shovel manufacturers was wiped out by a disruptive technology—hydraulics—that the leaders' customers and their economic structure had caused them initially to ignore. Although in disk drives such invasions of established markets occurred within a few years of the initial emergence of each disruptive technology, the triumph of hydraulic excavators took twenty years. Yet the disruptive invasion proved just as decisive and difficult to counter in excavators as those in the disk drive industry.[1]

LEADERSHIP IN SUSTAINING TECHNOLOGICAL CHANGE

From William Smith Otis' invention of the steam shovel in 1837 through the early 1920s, mechanical earthmoving equipment was steam-powered. A central boiler sent steam through pipes to small steam engines at each point where power was required in the machine. Through a system of pulleys, drums, and cables, these engines manipulated frontward-scooping buckets, as illustrated in Figure 3.1. Originally, steam shovels were mounted on rails and used to excavate earth in railway and canal construction. American excavator manufacturers were tightly clustered in northern Ohio and near Milwaukee.

In the early 1920s, when there were more than thirty-two steam shovel manufacturers based in the United States, the industry faced a major technological upheaval, as gasoline-powered engines were substituted for steam power.[2] This transition to gasoline power falls into the category that Henderson and Clark label radical technological transition. The fundamental technological concept in a key component (the engine) changed from steam to internal combustion, and the basic architecture of the product changed. Where steam shovels used steam pressure to power a set of steam engines to extend and retract the cables that actuated their

Figure 3.1   Cable-Actuated Mechanical Shovel Manufactured by Osgood General

Source: Osgood General photo in Herbert L. Nichols, Jr., *Moving the Earth: The Workbook of Excavation* (Greenwich, CT: North Castle, 1955).

buckets, gasoline shovels used a single engine and a very different system of gearing, clutches, drums, and brakes to wind and unwind the cable. Despite the radical nature of the technological change, however, gasoline technology had a *sustaining* impact on the mechanical excavator industry. Gasoline engines were powerful enough to enable contractors to move earth faster, more reliably, and at lower cost than any but the very largest steam shovels.

The leading innovators in gasoline engine technology were the industry's dominant firms, such as Bucyrus, Thew, and Marion. Twenty-three of the twenty-five largest makers of steam shovels successfully negotiated the transition to gasoline power.[3] As Figure 3.2 shows, there were a few entrant firms among the gasoline technology leaders in the 1920s, but the established firms dominated this transition.

Beginning in about 1928, the established manufacturers of gasoline-powered shovels initiated the next major, but less radical, sustaining technological transition—to shovels powered by diesel engines and electric motors. A further transition, made after World War II, introduced the

Figure 3.2   Manufacturers of Gasoline-Powered Cable Shovels, 1920–1934

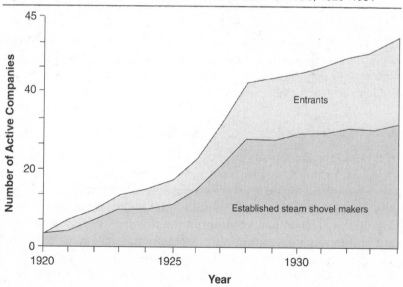

Source: Data are from the Historical Construction Equipment Association and from *The Thomas Register,* various years.

arched boom design, which allowed longer reach, bigger buckets, and better down-reaching flexibility. The established firms continued to embrace and succeed with each of these innovations.

Excavation contractors themselves actually pioneered a number of other important sustaining innovations, first modifying their own equipment in the field to make it perform better and then manufacturing excavators incorporating those features to sell to the broader market.[4]

THE IMPACT OF DISRUPTIVE HYDRAULICS TECHNOLOGY

The next major technological change precipitated widespread failure in the industry. Beginning shortly after World War II and continuing through the late 1960s, while the dominant source of power remained the diesel engine, a new mechanism emerged for extending and lifting the bucket: hydraulically actuated systems replaced the cable-actuated systems. Only four of the thirty or so established manufacturers of cable-actuated equipment in business in the 1950s (Insley, Koehring, Little Giant, and Link Belt) had successfully transformed themselves into sustainable hydraulic excavator manufacturers by the 1970s. A few others survived by withdrawing into making such equipment as huge, cable-actuated draglines for strip mining and dredging.[5] Most of the others failed. The firms that overran the excavation equipment industry at this point were all entrants into the hydraulics generation: J. I. Case, John Deere, Drott, Ford, J. C. Bamford, Poclain, International Harvester, Caterpillar, O & K, Demag, Leibherr, Komatsu, and Hitachi.[6] Why did this happen?

Performance Demanded in the Mechanical Excavator Market

Excavators are one of many types of earthmoving equipment. Some equipment, such as bulldozers, loaders, graders, and scrapers, essentially push, smooth, and lift earth. Excavators[7] have been used to dig holes and trenches, primarily in three markets: first and largest, the general excavation market, composed of contractors who dig holes for basements or civil engineering projects such as canal construction; second, sewer and piping contractors, who generally dig long trenches; and third, open pit or strip mining. In each of these markets, contractors have tended to measure the functionality of mechanical excavators by their reach or extension distance and by the cubic yards of earth lifted in a single scoop.[8]

In 1945, sewer and piping contractors used machines whose bucket capacity averaged about 1 cubic yard (best for digging relatively narrow trenches), while the average general excavation contractor used excavators that hefted 2½ cubic yards per scoop and mining contractors used shovels holding about 5 cubic yards. The average bucket capacity used in each of these markets increased at about 4 percent per year, a rate of increase constrained by other factors in the broader system-of-use. The logistical problems of transporting large machines into and out of typical construction sites, for example, helped limit the rate of increase demanded by contractors.

The Emergence and Trajectory of Improvement of Hydraulic Excavation

The first hydraulic excavator was developed by a British company, J. C. Bamford, in 1947. Similar products then emerged simultaneously in several American companies in the late 1940s, among them, the Henry Company, of Topeka, Kansas, and Sherman Products, Inc., of Royal Oak, Michigan. The approach was labeled "Hydraulically Operated Power Take-Off," yielding an acronym that became the name of the third entrant to hydraulic excavating in the late 1940s, HOPTO.[9]

Their machines were called *backhoes* because they were mounted on the back of industrial or farm tractors. Backhoes excavated by extending the shovel out, pushing it down into the earth,[10] curling or articulating the shovel under the slice of earth, and lifting it up out of the hole. Limited by the power and strength of available hydraulic pumps' seals, the capacity of these early machines was a mere ¼ cubic yard, as graphed in Figure 3.3. Their reach was also limited to about six feet. Whereas the best cable excavators could rotate a full 360 degrees on their track base, the most flexible backhoes could rotate only 180 degrees.

Because their capacity was so small and their reach so short, hydraulic excavators were of no use to mining, general excavation, or sewer contractors, who were demanding machines with buckets that held 1 to 4 cubic yards. As a result, the entrant firms had to develop a new application for their products. They began to sell their excavators as attachments for the back of small industrial and farm tractors made by Ford, J. I. Case, John Deere, International Harvester, and Massey Ferguson. Small residential contractors purchased these units to dig narrow ditches from water and sewer lines in the street to the foundations of houses under construction. These very small jobs had never warranted the expense or time required

Figure 3.3 Disruptive Impact of Hydraulics Technology in the Mechanical Excavator Market

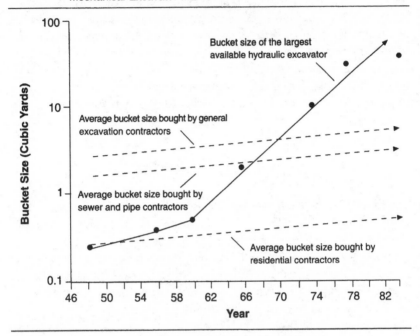

Source: Data are from the Historical Construction Equipment Association.

to bring in a big, imprecise, cable-actuated, track-driven shovel, so the trenches had always been dug by hand. Hydraulic backhoes attached to highly mobile tractors could do these jobs in less than an hour per house, and they became extremely popular with contractors building large tract subdivisions during the housing booms that followed World War II and the Korean War. These early backhoes were sold through tractor and implement dealerships accustomed to dealing with small customers.

The early users of hydraulic excavators were, in a word, *very* different from the mainstream customers of the cable shovel manufacturers—in size, in needs, and in the distribution channels through which they bought. They constituted a new value network for mechanical excavation. Interestingly, just as the performance of smaller-architecture disk drives was measured in different metrics than the performance of large drives (weight, ruggedness, and power consumption versus capacity and speed), the performance of the first backhoes was measured differently from the performance of cable-actuated equipment. The metrics featured most prominently in early product literature of hydraulic backhoes were shovel *width* (contractors wanted to dig narrow, shallow trenches) and the speed and maneuverability of the *tractor*. Figure 3.4, excerpted from an early product brochure from Sherman Products for its "Bobcat" hydraulic backhoe, illustrates this. Sherman called its Bobcat a "digger," showed it operating in tight quarters, and claimed it could travel over sod with minimum damage. The Bobcat was mounted on a Ford tractor. (Ford subsequently acquired the Sherman Bobcat line.) The featured attributes,

Figure 3.4 Hydraulic Backhoe Manufactured by Sherman Products

of course, were simply irrelevant to contractors whose bread was buttered by big earthmoving projects. These differences in the rank-ordering of performance attributes defined the boundaries of the industry's value networks.

The solid line in Figure 3.3 charts the rate of improvement in bucket size that hydraulics engineers were able to provide in the new excavator architecture. The maximum available bucket size had reached ⅜ cubic yard by 1955, ½ cubic yard by 1960, and 2 cubic yards by 1965. By 1974, the largest hydraulic excavators had the muscle to lift 10 cubic yards. This trajectory of improvement, which was far more rapid than the rate of improvement demanded in any of the excavator markets, carried this disruptive hydraulics technology upward from its original market through the large, mainstream excavation markets. The use of hydraulic excavators in general contracting markets was given a boost in 1954 when another entrant firm in Germany, Demag, introduced a track-mounted model that could rotate on its base a full 360 degrees.

THE RESPONSE TO HYDRAULICS BY THE ESTABLISHED EXCAVATOR MANUFACTURERS

Just as Seagate Technology was one of the first firms to develop prototype 3.5-inch drives, Bucyrus Erie, the leading cable shovel maker, was keenly aware of the emergence of hydraulic excavating technology. By 1950 (about two years after the first backhoe appeared) Bucyrus purchased a fledgling hydraulic backhoe company, the Milwaukee Hydraulics Corporation. Bucyrus faced precisely the same problem in marketing its hydraulic backhoe as Seagate had faced with its 3.5-inch drives: Its most powerful mainstream customers had no use for it.

Bucyrus Erie's response was a new product, introduced in 1951, called the "Hydrohoe." Instead of using three hydraulic cylinders, it used only two, one to curl the shovel into the earth and one to "crowd" or draw the shovel toward the cab; it used a cable mechanism to lift the shovel. The Hydrohoe was thus a hybrid of the two technologies, reminiscent of the early transoceanic steamships outfitted with sails.[11] There is no evidence, however, that the Hydrohoe's hybrid design resulted from Bucyrus engineers' being "stuck" in some sort of cable-based engineering paradigm. Rather, the cable lift mechanism was the *only* viable way at that time, based on the state of hydraulics technology, to give the Hydrohoe the bucket capacity and reach that Bucyrus marketers thought they needed to appeal to their existing customers' needs.

Figure 3.5 presents an excerpt from an early Hydrohoe product brochure. Note the differences from Sherman's marketing approach: Bucyrus labeled the Hydrohoe a "dragshovel," showed it in an open field, and claimed it could "get a heaping load on every pass"—all intended to

Figure 3.5 Hydrohoe Manufactured by Bucyrus Erie

Source: Brochure from Bucyrus Erie Company, South Milwaukee, Wisconsin, 1951.

appeal to general excavation contractors. Rather than commercialize the disruptive technology in the value network in which the current attributes of hydraulics were prized, Bucyrus tried to adapt the technology to fit its own value network. Despite this attempt, the Hydrohoe was still too limited in capacity and reach and did not sell well to Bucyrus' customers. Bucyrus kept its Hydrohoe on the market for over a decade, attempting periodically to upgrade its performance to make it acceptable to its customers, but the machine was never commercially successful. Ultimately, the company returned to the cable shovels that its customers needed.

Bucyrus Erie was the only maker of cable-actuated shovels known to have launched a hydraulic excavator between 1948 and 1961: All of the other manufacturers continued serving their established customers, well and prosperously.[12] In fact, the largest makers of cable-actuated excavators, Bucyrus Erie and Northwest Engineering, logged record profits until 1966—the point at which the disruptive hydraulics technology had squarely intersected with customers' needs in the sewer and piping segment. This is typical of industries facing a disruptive technology: The leading firms in the established technology remain financially strong until the disruptive technology is, in fact, in the midst of their mainstream market.

Between 1947 and 1965, twenty-three companies entered the mechanical excavation market with hydraulic products. Figure 3.6, which measures the total number of active entrants and established firms offering hydraulic excavators (net of the companies that had exited), shows how completely the entrants dominated the hydraulic excavator market.

In the 1960s, some of the strongest cable shovel makers introduced shovels with hydraulics. Almost all of these models were hybrids, however, like Bucyrus Erie's Hydrohoe, generally employing a hydraulic cylinder to articulate or curl the bucket and using cables to extend the bucket out and to lift the boom. When used in this way in the 1960s, hydraulics had a sustaining impact on the established manufacturers' products, improving their performance in the mainstream value networks. Some of the methods that engineers found to use hydraulics on the cable excavators were truly ingenious. All of this innovative energy, however, was targeted at existing customers.

The strategies employed by the excavator manufacturers during this period highlight an important choice that confronts companies encountering disruptive technological change. In general, the successful entrants accepted the capabilities of hydraulics technology in the 1940s and 1950s

Figure 3.6 Manufacturers of Hydraulic Excavators, 1948–1965

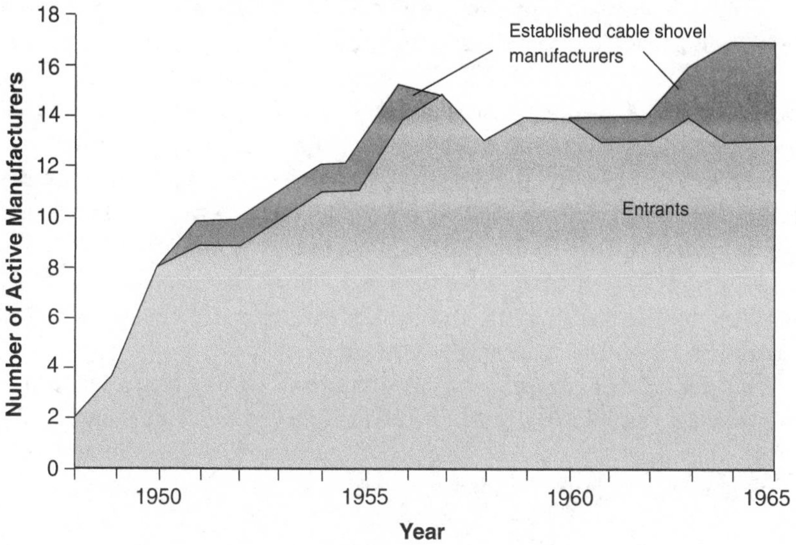

Source: Data are from the Historical Construction Equipment Association.

as a given and cultivated new market applications in which the technology, as it existed, could create value. And as a general rule, the established firms saw the situation the other way around: They took the *market's* needs as the given. They consequently sought to adapt or improve the technology in ways that would allow them to market the new technology to their existing customers as a sustaining improvement. The established firms steadfastly focused their innovative investments on their customers. Subsequent chapters will show that this strategic choice is present in most instances of disruptive innovation. Consistently, established firms attempt to push the technology into their established markets, while the successful entrants find a new market that values the technology.

Hydraulics technology ultimately *did* progress to the point where it could address the needs of mainstream excavation contractors. That progress was achieved, however, by the entrant companies, who had first found a market for the initial capabilities of the technology, accumulated design and manufacturing experience in that market, and then used that commercial platform to attack the value networks above them. The established firms lost this contest. Only four cable excavator companies—Insley,

Koehring, Little Giant, and Link Belt—remained as viable suppliers to excavation contractors by successfully but belatedly introducing lines of hydraulic excavators to defend their markets.[13]

Aside from these, however, the other leading manufacturers of big cable machines in the mainstream excavation markets never introduced a commercially successful hydraulic excavator. Although some had employed hydraulics to a modest degree as a bucket-curling mechanism, they lacked the design expertise and volume-based manufacturing cost position to compete as hydraulics invaded the mainstream. By the early 1970s, all of these firms had been driven from the sewer, piping, and general excavation markets by the entrants, most of which had refined their technological capabilities initially in the small-contractor market.[14]

This contrast in strategies for profiting from change characterizes the approaches employed by entrant and established firms in many of the other industries affected by disruptive technologies—particularly disk drives, steel, computers, and electric cars.

THE CHOICE BETWEEN CABLE AND HYDRAULICS

In the trajectory map of Figure 3.3, when hydraulics technology became capable of addressing the bucket-size needs of sewer and piping contractors (and a similar trajectory could be sketched for arm-reach), the competitive dynamics in the industry changed, and the mainstream excavation contractors changed the criteria by which they purchased their equipment. Even today, the cable-actuated architecture can attain much longer reach and greater lift than can hydraulic excavators: They have roughly parallel technology trajectories. But once *both* cable- and hydraulics-actuated systems could satisfy mainstream market requirements, excavation contractors could no longer base their choice of equipment on which had longer reach and greater bucket capacity. Both were good enough, and the fact that cable was better ceased to have competitive relevance.

Contractors found, however, that hydraulic machines were much less prone to breakdowns than cable-actuated excavators. In particular, those who had experienced the life-threatening snap of a cable while hefting a heavy bucket embraced reliable hydraulics quickly, as soon as it was capable of doing the job. Once both technologies were good enough in the basic capabilities demanded, therefore, the basis of product choice in the market shifted to reliability. Sewer and piping contractors began adopting hydraulic equipment rapidly beginning in the early 1960s, and general excavation contractors followed later in the decade.

CONSEQUENCES AND IMPLICATIONS OF THE HYDRAULICS ERUPTION

What went wrong within the companies that made cable-actuated excavators? Clearly, with the benefit of hindsight, they should have invested in hydraulics machines and embedded that piece of their organizations charged with making hydraulic products in the value network that needed them. But the dilemma in managing the disruptive technology in the heat of the battle is that nothing went wrong inside these companies. Hydraulics was a technology that their customers didn't need—indeed, couldn't use. Each cable shovel manufacturer was one of at least twenty manufacturers doing everything they could to steal each other's customers: If they took their eyes off their customers' next-generation needs, existing business would have been put at risk. Moreover, developing bigger, better, and faster cable excavators to steal share from existing competitors constituted a much more obvious opportunity for profitable growth than did a venture into hydraulic backhoes, given how small the backhoe market was when it appeared in the 1950s. So, as we have seen before, these companies did not fail because the technology wasn't available. They did not fail because they lacked information about hydraulics or how to use it; indeed, the best of them used it as soon as it could help their customers. They did not fail because management was sleepy or arrogant. They failed because hydraulics didn't make sense—until it was too late.

The patterns of success and failure we see among firms faced with sustaining and disruptive technology change are a natural or systematic result of *good* managerial decisions. That is, in fact, why disruptive technologies confront innovators with such a dilemma. Working harder, being smarter, investing more aggressively, and listening more astutely to customers are all solutions to the problems posed by new sustaining technologies. But these paradigms of sound management are useless—even counterproductive, in many instances—when dealing with disruptive technology.

NOTES

1. A summary of how this same mechanism might have affected a broader range of industries can be found in Richard S. Rosenbloom and Clayton

M. Christensen, "Technological Discontinuities, Organizational Capabilities, and Strategic Commitments," *Industrial and Corporate Change* (3), 1994, 655–686.

2. This information and the data used to calculate the graphs in this section were provided by Dimitrie Toth, Jr., and Keith Haddock, both National Directors of the Historical Construction Equipment Association. The association has a wealth of information about the earthmoving equipment industry in its archives, and Toth and Haddock were most gracious in sharing their knowledge and information with me. I am also indebted to them for their helpful comments on an earlier draft of this chapter. Other useful sources of information are Peter Grimshaw, *Excavators* (Poole, England: Blandford Press, 1985); The Olyslager Organisation, Inc., *Earthmoving Vehicles* (London: Frederick Warne & Co., Ltd., 1972); Harold F. Williamson and Kenneth H. Myers, *Designed for Digging: The First 75 Years of Bucyrus Erie Company* (Evanston, IL: Northwestern University Press, 1955); and J. L. Allhands, *Tools of the Earthmover* (Huntsville, TX: Sam Houston College Press, 1951).

3. Interestingly, the high success rate was only amongst the industry's twenty-five largest firms. Only one of the seven smallest steam shovel manufacturers survived this sustaining technology change to internal gasoline combustion. Almost no information is available about these companies other than what is provided by their product brochures. I suspect, however, that the fact that the large and mid-sized firms cruised through this transition while the small ones were killed indicates that resources played a part in the story, a conclusion that complements the theoretical perspectives summarized in chapter 2 above. Some sustaining technologies clearly are so expensive to develop and implement or so dependent on proprietary or scarce expertise that some companies simply cannot successfully manage the transition. I am indebted to Professor Richard Rosenbloom for sharing his perspective on this issue.

4. An example of this is the development of the first dragline, by Page, a Chicago area contractor. Page dug Chicago's system of canals, and invented the dragline in 1903 to do that job more effectively. Page draglines were later used extensively in digging the Panama Canal, alongside steam shovels made by Bucyrus Erie and Marion. This finding that customers were significant sources of sustaining innovations is consistent with Professor Eric von Hippel's findings; see *The Sources of Innovation* (New York: Oxford University Press, 1988).

5. The companies that survived the invasion of hydraulics in this way found safe haven in a particular high-end market. Bucyrus Erie and Marion, for example, became the dominant makers of the huge stripping shovels used in strip mines. Marion's model 6360 stripping shovel was the largest frontward-scooping shovel ever built, able to heft 180 cubic yards in its bucket. (An

advertisement showing Paul Bunyan standing aside the 6360 is one of the most stunning pieces of advertising art I have seen.) Harnischfeger is the world's largest maker of electric mining shovels, while Unit found a niche making the huge pedestal cranes used on offshore oil rigs. For a time, North-west survived by making draglines for dredging ocean shipping lanes. P & H and Lorain made huge cranes and draglines (all cable-actuated).

6. As the hydraulic excavator has matured, these companies have met with varying degrees of subsequent success. In 1996, the world's highest-volume excavator companies, Demag and O & K, were based in Germany.

7. Technically, excavators that scoop their buckets forward are power *shovels*. This was the dominant design from 1837 through the early 1900s, and persisted as a major market segment through much of this century. Excavators that pull earth backward toward the cab are *backhoes*. As the hydraulic excavator became the dominant design during the 1970s, both types came to be called excavators. Until hydraulic actuation required the booms to be permanently attached to the unit, contractors could attach different booms or arms to their basic power units so that the same unit could work as a shovel, backhoe, or crane. Similarly, different buckets, sometimes called *dippers,* could be attached to move different types of material.

8. The true measure of performance in excavation was the number of cubic yards of earth that could be moved per minute. This measure was so dependent upon operator skill and upon the type of earth being dug, however, that contractors adopted bucket size as the more robust, verifiable metric.

9. These British and American pioneers were followed by several European manufacturers, each of which was also an entrant to the excavator industry, including France's Poclain and Italy's Bruneri Brothers.

10. The ability to push the shovel into the earth was a major advantage to the hydraulics approach. The cable-actuated excavators that pulled earth toward the operator all had to rely on gravity to drive the teeth of the heavy shovel into the earth.

11. Makers of early hybrid ocean transports, which were steam-powered but still outfitted with sails, used the same rationale for their design as did the Bucyrus Erie engineers: Steam power still was not reliable enough for the transoceanic market, so steam power plants had to be backed up by conventional technology. The advent of steam-powered ships and their substitution for wind-powered ships in the transoceanic business is itself a classic study of disruptive technology. When Robert Fulton sailed the first steamship up the Hudson River in 1807, it underperformed transoceanic sailing ships on nearly every dimension of performance: It cost more per mile to operate; it was slower; and it was prone to frequent breakdowns. Hence, it could not be used in the transoceanic value network and could only be applied in a

different value network, inland waterways, in which product performance was measured very differently. In rivers and lakes, the ability to move against the wind or in the absence of a wind was the attribute most highly valued by ship captains, and along that dimension, steam outperformed sail. Some scholars (see, for example, Richard Foster, in *Innovation: The Attacker's Advantage* [New York: Summit Books, 1986]) have marveled at how myopic were the makers of sailing ships, who stayed with their aging technology until the bitter end, in the early 1900s, completely ignoring steam power. Indeed, not a single maker of sailing ships survived the industry's transition to steam power. The value network framework offers a perspective on this problem that these scholars seem to have ignored, however. It was not a problem of *knowing* about steam power or of having access to technology. The problem was that the customers of the sailing ship manufacturers, who were transoceanic shippers, could not use steam-powered ships until the turn of the century. To cultivate a position in steamship building, the makers of sailing ships would have had to engineer a major strategic reorientation into the inland waterway market, because that was the only value network where steam-powered vessels were valued throughout most of the 1800s. Hence, it was these firms' reluctance or inability to change strategy, rather than their inability to change technology, that lay at the root of their failure in the face of steam-powered vessels.

12. An exception to this is an unusual product introduced by Koehring in 1957: the Skooper combined cables and hydraulics to dig earth away from a facing wall; it did not dig down into the earth.

13. Bucyrus Erie does not fit easily into either of these groups. It introduced a large hydraulic excavator in the 1950s, but subsequently withdrew it from the market. In the late 1960s, it acquired the "Dynahoe" line of hydraulic loader-backhoes from Hy-Dynamic Corporation and sold them as utility machines to its general excavation customers, but, again, dropped this product line as well.

14. Caterpillar was a very late (but successful) entrant into the hydraulic excavation equipment industry, introducing its first model in 1972. Excavators were an extension of its line of dozers, scrapers, and graders. Caterpillar never participated in the excavation machine market when cable actuation was the dominant design.

CHAPTER **FOUR**

What Goes Up, Can't Go Down

 It is clear from the histories of the disk drive and excavator industries that the boundaries of value networks do not completely imprison the companies within them: There is considerable *upward* mobility into other networks. It is in restraining *downward* mobility into the markets enabled by disruptive technologies that the value networks exercise such unusual power. In this chapter we will explore these questions: Why could leading companies migrate so readily toward high-end markets, and why does moving downmarket appear to have been so difficult? Rational managers, as we shall see, can rarely build a cogent case for entering small, poorly defined low-end markets that offer only lower profitability. In fact, the prospects for growth and improved profitability in upmarket value networks often appear to be so much more attractive than the prospect of staying within the *current* value network, that it is not unusual to see well-managed companies leaving (or becoming uncompetitive with) their original customers as they search for customers at higher price points. In good companies, resources and energy coalesce most readily behind proposals to attack upmarket into higher-performance products that can earn higher margins.

Indeed, the prospects for improving financial performance by moving toward upmarket value networks are so strong that one senses a huge magnet in the northeast corner of the disk drive and excavator trajectory maps. This chapter examines the power of this "northeastern pull" by looking at evidence from the history of the disk drive industry. It then generalizes this framework by exploring the same phenomenon in the battle between minimill and integrated steel makers.

THE GREAT NORTHEAST MIGRATION IN DISK DRIVES

Figure 4.1 plots in more detail the upmarket movement of Seagate Technology, whose strategy was typical of most disk drive manufacturers. Recall that Seagate had spawned, and then grew to dominate, the value network for desktop computing. Its product position relative to capacity demanded in its market is mapped by vertical lines which span from the lowest- to the highest-capacity drives in its product line, in each of the years shown. The black rectangle on the line measuring each year's capacity span shows the median capacity of the drives Seagate introduced in each of those years.

Figure 4.1 Upmarket Migration of Seagate Products

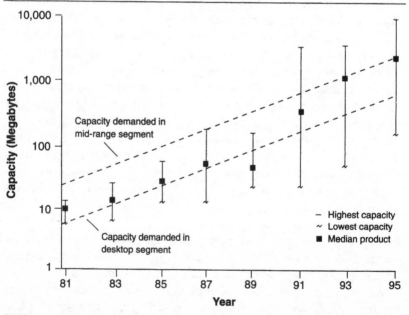

Source: Data are from various issues of *Disk/Trend Report*.

Between 1983 and 1985, the center of gravity of Seagate's product line was positioned squarely on the average capacity demanded in the desktop segment. It was between 1987 and 1989 that the disruptive 3.5-inch form invaded the desktop market from below. Seagate responded to that attack, not by fighting the disruptive technology head-on, but by retreating up-market. It continued to offer models in the capacity ranges the desktop PC market demanded, but by 1993 the focus of its energy had clearly shifted to the market for mid-range computers, such as file servers and engineering workstations.

Indeed, disruptive technologies have such a devastating impact because the firms that first commercialized each generation of disruptive disk drives chose *not* to remain contained within their initial value network. Rather, they reached as far upmarket as they could in each new product generation, until their drives packed the capacity to appeal to the value networks above them. It is this upward mobility that makes disruptive technologies so dangerous to established firms—and so attractive to entrants.

VALUE NETWORKS AND CHARACTERISTIC COST STRUCTURES

What lies behind this asymmetric mobility? As we have already seen, it is driven by resource allocation processes that direct resources toward new product proposals that promise higher margins and larger markets. These are almost always better in the northeast portions of trajectory maps (such as Figures 1.7 and 3.3) than in the southeast. The disk drive manufacturers migrated to the northeast corner of the product-market map because the resource allocation processes they employed took them there.

As we saw in chapter 2, a characteristic of each value network is a particular cost structure that firms within it must create if they are to provide the products and services in the priority their customers demand. Thus, as the disk drive makers became large and successful within their "home" value network, they developed a very specific economic character: tuning their levels of effort and expenses in research, development, sales, marketing, and administration to the needs of their customers and the challenges of their competitors. Gross margins tended to evolve in each value network to levels that enabled the better disk drive makers to make money, given these costs of doing business.

In turn, this gave these companies a very specific model for improving profitability. Generally, they found it difficult to improve profitability by hacking out cost while steadfastly standing in their mainstream market: The research, development, marketing, and administrative costs they were incurring were all critical to remaining competitive in their mainstream business. Moving upmarket toward higher-performance products that promised higher gross margins was usually a more straightforward path to profit improvement. Moving downmarket was anathema to that objective.

The obviousness of the path toward profit improvement is shown in Figure 4.2. The three bars on the left depict the size of the desktop, minicomputer, and mainframe computer value networks in 1981 and are labeled with the characteristic margins enjoyed by disk drive makers in each of those networks. Gross margins are clearly higher in higher-end markets, compensating manufacturers for the higher levels of overhead characteristic of those businesses.

The differences in the size of these markets and the characteristic cost structures across these value networks created serious asymmetries in the combat among these firms. Firms making 8-inch drives for the minicomputer market, for example, had cost structures requiring gross margins of 40 percent. Aggressively moving downmarket would have pitted them against foes who had honed their cost structures to make money at 25 percent gross margins. On the other hand, moving upmarket enabled them to take a relatively lower-cost structure into a market that was accustomed to giving its suppliers 60 percent gross margins. Which direction made sense? A similar asymmetry faced the makers of 5.25-inch drives in 1986, as they decided whether to spend their resources building a position in the emerging market for 3.5-inch drives in portable computers or to move up toward the minicomputer and mainframe companies.

Committing development resources to launch higher-performance products that could garner higher gross margins generally both offered greater returns and caused less pain. As their managers were making repeated decisions about which new product development proposals they should fund and which they should shelve, proposals to develop higher-performance products targeted at the larger, higher-margin markets immediately above them always got the resources. In other words, sensible resource allocation processes were at the root of companies' upward mobility and downmarket immobility across the boundaries of the value networks in the disk drive industry.

The hedonic regression analysis summarized in chapter 2 showed that

Figure 4.2 Views Upmarket and Downmarket for Established Disk Drive Manufacturers

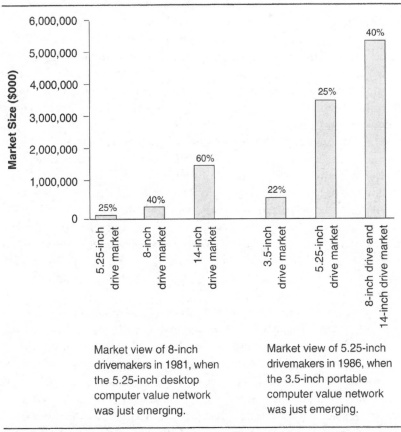

Market view of 8-inch drivemakers in 1981, when the 5.25-inch desktop computer value network was just emerging.

Market view of 5.25-inch drivemakers in 1986, when the 3.5-inch portable computer value network was just emerging.

Source: Data are from various issues of *Disk/Trend Report*, corporate annual reports, and data provided in personal interviews.
Note: Percentages above each bar indicate typical gross margins in each value network.

higher-end markets consistently paid significantly higher prices for incremental megabytes of capacity. Why would anyone opt to sell a megabyte for less when it could be sold for more? The disk drive companies' migration to the northeast was, as such, highly rational.

Other scholars have found evidence in other industries that as companies leave their disruptive roots in search of greater profitability in the market tiers above them, they gradually come to acquire the cost structures required to compete in those upper market tiers.[1] This exacerbates their problem of downward immobility.

RESOURCE ALLOCATION AND UPWARD MIGRATION

Further insight into this asymmetric mobility across value networks comes from comparing two different descriptive models of how resources are allocated. The first model describes resource allocation as a rational, top-down decision-making process in which senior managers weigh alternative proposals for investment in innovation and put money into those projects that they find to be consistent with firm strategy and to offer the highest return on investment. Proposals that don't clear these hurdles are killed.

The second model of resource allocation, first articulated by Joseph Bower,[2] characterizes resource allocation decisions much differently. Bower notes that most proposals to innovate are generated from deep within the organization not from the top. As these ideas bubble up from the bottom, the organization's middle managers play a critical but invisible role in screening these projects. These managers can't package and throw their weight behind every idea that passes by; they need to decide which are the best, which are most likely to succeed, and which are most likely to be approved, given the corporate financial, competitive, and strategic climate.

In most organizations, managers' careers receive a big boost when they play a key sponsorship role in very successful projects—and their careers can be permanently derailed if they have the bad judgment or misfortune to back projects that fail. Middle managers aren't penalized for *all* failures, of course. Projects that fail because the technologists couldn't deliver, for example, often are not (necessarily) regarded as failures at all, because a lot is learned from the effort and because technology development is generally regarded as an unpredictable, probabilistic endeavor. But projects that fail because the *market* wasn't there have far more serious implications for managers' careers. These tend to be much more expensive and public failures. They generally occur after the company has made full investments in product design, manufacturing, engineering, marketing, and distribution. Hence, middle managers—acting in both their own and the company's interest—tend to back those projects for which market demand seems most assured. They then work to package the proposals for their chosen projects in ways geared to win senior management approval. As such, while senior managers may *think* they're making the resource allocation decisions, many of the really critical resource allocation decisions have actually been made long before senior management gets involved: Middle managers have made their decisions about which projects they'll back and carry to senior management—and which they will allow to languish.

Consider the implications of this for a successful firm's downward and upward mobility from its initial value network in this hypothetical example. In the same week, two respected employees, one from marketing, the other from engineering, run two very different ideas for new products past their common manager two levels above them in the organization. The marketer comes first, with an idea for a higher-capacity, higher-speed model. The two-levels-up manager starts her interrogation:

> "Who's going to buy it?"
>
> "Well, there's a whole segment in the workstation industry—they buy over $600 million in drives each year—that we've just never been able to reach because our capacity points just don't reach that high. I think this product just might get us there."
>
> "Have you run this idea past any potential customers?"
>
> "Yeah, I was in California last week. They all said they wanted prototypes as soon as they could get them. There's a design window opening up in nine months. They've been working with their current supplier [competitor X] to get something ready, but someone we just hired from competitor X said they're having lots of trouble meeting the specs. I really think we can do it."
>
> "But does *engineering* think we can do it?"
>
> "They say it'll be a stretch, but you know them. They always say that."
>
> "What kind of margins are we looking at up there?"
>
> "That's what really excites me about this. If we can build it in our current factory, given the price per megabyte competitor X has been getting, I think we can get close to 35 percent."

Compare that conversation to the manager's interchange with the engineer whose idea is for a cheaper, smaller, slower, lower-capacity disruptive disk drive.

> "Who's going to buy it?"
>
> "Well, I'm not sure, but there's *got* to be a market out there *somewhere* for it. People are always wanting things smaller and less expensive. I could see them using it in fax machines, printers, maybe."
>
> "Have you run this idea past any potential customers?"
>
> "Yeah, when I was at the last trade show I sketched the idea out for one of our current customers. He said he was interested, but couldn't see how they could really use it. Today you really need 270 MB to run everything, and there's just no way we could get that kind of capacity on this thing—at least not for a while. His response doesn't surprise me, really."

"How about the guys who make fax machines? What do they think?"

"Well, they say they don't know. Again, it's an intriguing idea, but they already have their product plans pretty well set, and none of them use disk drives."

"You think we could make money on this project?"

"Well, I think so, but that depends on how we could price it, of course."

Which of the two projects will the two-levels-up manager back? In the tug-of-war for development resources, projects targeted at the explicit needs of current customers or at the needs of existing users that a supplier has not yet been able to reach will *always* win over proposals to develop products for markets that do not exist. This is because, in fact, the best resource allocation systems are designed precisely to weed out ideas that are unlikely to find large, profitable, receptive markets. Any company that *doesn't* have a systematic way of targeting its development resources toward customers' needs, in fact, will fail.[3]

The most vexing managerial aspect of this problem of asymmetry, where the easiest path to growth and profit is up, and the most deadly attacks come from below, is that "good" management—working harder and smarter and being more visionary—doesn't solve the problem. The resource allocation process involves thousands of decisions, some subtle and some explicit, made every day by hundreds of people, about how their time and the company's money ought to be spent. Even when a senior manager decides to pursue a disruptive technology, the people in the organization are likely to ignore it or, at best, cooperate reluctantly if it doesn't fit *their* model of what it takes to succeed as an organization and as individuals within an organization. Well-run companies are not populated by yes-people who have been taught to carry out mindlessly the directives of management. Rather, their employees have been trained to understand what is good for the company and what it takes to build a successful career within the company. Employees of great companies exercise initiative to serve customers and meet budgeted sales and profits. It is very difficult for a manager to motivate competent people to energetically and persistently pursue a course of action that they think makes no sense. An example from the history of the disk drive industry illustrates the impact of such employee behavior.

THE CASE OF THE 1.8-INCH DISK DRIVE

Managers in disk drive companies were very generous in helping me conduct the research reported in this book, and, as the results began emerging in 1992, I began feeding back the published papers that summarized what I was learning. I was particularly interested in whether the framework summarized in Figure 1.7 would have an impact on their decisions regarding the 1.8-inch drive, which was just then emerging as the industry's most recent disruptive technology. For industry outsiders, of course, the conclusion was obvious: "How many times does this have to happen before these guys learn?! Of course they've got to do it." The guys did, in fact, learn. By the end of 1993, each of the leading drive makers had developed 1.8-inch models and had them ready for introduction if and when the market developed.

In August 1994, I was visiting the CEO of one of the largest disk drive companies and asked him what his firm was doing about the 1.8-inch drive. This clearly touched a hot button. He pointed to a shelf in his office where a sample 1.8-inch drive was perched. "You see that?" he demanded. "That's the *fourth generation* of 1.8-inch drives we've developed—each one with more capacity than the last. But we haven't sold any. We want to be ready when the market is there, but there just isn't a market for them yet."

I countered by reminding him that *Disk/Trend Report,* a highly regarded market research publication that was the source of much of the data used in my study, had measured the 1993 market at $40 million, was projecting 1994 sales to be $80 million, and forecast 1995 volume at $140 million.

"I know that's what they think," he responded. "But they're wrong. There isn't a market. We've had that drive in our catalog for 18 months. Everyone knows we've got it, but nobody wants it. The market just isn't there. We just got way ahead of the market." I had no other basis for pressing my point with this manager, who is one of the most astute managers I've ever met. Our conversation moved to other issues.

About a month later I was leading a case discussion in the Harvard MBA program's technology and operations management course about the development of a new engine at Honda. One of the students in the class had previously worked in Honda's research and development organization, so I asked him to take a few minutes to tell the class what it was like working there. It turned out that he had been working on dashboard mapping and navigation systems. I couldn't resist interrupting his talk by asking, "How do you store all that data for the maps?"

Said the student: "We found a little 1.8-inch disk drive and put it in there. It's really neat—almost a solid-state device, with very few moving parts. Really rugged."

"Who do you buy them from?" I pressed.

"It's kind of funny," he replied. "You can't buy them from any of the big disk drive companies. We get them from a little startup company somewhere in Colorado—I can't remember the name."

I have since reflected on why the head of this company would insist so stubbornly that there was no market for 1.8-inch drives, even while there was, and why my student would say the big drive makers didn't sell these drives, even though they were trying. The answer lies in the northeast-southeast problem, and in the role that the hundreds of well-trained decision makers in a good company play in funneling resources and energy into those projects they perceive will bring the company the greatest growth and profit. The CEO had decided that the company was going to catch this next disruptive wave early and had shepherded the project through to a successful, economical design. But among the employees, there was nothing about an $80 million, low-end market that solved the growth and profit problems of a multibillion dollar company—especially when capable competitors were doing all they could to steal away the customers providing those billions. (The revenue figure is disguised.) And way at the other end of the company, there was nothing about supplying prototype quantities of 1.8-inch drives to an automaker that solved the problem of meeting the 1994 quotas of salespeople whose contacts and expertise were based so solidly in the computer industry.

For an organization to accomplish a task as complex as launching a new product, logic, energy, and impetus must all coalesce behind the effort. Hence, it is not just the *customers* of an established firm that hold it captive to their needs. Established firms are also captive to the financial structure and organizational culture inherent in the value network in which they compete—a captivity that can block any rationale for timely investment in the next wave of disruptive technology.

VALUE NETWORKS AND MARKET VISIBILITY

The impetus to drift upmarket can be particularly powerful when a firm's customers themselves are migrating upmarket. In such circumstances, suppliers of an intermediate component such as a disk drive may not sense their northeasterly migration because they are embedded among competitors and customers experiencing a similar drift.

In this light, we can see how easy it would have been for the leading 8-inch disk drive makers—Priam, Quantum, and Shugart—to miss the 5.25-inch generation of drives. Not a single one of their core customers, for example, Digital Equipment, Prime Computer, Data General, Wang Laboratories, and Nixdorf, successfully introduced a desktop computer. Instead, each was moving upmarket *itself* toward ever higher performance segments of their markets, trying to win the business of customers who historically had used mainframes. Similarly, not a single one of the customers of the 14-inch drive makers—mainframe makers such as Univac, Burroughs, NCR, ICL, Siemens, and Amdahl—ever made a bold enough move downmarket into minicomputers to become a significant player there.

Three factors—the promise of upmarket margins, the simultaneous upmarket movement of many of a company's customers, and the difficulty of cutting costs to move downmarket profitably—together create powerful barriers to downward mobility. In the internal debates about resource allocation for new product development, therefore, proposals to pursue disruptive technologies generally lose out to proposals to move upmarket. In fact, cultivating a systematic approach to weeding out new product development initiatives that would likely lower profits is one of the most important achievements of any well-managed company.

An important strategic implication of this rational pattern of upmarket movement is that it can create vacuum in low-end value networks that draws in entrants with technologies and cost structures better suited to competition. One of these powerful downmarket voids occurred in the steel industry, for example, when entrant companies employing disruptive minimill process technology entered through low-end beachheads; they have attacked relentlessly upmarket ever since.

THE NORTHEASTERLY MIGRATION
OF INTEGRATED STEEL

Minimill steel making first became commercially viable in the mid-1960s. Employing widely available and familiar technology and equipment, mini-mills melt scrap steel in electric arc furnaces, continuously cast it into intermediate shapes called billets, and then roll those into products such as bars, rods, beams, or sheets. They are called *minimills* because the scale at which they produce cost-competitive molten steel from scrap is less than one-tenth of the scale required for an integrated mill to produce cost-competitive molten steel from iron ore in blast and basic oxygen furnaces. (Integrated mills take their name from the integrated process of transforming iron ore, coal, and limestone into final steel shapes.) Integrated mills and minimills look much the same in their processes of continuous casting and rolling operations. Scale is the only difference: The output of efficiently sized blast furnaces requires that integrated mills' casting and rolling operations must be much greater than those of the minimills.

North America's steel minimills are the most efficient, lowest-cost steel makers in the world. In 1995, the most efficient minimill required 0.6 labor-hours per ton of steel produced; the best integrated mill required 2.3 labor-hours. In the product categories in which they compete, the average minimill can make product of equivalent quality, on a fully costed basis, at about a 15 percent lower cost than the average integrated mill. In 1995, it cost about $400 million to build a cost-competitive steel minimill and about $6 billion to build a cost-competitive integrated mill.[4] In terms of capital cost per ton of steel making capacity, integrated mills are more than four times as costly to build.[5] As a result, minimills' share of the North American market has grown from nothing in 1965 to 19 percent in 1975, 32 percent in 1985, and 40 percent in 1995. Experts predict they will account for half of all steel production by the turn of the century.[6] Minimills virtually dominate the North American markets for rods, bars, and structural beams.

Yet not a single one of the world's major integrated steel companies to date has built a mill employing minimill technology. Why would none of them do something that makes so much sense? The explanation forwarded most frequently by the business press, especially in the United States, is that the managers of the integrated companies are conservative, backward-looking, risk-averse, and incompetent. Consider these indictments.

Last year, U.S. Steel Corp. closed fifteen of its facilities, claiming they had become "noncompetitive." Three years ago, Bethlehem Steel Corp. shuttered major portions of its plants in Johnstown, PA, and Lackawanna, NY. . . . The closing of these major steel complexes is the final dramatic concession from today's chief executives that management has not been doing its job. It represents decades of maximizing profits to look good for the short term.[7]

If the U.S. steel industry were as productive in tons per man-hour as it is in rhetoric per problem, it would be a top-notch performer.[8]

Surely there is some credibility to such accusations. But managerial incompetence cannot be a complete answer for the failure of North American integrated mills to counter the conquest by minimills of vast portions of the steel industry. *None* of what most experts regard as the best-managed and most successful of the world's integrated steel makers—including Nippon, Kawasaki, and NKK in Japan; British Steel and Hoogovens in Europe; and Pohang Steel in Korea—has invested in minimill technology even though it is demonstrably the lowest-cost technology in the world.

At the same time, in the last decade the management teams at integrated mills have taken aggressive steps to increase mill efficiency. USX, for example, improved the efficiency of its steel making operations from more than nine labor-hours per ton of steel produced in 1980 to just under three hours per ton in 1991. It accomplished this by ferociously attacking the size of its workforce, paring it from more than 93,000 in 1980 to fewer than 23,000 in 1991, and by investing more than $2 billion in modernizing its plant and equipment. Yet all of this managerial aggressiveness was targeted at conventional ways of making steel. How can this be?

Minimill steelmaking is a disruptive technology. When it emerged in the 1960s, because it used scrap steel, it produced steel of marginal quality. The properties of its products varied according to the metallurgical composition and impurities of the scrap. Hence, about the only market that minimill producers could address was that for steel reinforcing bars (rebars)—right at the bottom of the market in terms of quality, cost, and margins. This market was the least attractive of those served by established steel makers. And not only were margins low, but customers were the least loyal: They would switch suppliers at will, dealing with whoever offered the lowest price. The integrated steel makers were almost relieved to be rid of the rebar business.

The minimills, however, saw the rebar market quite differently. They had very different cost structures than those of the integrated mills: little depreciation and no research and development costs, low sales expenses (mostly telephone bills), and minimal general managerial overhead. They could sell by telephone virtually all the steel they could make—and sell it profitably.

Once they had established themselves in the rebar market, the most aggressive minimills, especially Nucor and Chaparral, developed a very different view of the overall steel market than the view that the integrated mills held. Whereas the downmarket rebar territory they seized had looked singularly unattractive to their integrated competitors, the minimills' view *upmarket* showed that opportunities for greater profits and expanded sales were all above them. With such incentive, they worked to improve the metallurgical quality and consistency of their products and invested in equipment to make larger shapes.

As the trajectory map in Figure 4.3 indicates, the minimills next attacked the markets for larger bars, rods, and angle irons immediately above them. By 1980, they had captured 90 percent of the rebar market and held about 30 percent of the markets for bars, rods, and angle irons. At the time of the minimills' attack, the bar, rod, and angle iron shapes brought the lowest margins in the integrated mills' product lines. As a consequence, the integrated steel makers were, again, almost relieved to be rid of the business, and by the mid-1980s this market belonged to the minimills.

Once their position in the market for bars, rods, and angle irons seemed secure, the minimills continued their march upmarket, this time toward structural beams. Nucor did so from a new minimill plant in Arkansas, and Chaparral launched its attack from a new mill adjacent to its first

Figure 4.3 The Progress of Disruptive Minimill Steel Technology

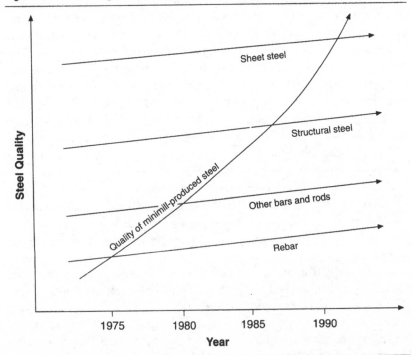

one in Texas. The integrated mills were driven from this market by the minimills as well. In 1992, USX closed its South Chicago structural steel mill, leaving Bethlehem as the only integrated North American structural steel maker. Bethlehem closed its last structural beam plant in 1995, leaving the field to the minimills.

An important part of this story is that, throughout the 1980s, as they were ceding the bar and beam business to the minimills, the integrated steel makers experienced dramatically improving profit. Not only were these firms attacking cost, they were forsaking their lowest-margin products and focusing increasingly on high-quality rolled sheet steel, where quality-sensitive manufacturers of cans, cars, and appliances paid premium prices for metallurgically consistent steel with defect-free surfaces. Indeed, the lion's share of integrated mills' investments in the 1980s had been targeted at improving their ability to provide the most demanding customers in these three markets with the highest-quality product and to do so profitably. Sheet steel markets were an attractive haven for the integrated producers in part because they were protected from minimill competition. It cost about $2 billion to build a state-of-the-art, cost-competitive sheet steel rolling mill, and this capital outlay simply had been too much for even the largest of the minimills.

Targeting the premium end of the market pleased the integrated mills' investors: For example, Bethlehem Steel's market value had leapt from $175 million in 1986 to $2.4 billion in 1989. This represented a very attractive return on the $1.3 billion the company invested in R&D and plant and equipment during this period. The business press generously acknowledged these aggressive, well-placed investments.

> Walter Williams (Bethlehem's CEO) has worked wonders. Over the past three years he mounted a highly personal campaign to improve the quality and productivity of Bethlehem's basic steel business. Bethlehem's metamorphosis has outclassed even its major U.S. competitors—which as a whole are now producing at lower costs than their Japanese rivals and are fast closing the quality gap. Customers notice the difference. *"It's nothing short of miraculous,"* says a top purchaser of sheet steel at Campbell Soup. [Italics added.][9]

Another analyst made similar observations.

> While almost no one was looking, a near miracle occurred: Big Steel is making a quiet comeback. Gary Works (US Steel) is back in the black . . .

pouring out a glowing river of molten iron at the rate of 3 million tons per year—a North American record. Union-management problem-solving teams are everywhere. Instead of making steel in all shapes and sizes, *Gary has focused almost entirely on higher-value flat-rolled steel.* [Italics added.][10]

Almost all of us would agree that these remarkable recoveries were the fruits of good management. But where will good management in this *genre* lead these firms?

MINIMILL THIN-SLAB CASTING FOR SHEET STEEL

While integrated steel makers were busy engineering their recoveries, more disruptive clouds began gathering on the horizon. In 1987, a German supplier of equipment for the steel industry, Schloemann-Siemag AG, announced that it had developed what it called "continuous thin-slab casting" technology—a way for steel to be continuously cast from its molten state into long, thin slabs that could be transported directly, without cooling, into a rolling mill. Rolling the white-hot, already thin slab of steel to the final thickness of coiled sheet steel was much simpler than the traditional task mastered by the integrated mills of reheating and rolling sheet from thick ingots or slabs. Most important, a cost-competitive continuous thin-slab casting and rolling mill could be built for less than $250 million—one-tenth the capital cost of a traditional sheet mill and a relatively manageable investment for a minimill steel maker. At this scale, an electric arc furnace could easily supply the required quantity of molten steel. Moreover, thin-slab casting promised at least a 20 percent reduction in the total cost of making sheet steel.

Because of its promise, thin-slab casting was carefully evaluated by every major player in the steel industry. Some integrated mills, such as USX, worked very hard to justify installation of a thin-slab facility.[11] In the end, however, it was minimill Nucor Steel, rather than the integrated mills, that made the bold move into thin-slab casting. Why?

At the outset, thin-slab casting technology could not offer the smooth, defect-free surface finish required by the integrated mills' mainstream customers (makers of cans, cars, and appliances). The only markets were those such as construction decking and corrugated steel for culverts, pipes, and Quonset huts, in which users were more sensitive to price than to surface blemishes. Thin-slab casting was a disruptive technology. Furthermore, large, capable, and hungry integrated competitors were busy trying to rob each other's most profitable business with the large auto, appliance, and can companies. It made no sense for them to target capital investment at thin-slab casting, positioned as it was in the least-profitable, most price-competitive and commodity-like end of their business. Indeed, after seriously considering between 1987 and 1988 whether to invest in thin-slab casting at an amount then projected to be about $150 million, both Bethlehem and USX elected instead to invest in conventional thick-slab continuous casters at a cost of $250 million to protect and enhance the profitability of the business with their mainstream customers.

Not surprisingly, Nucor saw the situation another way. Unencumbered by the demands of profitable customers in the sheet steel business and benefiting from a cost structure forged at the bottom of the industry, Nucor fired up the world's first continuous thin-slab casting facility in Crawfordsville, Indiana, in 1989, and constructed a second mill in Hickman, Arkansas, in 1992. It increased its capacity at both sites by 80 percent in 1995. Analysts estimate that Nucor had captured 7 percent of the massive North American sheet market by 1996—hardly enough to concern the integrated mills, because Nucor's success has been limited to the commoditized, least-profitable end of their product line. Of course, in its effort to win higher-margin business with higher-quality products from these mills, Nucor has already improved the surface quality of its sheet steel substantially.

Thus, the integrated steel companies' march to the profitable northeast corner of the steel industry is a story of aggressive investment, rational decision making, close attention to the needs of mainstream customers, and record profits. It is the same innovator's dilemma that confounded the leading providers of disk drives and mechanical excavators: Sound managerial decisions are at the very root of their impending fall from industry leadership.

NOTES

1. This process of moving to higher tiers of the market and then adding the costs to support business at that level was described by Professor Malcom P. McNair, of the Harvard Business School, in a way that strikingly parallels the disk drive story. Writing in a history of retailing, McNair describes how successive waves of retailers entered the field with disruptive technologies (though he does not use the term):

   The wheel always revolves, sometimes slowly, sometimes more rapidly, but it does not stand still. The cycle frequently begins with the bold new concept, the innovation. Somebody gets a bright new idea. There is a John Wanamaker, a George Hartford (A&P), a Frank Woolworth, a W. T. Grant, a General Wood (Sears), a Michael Cullen (supermarkets), a Eugene Ferkauf. Such an innovator has an idea for a new kind of distributive enterprise. At the outset he is in bad odor, ridiculed, scorned, condemned as "illegitimate." Bankers and investors are leery of him. But he attracts the public on the basis of the price appeal made possible by the low operating costs inherent in his innovation. As he goes along he trades up, improves the quality of his merchandise, improves the appearance and standing of his store, attains greater respectability. . . .

During this process of growth the institution rapidly becomes respectable in the eyes of both consumers and investors, but at the same time its capital investment increases and its operating costs tend to rise. Then the institution enters the stage of maturity. . . . The maturity phase soon tends to be followed by topheaviness . . . and eventual vulnerability. Vulnerability to what? Vulnerability to the next fellow who has a bright idea and who starts his business on a low-cost basis, slipping in under the umbrella that the old-line institutions have hoisted.

See Malcom P. McNair, "Significant Trends and Developments in the Post-War Period," in Albert B. Smith, ed., *Competitive Distribution in a Free High-Level Economy and Its Implications for the University* (Pittsburgh: University of Pittsburgh Press, 1958) 17–18. In other words, the very costs required to become competitive in higher-end markets restrict downward mobility and create further incentive to move upmarket.

2. Joseph Bower, *Managing the Resource Allocation Process* (Homewood, IL: Richard D. Irwin, 1970).

3. The use of the term *systematic* in this sentence is important, because most resource allocation systems work in a systematic way—whether the system is formal or informal. It will be shown later in this book that a key to managers' ability to confront disruptive technology successfully is their ability to intervene and make resource allocation decisions personally and persistently. Allocation systems are designed to weed out just such proposals as disruptive technologies. An excellent description of this dilemma can be found in Roger Martin, "Changing the Mind of the Corporation," *Harvard Business Review*, November–December 1993, 81–94.

4. Because of slow growth in steel demand in many of the world's markets, fewer large integrated steel mills are being built in the 1990s. Those integrated mills that are being built these days are in high-growth, rapidly developing countries such as Korea, Mexico, and Brazil.

5. Professor Thomas Eagar of the Department of Materials Science at the Massachusetts Institute of Technology provided these estimates.

6. "The U.S. Steel Industry: An Historical Overview," *Goldman Sachs U.S. Research Report*, 1995.

7. "What Caused the Decline," *Business Week*, June 30, 1980, 74.

8. Donald B. Thompson, "Are Steel's Woes Just Short-term," *Industry Week*, February 22, 1982, 31.

9. Gregory L. Miles, "Forging the New Bethlehem," *Business Week*, June 5, 1989, 108–110.

10. Seth Lubove and James R. Norman, "New Lease on Life," *Forbes*, May 9, 1994, 87.

11. The experience of the team at U.S. Steel charged with evaluating continuous thin-slab casting technology is chronicled in the Harvard Business School teaching case "Continuous Casting Investments at USX Corporation," No. 697-020.

Part **Two**

MANAGING DISRUPTIVE TECHNOLOGICAL CHANGE

In the search for reasons why so many strong companies in three very different industries stumbled or failed, the research summarized in the preceding chapters casts doubt on several conventional explanations other researchers have offered. It wasn't the case that the leading companies' engineers tended to get stuck in a particular technological paradigm or ignored innovations that were "not invented here." The cause of failure could not be solely attributed to established firms' inadequate competence in new technological fields or their inability to stay atop their industry's "technological mudslide." Of course, these problems do afflict some companies. But as a general rule, the evidence is very strong that as long as the new technology was required to address the needs of their customers, established firms were able to muster the expertise, capital, suppliers, energy, and rationale to develop and implement the requisite technology both competitively and effectively. This has been true for incremental as well as radical advances; for projects that consumed months as well as those lasting more than a decade; in fast-paced disk drives, in the slower-paced mechanical excavator industry, and in the process-intensive steel industry.

Probably the most important outcome of this attempt to define the problem is that it ruled out poor management as a root cause. Again, this is not to say that good and bad management aren't key factors affecting the fortunes of firms. But as a general explanation, the managers of the companies studied here had a great track record in understanding customers' future needs, identifying which technologies could best address those needs, and in investing to develop and implement them. It was only when confronted with disruptive technology that they failed. There had, therefore, to be a reason why good managers consistently made wrong decisions when faced with disruptive technological change.

The reason is that *good management itself* was the root cause. Managers played the game the way it was supposed to be played. The very decision-making and resource-allocation processes that are key to the success of established companies are the very processes that reject disruptive technologies: listening carefully to customers; tracking competitors' actions carefully; and investing resources to design and build higher-performance, higher-quality products that will yield greater profit. These are the reasons why great firms stumbled or failed when confronted with disruptive technological change.

Successful companies *want* their resources to be focused on activities that address customers' needs, that promise higher profits, that are technologically feasible, and that help them play in substantial markets. Yet, to expect the processes that accomplish these things *also* to do something like nurturing disruptive technologies—to focus resources on proposals that customers reject, that offer lower profit, that underperform existing technologies and can only be sold in insignificant markets—is akin to flapping one's arms with wings strapped to them in an attempt to fly. Such expectations involve fighting some fundamental tendencies about the way successful organizations work and about how their performance is evaluated.

Part Two of this book is built upon detailed case studies of a few companies that succeeded, and many more that failed, when faced with disruptive technological change. Just as in our analogy to man's finally learning to fly when aviators ultimately came to understand and either harness or accommodate some fundamental laws of nature, these case studies show that those executives who succeeded tended to manage by a very different set of rules than those that failed. There were, in fact, five fundamental principles of organizational nature that managers in the successful firms consistently recognized and harnessed. The firms that lost their battles with disruptive technologies chose to ignore or fight them. These principles are:

1. Resource dependence: Customers effectively control the patterns of resource allocation in well-run companies.

2. Small markets don't solve the growth needs of large companies.

3. The ultimate uses or applications for disruptive technologies are unknowable in advance. Failure is an intrinsic step toward success.

4. Organizations have capabilities that exist independently of the capabilities of the people who work within them. Organizations' capabilities reside in their processes and their values—and the very processes and values that constitute their core capabilities within the current business model also define their disabilities when confronted with disruption.

5. Technology supply may not equal market demand. The attributes that make disruptive technologies unattractive in established markets often are the very ones that constitute their greatest value in emerging markets.

How did the successful managers harness these principles to their advantage?

1. They embedded projects to develop and commercialize disruptive technologies within an organization whose customers needed them. When managers aligned a disruptive innovation with the "right" customers, customer demand increased the probability that the innovation would get the resources it needed.

2. They placed projects to develop disruptive technologies in organizations small enough to get excited about small opportunities and small wins.

3. They planned to fail early and *inexpensively* in the search for the market for a disruptive technology. They found that their markets generally coalesced through an iterative process of trial, learning, and trial again.

4. They utilized some of the *resources* of the mainstream organization to address the disruption, but they were careful *not* to leverage its processes and values. They created different ways of working within an organization whose values and cost structure were turned to the disruptive task at hand.

5. When commercializing disruptive technologies, they found or developed new *markets* that valued the attributes of the disruptive

products, rather than search for a technological breakthrough so that the disruptive product could compete as a sustaining technology in mainstream markets.

Chapters 5 through 9 in Part Two describe in more detail how managers can address and harness these four principles. Each chapter starts by examining how harnessing or ignoring these principles affected the fortunes of disk drive companies when disruptive technologies were emerging.[1] Each chapter then branches into an industry with very different characteristics, to show how the same principles drove the success and failure of firms confronted with disruptive technologies there.

The sum of these studies is that while disruptive technology can change the dynamics of industries with widely varying characteristics, the drivers of success or failure when confronted by such technology are consistent across industries.

Chapter 10 shows how these principles can be used by illustrating how managers might apply them in a case study of a particularly vexing technology—the electric vehicle. Chapter 11 then reviews the principal findings of the book.

NOTES

1. The notion that we exercise power most effectively when we understand the physical and psychological laws that define the way the world works and then position or align ourselves in harmony with those laws, is of course not new to this book. At a light-hearted level, Stanford Professor Robert Burgelman, whose work is extensively cited in ths book, once dropped his pen onto the floor in a lecture. He muttered as he stooped to pick it up, "I hate gravity." Then, as he walked to the blackboard to continue his line of thought, he added, "But do you know what? Gravity doesn't care! It will always pull things down, and I may as well plan on it."

At a more serious level, the desirability of aligning our actions with the amore powerful laws of nature, society, and psychology, in order to lead a productive life, is a central theme in many works, particularly the ancient Chinese classic, *Tao te Ching*.

CHAPTER FIVE

Give Responsibility for Disruptive Technologies to Organizations Whose Customers Need Them

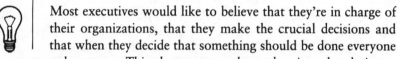 Most executives would like to believe that they're in charge of their organizations, that they make the crucial decisions and that when they decide that something should be done everyone snaps to and executes. This chapter expands on the view already introduced: that in practice, it is a company's *customers* who effectively control what it can and cannot do. As we have seen in the disk drive industry, companies were willing to bet enormous amounts on technologically risky projects when it was clear that their customers needed the resulting products. But they were unable to muster the wherewithal to execute much simpler disruptive projects if existing, profitable customers didn't need the products.

This observation supports a somewhat controversial theory called *resource dependence*, propounded by a minority of management scholars,[1] which posits that companies' freedom of action is limited to satisfying the needs of those entities outside the firm (customers and investors, primarily) that give it the resources it needs to survive. Drawing heavily upon concepts from biological evolution, resource dependence theorists assert that organizations will survive and prosper only if their staffs and systems serve the needs of customers and investors by providing them with the products, services, and profit they require. Organizations that do not will ultimately die off, starved of the revenues they need to survive.[2]

Hence, through this survival-of-the-fittest mechanism, those firms that rise to prominence in their industries generally will be those whose people and processes are most keenly tuned to giving their customers what they want. The controversy with this theory arises when its proponents conclude that managers are *powerless* to change the courses of their firms against the dictates of their customers. Even if a manager has a bold vision to take her or his company in a very different direction, the power of the customer-focused people and processes in any company well-adapted to survival in its competitive environment will reject the manager's attempts to change direction. Therefore, because they provide the resources upon which the firm is dependent, it is the customers, rather than the managers, who really determine what a firm will do. It is forces outside the organization, rather than the managers within it, that dictate the company's course. Resource dependence theorists conclude that the real role of managers in companies whose people and systems are well-adapted to survival is, therefore, only a symbolic one.

For those of us who have managed companies, consulted for management, or taught future managers, this is a most disquieting thought. We are there to manage, to make a difference, to formulate and implement strategy, to accelerate growth and improve profits. Resource dependence violates our very reason for being. Nonetheless, the findings reported in this book provide rather stunning support for the theory of resource dependence—especially for the notion that the customer-focused resource allocation and decision-making processes of successful companies are far more powerful in directing investments than are executives' decisions.

Clearly, customers wield enormous power in directing a firm's investments. What, then, should managers do when faced with a disruptive technology that the company's customers explicitly do not want? One option is to convince everyone in the firm that the company should pursue it anyway, that it has long-term strategic importance despite rejection by the customers who pay the bills and despite lower profitability than the upmarket alternatives. The other option would be to create an independent organization and embed it among emerging customers that *do* need the technology. Which works best?

Managers who choose the first option essentially are picking a fight with a powerful tendency of organizational nature—that customers, not managers, essentially control the investment patterns of a company. By contrast, managers who choose the second option align themselves with this tendency, harnessing rather than fighting its power. The cases presented in this chapter provide strong evidence that the second option offers far higher probabilities of success than the first.

INNOVATION AND RESOURCE ALLOCATION

The mechanism through which customers control the investments of a firm is the resource allocation process—the process that determines which initiatives get staff and money and which don't. Resource allocation and innovation are two sides of the same coin: Only those new product development projects that do get adequate funding, staffing, and management attention have a chance to succeed; those that are starved of resources will languish. Hence, the patterns of innovation in a company will mirror quite closely the patterns in which resources are allocated.

Good resource allocation processes are designed to weed out proposals that customers don't want. When these decision-making processes work well, if customers don't want a product, it won't get funded; if they do want it, it will. This is how things *must* work in great companies. They *must* invest in things customers want—and the better they become at doing this, the more successful they will be.

As we saw in chapter 4, resource allocation is not simply a matter of top-down decision making followed by implementation. Typically, senior managers are asked to decide whether to fund a project only after many others at lower levels in the organization have already decided which types of project proposals they want to package and send on to senior management for approval and which they don't think are worth the effort. Senior managers typically see only a well-screened subset of the innovative ideas generated.[3]

And even after senior management has endorsed funding for a particular project, it is rarely a "done deal." Many crucial resource allocation decisions are made after project approval—indeed, after product launch—by mid-level managers who set priorities when multiple projects and products compete for the time of the same people, equipment, and vendors. As management scholar Chester Barnard has noted:

> From the point of view of the relative importance of specific decisions, those of executives properly call for first attention. But from the point of view of aggregate importance, it is not decisions of executives, but of *non-executive participants* in organizations which should enlist major interest. [Italics added.][4]

So how do non-executive participants make *their* resource allocation decisions? They decide which projects they will propose to senior management and which they will give priority to, based upon their understanding of what types of customers and products are most profitable to the company. Tightly coupled with this is their view of how their sponsorship of different proposals will affect their own career trajectories within the company, a view that is formed heavily by their understanding of what customers want and what types of products the company needs to sell more of in order to be more profitable. Individuals' career trajectories can soar when they sponsor highly profitable innovation programs. It is through these mechanisms of seeking corporate profit and personal success, therefore, that customers exert a profound influence on the process of resource allocation, and hence on the patterns of innovation, in most companies.

SUCCESS IN DISRUPTIVE DISK DRIVE TECHNOLOGY

It is possible to break out of this system of customer control, however. Three cases in the history of the disk drive industry demonstrate how managers can develop strong market positions in a disruptive technology. In two cases, managers harnessed, rather than fought, the forces of resource dependence: They spun out independent companies to commercialize the disruptive technology. In the third, the manager chose to fight these forces, and survived the project, exhausted.

Quantum and Plus Development

As we have seen, Quantum Corporation, a leading maker of 8-inch drives sold in the minicomputer market in the early 1980s, completely missed the advent of 5.25-inch drives: It introduced its first versions nearly four years after those drives first appeared in the market. As the 5.25-inch pioneers began to invade the minicomputer market from below, for all the reasons already described, Quantum's sales began to sag.

In 1984 several Quantum employees saw a potential market for a thin 3.5-inch drive plugged into an expansion slot in IBM XT- and AT-class desktop computers—drives that would be sold to personal computer users rather than the OEM minicomputer manufacturers that had accounted for all of Quantum's revenue. They determined to leave Quantum and start a new firm to commercialize their idea.

Rather than let them leave unencumbered, however, Quantum's executives financed and retained 80 percent ownership of this spinoff venture, called Plus Development Corporation, and set the company up in different facilities. It was a completely self-sufficient organization, with its own executive staff and all of the functional capabilities required in an independent company. Plus was extremely successful. It designed and marketed its drives but had them manufactured under contract by Matsushita Kotobuki Electronics (MKE) in Japan.

As sales of Quantum's line of 8-inch drives began to evaporate in the mid-1980s, they were offset by Plus's growing "Hardcard" revenues. By 1987, sales of Quantum's 8- and 5.25-inch products had largely disappeared. Quantum then purchased the remaining 20 percent of Plus, essentially closed down the old corporation, and installed Plus's executives in Quantum's most senior positions. They then reconfigured Plus's 3.5-inch products to appeal to OEM desktop computer makers, such as Apple, just as the capacity vector for 3.5-inch drives was invading the desktop market, as shown in the disk drive trajectory map in Figure 1.7. Quantum, thus reconstituted as a 3.5-inch drive maker, has aggressively adopted sustaining component technology innovations, moving upmarket toward engineering workstations, and has also successfully negotiated the sustaining architectural innovation into 2.5-inch drives. By 1994 the new Quantum had become the largest unit-volume producer of disk drives in the world.[5]

Control Data in Oklahoma

Control Data Corporation (CDC) effected the same self-reconstitution—once. CDC was the dominant manufacturer of 14-inch drives sold into the OEM market between 1965 and 1982; its market share fluctuated between 55 and 62 percent. When the 8-inch architecture emerged in the late 1970s, however, CDC missed it—by three years. The company never captured more than a fraction of the 8-inch market, and those 8-inch drives that it did sell were sold almost exclusively to defend its established customer base of mainframe computer manufacturers. The reason was resources and managerial emphasis: Engineers and marketers at the company's principal Minneapolis facility kept getting pulled off the 8-inch program to resolve problems in the launch of next-generation 14-inch products for CDC's mainstream customers.

CDC launched its first 5.25-inch model two years after Seagate's pioneering product appeared in 1980. This time, however, CDC located its 5.25-inch effort in Oklahoma City. This was done, according to one manager, "not to escape CDC's Minneapolis engineering culture, but to isolate the [5.25-inch product] group from the company's mainstream customers." Although it was late in the market and never regained its former dominant position, CDC's foray into 5.25-inch drives was profitable, and at times the firm commanded a 20 percent share of higher-capacity 5.25-inch drives.

Micropolis: Transition by Managerial Force

Micropolis Corporation, an early disk drive leader founded in 1978 to make 8-inch drives, was the only other industry player to successfully make the transition to a disruptive platform. It did not use the spin-out strategy that had worked for Quantum and Control Data, however, choosing instead to manage the change from within the mainstream company. But even this exception supports the rule that customers exert exceptionally powerful influence over the investments that firms can undertake successfully.

Micropolis began to change in 1982, when founder and CEO Stuart Mabon intuitively perceived the trajectories of market demand and technology supply mapped in Figure 1.7 and decided that the firm should become primarily a maker of 5.25-inch drives. While initially hoping to keep adequate resources focused on developing its next generation of 8-inch drives so that Micropolis could straddle both markets,[6] he assigned the company's premier engineers to the 5.25-inch program. Mabon recalls that it took "100 percent of my time and energy for eighteen months" to keep adequate resources focused on the 5.25-inch program, because the organization's own mechanisms allocated resources to where the customers were—8-inch drives.

By 1984, Micropolis had failed to keep pace with competition in the minicomputer market for disk drives and withdrew its remaining 8-inch models. With Herculean effort, however, it did succeed in its 5.25-inch programs. Figure 5.1 shows why this struggle occurred: In making the transition, Micropolis assumed a position on a very different technological trajectory. It had to walk away from every one of its major customers and replace the lost revenues with sales of the new product line to an entirely different group of desktop computer makers. Mabon remembers the experience as the most exhausting of his life.

Figure 5.1   Technology Transition and Market Position at Micropolis Corporation

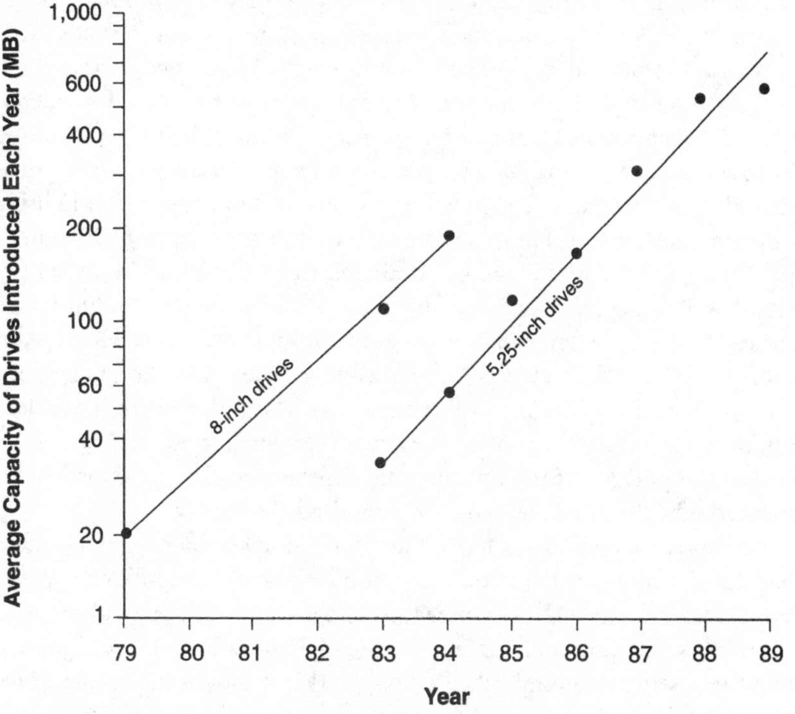

Source: Data are from various issues of *Disk/Trend Report.*

Micropolis finally introduced a 3.5-inch product in 1993. That was the point at which the product had progressed to pack more than 1 gigabyte in the 3.5-inch platform. At that level, Micropolis could sell the 3.5-inch drive to its existing customers.

DISRUPTIVE TECHNOLOGIES AND THE THEORY OF RESOURCE DEPENDENCE

The struggles recounted earlier of Seagate Technology's attempts to sell 3.5-inch drives and of Bucyrus Erie's failed attempt to sell its early Hydrohoe only to its mainstream customers illustrate how the theory of resource dependence can be applied to cases of disruptive technologies. In both instances, Seagate and Bucyrus were among the first in their industries to develop these disruptive products. But despite senior managers' decisions to introduce them, the impetus or organizational energy required to launch the products aggressively into the appropriate value networks simply did not coalesce—until customers needed them.

Should we then accept the corollary stipulated by resource-dependence theorists that managers are merely powerless individuals? Hardly. In the Introduction, exploring the image of how people learned to fly, I noted that all attempts had ended in failure as long as they consisted of fighting fundamental laws of nature. But once laws such as gravity, Bernoulli's principle, and the notions of lift, drag and resistance began to be understood, and flying machines were designed that accounted for or harnessed those laws, people flew quite successfully. By analogy, this is what Quantum and Control Data did. By embedding independent organizations within an entirely different value network, where they were dependent upon the appropriate set of customers for survival, those managers harnessed the powerful forces of resource dependence. The CEO of Micropolis fought them, but he won a rare and costly victory.

Disruptive technologies have had deadly impact in many industries besides disk drives, mechanical excavators, and steel.[7] The following pages summarize the effect of disruptive technologies in three other industries—computers, retailing, and printers—to highlight how the only companies in those industries that established strong market positions in the disruptive technologies were those which, like Quantum and Control Data, harnessed rather than fought the forces of resource dependence.

DEC, IBM, AND THE PERSONAL COMPUTER

Quite naturally, the computer industry and the disk drive industry have parallel histories, because value networks of the latter are embedded in those of the former. In fact, if the axes and intersecting trajectories depicted on the disk drive trajectory map in Figure 1.7 were relabeled with computer-relevant terms, it would summarize equally well the failure of leading computer industry firms. IBM, the industry's first leader, sold its mainframe computers to the central accounting and data processing departments of large organizations. The emergence of the minicomputer represented a disruptive technology to IBM and its competitors. Their customers had no use for it; it promised lower, not higher, margins; and the market initially was significantly smaller. As a result, the makers of mainframes ignored the minicomputer for years, allowing a set of entrants—Digital Equipment, Data General, Prime, Wang, and Nixdorf—to create and dominate that market. IBM ultimately introduced its own line of minicomputers, but it did so primarily as a defensive measure, when the capabilities of minicomputers had advanced to the point that they were performance-competitive with the computing needs of some of IBM's customers.

Similarly, none of the makers of minicomputers became a significant factor in the desktop personal computer market, because to them the desktop computer was a disruptive technology. The PC market was created by another set of entrants, including Apple, Commodore, Tandy, and IBM. The minicomputer makers were exceptionally prosperous and highly regarded by investors, the business press, and students of good management—until the late 1980s, when the technological trajectory of the desktop computer intersected with the performance demanded by those who had previously bought minicomputers. The missile-like attack of the desktop computer from below severely wounded every minicomputer maker. Several of them failed. None established a viable position in the desktop personal computer value network.

A similar sequence of events characterized the emergence of the portable computer, where the market was created and dominated by a set of entrants like Toshiba, Sharp, and Zenith. Apple and IBM, the leading desktop makers, did not introduce portable models until the portables' performance trajectory intersected with the computing needs of their customers.

Probably none of these firms has been so deeply wounded by disruptive technology as Digital Equipment. DEC fell from fortune to folly in just a few years, as stand-alone workstations and networked desktop computers obviated most customers' needs for minicomputers almost overnight.

DEC didn't stumble for lack of trying, of course. Four times between 1983 and 1995 it introduced lines of personal computers targeted at consumers, products that were technologically much simpler than DEC's minicomputers. But four times it failed to build businesses in this value network that were perceived within the company as profitable. Four times it withdrew from the personal computer market. Why? DEC launched all four forays from within the mainstream company.[8] For all of the reasons so far recounted, even though executive-level decisions lay behind the move into the PC business, those who made the day-to-day resource allocation decisions in the company never saw the sense in investing the necessary money, time, and energy in low-margin products that their customers didn't want. Higher-performance initiatives that promised up-scale margins, such as DEC's super-fast Alpha microprocessor and its adventure into mainframe computers, captured the resources instead.

In trying to enter the desktop personal computing business from within its mainstream organization, DEC was forced to straddle the two different cost structures intrinsic to two different value networks. It simply couldn't hack away enough overhead cost to be competitive in low-end personal computers because it needed those costs to remain competitive in its higher-performance products.

Yet IBM's success in the first five years of the personal computing industry stands in stark contrast to the failure of the other leading mainframe and minicomputer makers to catch the disruptive desktop computing wave. How did IBM do it? It created an autonomous organization in Florida, far away from its New York state headquarters, that was free to procure components from any source, to sell through its own channels, and to forge a cost structure appropriate to the technological and competitive requirements of the personal computing market. The organization was free to succeed along metrics of success that were relevant to the personal computing market. In fact, some have argued that IBM's subsequent decision to link its personal computer division much more closely to its mainstream organization was an important factor in IBM's difficulties in maintaining its profitability and market share in the personal computer industry. It seems to be very difficult to manage the peaceful, unambiguous coexistence of two cost structures, and two models for how to make money, within a single company.

The conclusion that a single organization might simply be incapable of competently pursuing disruptive technology, while remaining competitive in mainstream markets, bothers some "can-do" managers—and, in fact, most managers try to do exactly what Micropolis and DEC did: maintain their competitive intensity in the mainstream, while simultaneously trying to pursue disruptive technology. The evidence is strong that such efforts rarely succeed; position in one market will suffer unless two separate organizations, embedded within the appropriate value networks, pursue their separate customers.

KRESGE, WOOLWORTH, AND DISCOUNT RETAILING

In few industries has the impact of disruptive technology been felt so pervasively as in retailing, where discounters seized dominance from traditional department and variety stores. The technology of discount retailing was disruptive to traditional operations because the quality of service and selection offered by discounters played havoc with the accustomed metrics of quality retailing. Moreover, the cost structure required to compete profitably in discount retailing was fundamentally different than that which department stores had developed to compete within their value networks.

The first discount store was Korvette's, which began operating a number of outlets in New York in the mid-1950s. Korvette's and its imitators operated at the very low end of retailing's product line, selling nationally known brands of standard hard goods at 20 to 40 percent below department store prices. They focused on products that "sold themselves" because customers already knew how to use them. Relying on national brand image to establish the value and quality of their products, these discounters eliminated the need for knowledgeable salespeople; they also focused on the group of customers least attractive to mainstream retailers: "young wives of blue collar workers with young children."[9] This was counter to the upscale formulas department stores historically had used to define quality retailing and to improve profits.

Discounters didn't accept lower profits than those of traditional retailers, however; they just earned their profits through a different formula. In the simplest terms, retailers cover their costs through the gross margin, or markup, they charge over the cost of the merchandise they sell. Traditional department stores historically marked merchandise up by 40 percent and turned their inventory over four times in a year—that is, they earned 40 percent on the amount they invested in inventory, four times during the year, for a total return on inventory investment of 160 percent. Variety stores earned somewhat lower profits through a formula similar to that used by the department stores. Discount retailers earned a return on inventory investment similar to that of department stores, but through a different model: low gross margins and high inventory turns. Table 5.1 summarizes the three positions.

The history of discount retailing vividly recalls the history of minimill steel making. Just like the minimills, discounters took advantage of their cost structure to move upmarket and seize share from competing traditional retailers at a stunning rate: first at the low end, in brand-name hard goods such as hardware, small appliances, and luggage, and later in territory further to the northeast such as home furnishings and clothing. Figure 5.2 illustrates how stunning the discounters' invasion was: Their

Table 5.1 Different Pathways to Profits

Retailer Type	Company Example	Typical Gross Margins	Typical Inventory Turns	Return on Inventory Investment*
Department stores	R. H. Macy	40%	4x	160%
Variety stores	F. W. Woolworth	36%	4x	144%
Discount retailers	Kmart	20%	8x	160%

*Calculated as Margins x Turns, in other words, the total of the margins earned through successive turnovers each year.
Source: Annual corporate reports of many companies in each category for various years.

Figure 5.2 Gains in Discount Retailers' Market Share, 1960–1966

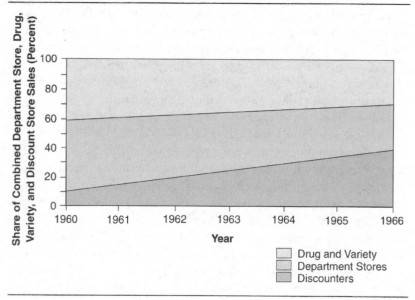

Source: Data are from various issues of *Discount Merchandiser*.

share of retailing revenues in the categories of goods they sold rose from 10 percent in 1960 to nearly 40 percent a scant six years later.

Just as in disk drives and excavators, a few of the leading traditional retailers—notably S. S. Kresge, F. W. Woolworth, and Dayton Hudson—saw the disruptive approach coming and invested early. None of the other major retail chains, including Sears, Montgomery Ward, J. C. Penney, and R. H. Macy, made a significant attempt to create a business in discount retailing. Kresge (with its Kmart chain) and Dayton Hudson (with the Target chain) succeeded.[10] They both created focused discount retailing organizations that were independent from their traditional business. They recognized and harnessed the forces of resource dependence. By contrast, Woolworth failed in its venture (Woolco), trying to launch it from within the F. W. Woolworth variety store company. A detailed comparison of the approaches of Kresge and Woolworth, which started from very similar positions, lends additional insight into why establishing independent organizations to pursue disruptive technology seems to be a necessary condition for success.

S. S. Kresge, then the world's second largest variety store chain, began studying discount retailing in 1957, while discounting was still in its infancy. By 1961, both Kresge and its rival F. W. Woolworth (the world's largest variety store operator) had announced initiatives to enter discount retailing. Both firms opened stores in 1962, within three months of each other. The performance of the Woolco and Kmart ventures they launched, however, subsequently differed dramatically. A decade later, Kmart's sales approached $3.5 billion while Woolco's sales were languishing unprofitably at $0.9 billion.[11]

In making its commitment to discount retailing, Kresge decided to exit the variety store business entirely: In 1959 it hired a new CEO, Harry Cunningham, whose sole mission was to convert Kresge into a discounting powerhouse. Cunningham, in turn, brought in an entirely new management team, so that by 1961 there "was not a single operating vice president, regional manager, assistant regional manager, or regional merchandise manager who was not new on the job."[12] In 1961 Cunningham stopped opening any new variety stores, embarking instead on a program of closing about 10 percent of Kresge's existing variety operations each year. This represented a wholesale refocusing of the company on discount retailing.

Woolworth, on the other hand, attempted to support a program of sustaining improvements in technology, capacity, and facilities in its core variety store businesses while simultaneously investing in disruptive discounting. The managers charged with improving the performance of Woolworth's variety stores were also charged with building "the largest chain of discount houses in America." CEO Robert Kirkwood asserted that Woolco "would not conflict with the company's plans for growth and expansion in the regular variety store operations," and that no existing stores would be converted to a discount format.[13] Indeed, as discount retailing hit its most frenzied expansion phase in the 1960s, Woolworth was opening new variety stores at the pace it had set in the 1950s.

Unfortunately (but predictably), Woolworth proved unable to sustain within a single organization the two different cultures, and two different models of how to make a profit, that were required to be successful in variety and discount retailing. By 1967 it had dropped the term "discount" from all Woolco advertising, adopting the term "promotional department store" instead. Although initially Woolworth had set up a separate administrative staff for its Woolco operation, by 1971 more rational, cost-conscious heads had prevailed.

> In a move designed to increase sales per square foot in both Woolco and Woolworth divisions, the two subsidiaries have been consolidated operationally on a regional basis. Company officials say the consolidation—which involves buying offices, distribution facilities and management personnel at the regional level—will help both to develop better merchandise and more efficient stores. Woolco will gain the benefits of Woolworth's buying resources, distribution facilities and additional expertise in developing specialty departments. In return, Woolworth will gain Woolco's knowhow in locating, designing, promoting and operating large stores over 100,000 sq. ft.[14]

What was the impact of this cost-saving consolidation? It provided more evidence that two models for how to make money cannot peacefully coexist within a single organization. Within a year of this consolidation, Woolco had increased its markups such that its gross margins were the highest in the discount industry—about 33 percent. In the process, its inventory turns fell from the 7x it originally had achieved to 4x. The formula for profit that had long sustained F. W. Woolworth (35 percent margins for four inventory turns or 140 percent return on inventory investment) was ultimately demanded of Woolco as well. (See Figure 5.3.) Woolco was no longer a discounter—in name or in fact. Not surprisingly, Woolworth's venture into discount retailing failed: It closed its last Woolco store in 1982.

Woolworth's organizational strategy for succeeding in disruptive discount retailing was the same as Digital Equipment's strategy for launching its personal computer business. Both founded new ventures within the mainstream organization that had to earn money by mainstream rules,

Figure 5.3   Impact of the Integration of Woolco, and F. W. Woolworth on the Way
Woolco Attempted to Make Money

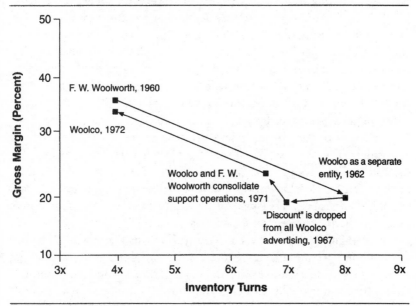

Source: Data are from various annual reports of F. W. Woolworth Company and from various issues
of *Discount Merchandiser*.

and neither could achieve the cost structure and profit model required to succeed in the mainstream value network.

SURVIVAL BY SUICIDE: HEWLETT-PACKARD'S LASER JET AND INK-JET PRINTERS

Hewlett-Packard's experience in the personal computer printer business illustrates how a company's pursuit of a disruptive technology by spinning out an independent organization might entail, in the end, killing another of its business units.

Hewlett-Packard's storied success in manufacturing printers for personal computers becomes even more remarkable when one considers its management of the emergence of bubble-jet or ink-jet technology. Beginning in the mid-1980s, HP began building a huge and successful business around laser jet printing technology. The laser jet was a discontinuous improvement over dot-matrix printing, the previously dominant personal computer printing technology, and HP built a commanding market lead.

When an alternative way of translating digital signals into images on paper (ink-jet technology) first appeared, there were vigorous debates about whether laser jet or ink jet would emerge as the dominant design in personal printing. Experts lined up on both sides of the question, offering HP extensive advice on which technology would ultimately become the printer of choice on the world's desktops.[15]

Although it was never framed as such in the debates of the time, ink-jet printing was a disruptive technology. It was slower than the laser jet, its resolution was worse, and its cost per printed page was higher. But the printer itself was smaller and potentially much less expensive than the laser jet. At these lower prices, it promised lower gross margin dollars per unit than the laser jet. Thus, the ink-jet printer was a classic disruptive product, relative to the laser jet business.

Rather than place its bet exclusively with one or the other, and rather than attempt to commercialize the disruptive ink-jet from within the existing printer division in Boise, Idaho, HP created a completely autonomous organizational unit, located in Vancouver, Washington, with responsibility for making the ink-jet printer a success. It then let the two businesses compete against each other. Each has behaved classically. As shown in Figure 5.4, the laser jet division has moved sharply upmarket, in a strategy reminiscent of 14-inch drives, mainframe computers, and integrated steel mills. HP's laser jet printers can print at high speeds with exceptional resolution; handle hundreds of fonts and complicated graphics; print on two sides of the page; and serve multiple users on a network. They have also gotten larger physically.

The ink-jet printer isn't as good as the laser jet and may never be. But the critical question is whether the ink jet could ever be as good a printer as the personal desktop computing *market* demands. The answer appears to be yes. The resolution and speed of ink-jet printers, while still inferior to those of laser jets, are now clearly good enough for many students, professionals, and other un-networked users of desktop computers.

HP's ink-jet printer business is now capturing many of those who would formerly have been laser jet users. Ultimately, the number of users at the highest-performance end of the market, toward which the laser jet division is headed, will probably become small. One of HP's businesses may, in the end, have killed another. But had HP not set up its ink-jet business as a separate organization, the ink-jet technology would probably have

Figure 5.4   Speed Improvement in InkJet and LaserJet Printers

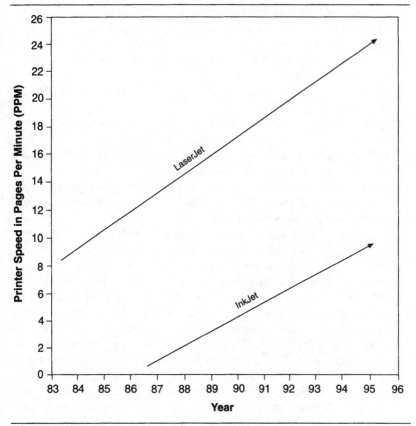

Source: Hewlett-Packard product brochures, various years.

languished within the mainstream laser jet business, leaving one of the other companies now actively competing in the ink-jet printer business, such as Canon, as a serious threat to HP's printer business. And by staying in the laser business, as well, HP has joined IBM's mainframe business and the integrated steel companies in making a *lot* of money while executing an upmarket retreat.[16]

NOTES

1. The theory of resource dependence has been most thoroughly argued by Jeffrey Pfeffer and Gerald R. Salancik in *The External Control of Organizations: A Resource Dependence Perspective* (New York: Harper & Row, 1978).

2. This implies that, in managing business under both normal conditions and conditions of assault by a disruptive technology, the choice of which customers the firm will serve has enormous strategic consequences.

3. Joseph L. Bower, in *Managing the Resource Allocation Process* (Homewood, IL: Richard D. Irwin, 1972), presents an elegant and compelling picture of the resource allocation process.

4. Chester Barnard, *The Functions of the Executive* (Cambridge, MA: Harvard University Press, 1938), 190–191.

5. Quantum's spin-out of the Hardcard effort and its subsequent strategic reorientation is an example of the processes of strategy change described by Robert Burgelman, in "Intraorganizational Ecology of Strategy-Making and Organizational Adaptation: Theory and Field Research," *Organization Science* (2), 1991, 239–262, as essentially a process of natural selection through which suboptimal strategic initiatives lose out to optimal ones in the internal competition for corporate resources.

6. The failure of Micropolis to maintain simultaneous competitive commitments to both its established technology and the new 5.25-inch technology is consistent with the technological histories recounted by James Utterback, in *Mastering the Dynamics of Innovation* (Boston: Harvard Business School Press, 1994). Utterback found that firms that attempted to develop radically new technology almost always tried to maintain simultaneous commitment to the old and that they almost always failed.

7. A set of industries in which disruptive technologies are believed to have played a role in toppling leading firms is presented by Richard S. Rosenbloom and Clayton M. Christensen in "Technological Discontinuities, Organizational Capabilities, and Strategic Commitments," *Industrial and Corporate Change* (3), 1994, 655–685.

8. In the 1990s, DEC finally set up a Personal Computer Division in its attempt to build a significant personal computer business. It was not as autonomous from DEC's mainstream business; however, the Quantum and Control Data spin-outs were. Although DEC set up specific performance metrics for the PC division, it was still held, *de facto*, to corporate standards for gross margins and revenue growth.

9. "Harvard Study on Discount Shoppers," *Discount Merchandiser*, September, 1963, 71.

10. When this book was being written, Kmart was a crippled company, having been beaten in a game of strategy and operational excellence by WalMart. Nonetheless, during the preceding two decades, Kmart had been a highly successful retailer, creating extraordinary value for Kresge shareholders. Kmart's present competitive struggles are unrelated to Kresge's strategy in meeting the original disruptive threat of discounting.

11. A detailed contrast between the Woolworth and Kresge approaches to dis-

count retailing can be found in the Harvard Business School teaching case. "The Discount Retailing Revolution in America," No. 695-081.

12. See Robert Drew-Bear, "S. S. Kresge's Kmarts," *Mass Merchandising: Revolution and Evolution* (New York: Fairchild Publications, 1970), 218.

13. F. W. Woolworth Company Annual Report, 1981, p. 8.

14. "Woolco Gets Lion's Share of New Space," *Chain Store Age,* November, 1972, E27. This was an extraordinarily elegant, rational argument for the consolidation, clearly crafted by a corporate spin-doctor extraordinaire. Never mind that no Woolworth stores approached 100,000 square feet in size!

15. See, for example, "The Desktop Printer Industry in 1990," Harvard Business School, Case No. 9-390-173.

16. Business historian Richard Tedlow noted that the same dilemma had confronted A&P's executives as they deliberated whether to adopt the disruptive supermarket retailing format:

> The supermarket entrepreneurs competed against A&P not by doing better what A&P was the best company in the world at doing, but by doing something that A&P did not want to do at all. The greatest entrepreneurial failure in this story is Kroger. This company was second in the market, and one of its own employees (who left to found the world's first supermarket) knew how to make it first. Kroger executives did not listen. Perhaps it was lack of imagination or perhaps, like the executives at A&P, those at Kroger also had too much invested in the standard way of doing business. If the executives at A&P endorsed the supermarket revolution, they were ruining their own distribution system. That is why they sat by paralyzed, unable to act until it was almost too late. In the end, A&P had little choice. The company could ruin its own system, or see others do it.

See Richard Tedlow, *New and Improved: The Story of Mass Marketing in America* (Boston: Harvard Business School Press, 1996).

CHAPTER SIX

Match the Size of the Organization to the Size of the Market

Managers who confront disruptive technological change must be leaders, not followers, in commercializing disruptive technologies. Doing so requires implanting the projects that are to develop such technologies in commercial organizations that match in size the market they are to address. These assertions are based on two key findings of this study: that leadership is more crucial in coping with disruptive technologies than with sustaining ones, and that small, emerging markets cannot solve the near-term growth and profit requirements of large companies.

The evidence from the disk drive industry shows that creating new markets is significantly *less* risky and *more* rewarding than entering established markets against entrenched competition. But as companies become larger and more successful, it becomes even more difficult to enter emerging markets early enough. Because growing companies need to add increasingly large chunks of new revenue each year just to maintain their desired rate of growth, it becomes less and less possible that small markets can be viable as vehicles through which to find these chunks of revenue. As we shall see, the most straightforward way of confronting this difficulty is to implant projects aimed at commercializing disruptive technologies in organizations small enough to get excited about small-market opportunities, and to do so on a regular basis even while the mainstream company is growing.

ARE THE PIONEERS *REALLY* THE ONES WITH ARROWS IN THEIR BACKS?

A crucial strategic decision in the management of innovation is whether it is important to be a leader or acceptable to be a follower. Volumes have been written on first-mover advantages, and an offsetting amount on the wisdom of waiting until the innovation's major risks have been resolved by the pioneering firms. "You can always tell who the pioneers were," an old management adage goes. "They're the ones with the arrows in their backs." As with most disagreements in management theory, neither position is always right. Indeed, some findings from the study of the disk drive industry give some insight into when leadership is critical and when followership makes better sense.

Leadership in Sustaining Technologies May Not Be Essential

One of the watershed technologies affecting the pace at which disk drive makers have increased the recording density of their drives was the thin-film read/write head. We saw in chapter 1 that despite the radically different, competence-destroying character of the technology, the $100 million and five-to-fifteen year expense of developing it, the firms that led in this technology were the leading, established disk drive manufacturers.

Because of the risk involved in the technology's development and its potential importance to the industry, the trade press began speculating in the late 1970s about which competitor would lead with thin-film heads. How far might conventional ferrite head technology be pushed? Would any drive makers get squeezed out of the industry race because they placed a late or wrong bet on the new head technology? Yet, it turned out, whether a firm led or followed in this innovation did *not* make a substantial difference in its competitive position. This is illustrated in Figures 6.1 and 6.2.

Figure 6.1 shows when each of the leading firms introduced its first model employing thin-film head technology. The vertical axis measures the recording density of the drive. The bottom end of the line for each firm denotes the maximum recording density it had achieved before it introduced a model with a thin-film head. The top end of each line indicates the density of the first model each company introduced with a thin-film head. Notice the wide disparity in the points at which the firms felt it was important to introduce the new technology. IBM led the industry,

Figure 6.1   Points at Which Thin-Film Technology Was Adopted by Leading
Manufacturers, Relative to the Capabilities of Ferrite/Oxide Technology
at the Time of the Switch

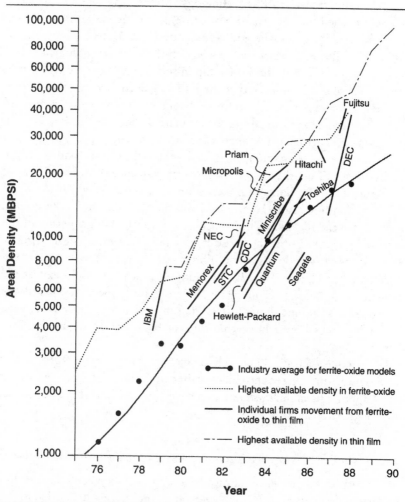

introducing its new head when it had achieved 3 megabits (Mb) per square inch. Memorex and Storage Technology similarly took a leadership posture with respect to this technology. At the other end, Fujitsu and Hitachi pushed the performance of conventional ferrite heads nearly ten times beyond the point where IBM first introduced the technology, choosing to be followers, rather than leaders, in thin-film technology.

What benefit, if any, did leadership in this technology give to the pioneers? There is no evidence that the leaders gained any significant competitive advantage over the followers; none of the firms that pioneered thin-film technology gained significant market share on that account. In addition, pioneering firms appear not to have developed any sort of learning advantage enabling them to leverage their early lead to attain higher levels of density than did followers. Evidence of this is displayed in Figure 6.2. The horizontal axis shows the order in which the firms adopted thin-film heads. Hence, IBM was the first, Memorex, the second, and Fujitsu the fifteenth. The vertical axis gives the rank ordering of the recording density of the most advanced model marketed by each firm in 1989. If the early adopters of thin-film heads enjoyed some sort of experience-based advantage over the late adopters, then we would expect the points in the chart to slope generally from the upper left toward the lower right. The chart shows instead that there is no relationship between leadership and followership in thin-film heads and any subsequent technological edge.[1]

Each of the other sustaining technologies in the industry's history present a similar picture. There is no evidence that any of the leaders in developing and adopting sustaining technologies developed a discernible competitive advantage over the followers.[2]

Leadership in Disruptive Technologies Creates Enormous Value

In contrast to the evidence that leadership in sustaining technologies has historically conferred little advantage on the pioneering disk drive firms, there is strong evidence that leadership in disruptive technology has been *very* important. The companies that entered the new value networks enabled by disruptive generations of disk drives within the first two years after those drives appeared were six times more likely to succeed than those that entered later.

Eighty-three companies entered the U.S. disk drive industry between 1976 and 1993. Thirty-five of these were diversified concerns, such as

Figure 6.2 Relationship between Order of Adoption of Thin-Film Technology and Areal Density of Highest-Performance 1989 Model

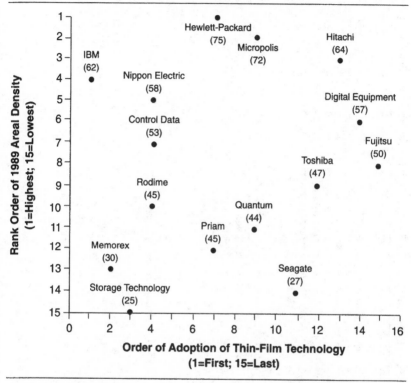

Source: Clayton M. Christensen, "Exploring the Limits of the Technology S-Curve. Part I: Component Technologies," *Production and Operations Management* 1, no. 4 (Fall 1992): 347. Reprinted by permission.

Memorex, Ampex, 3M, and Xerox, that made other computer peripheral equipment or other magnetic recording products. Forty-eight were independent startup companies, many being financed by venture capital and headed by people who previously had worked for other firms in the industry. These numbers represent the complete census of all firms that ever were incorporated and/or were known to have announced the design of a hard drive, whether or not they actually sold any. It is not a statistical sample of firms that might be biased in favor or against any type of firm.

The entry strategies employed by each of these firms can be characterized along the two axes in Table 6.1. The vertical axis describes *technology* strategies, with firms at the bottom using only proven technologies in their

Table 6.1 Disk Drive Companies Achieving $100 Million in Annual Revenues in at Least One Year Between 1976 and 1994

Technology Strategy at Entry

New Technology — Established Market

Type of Firm	S	F	N	T	% Success	Sales ($millions)
Start-ups	0	7	3	10	0%	$235.3
Related-Technology	0	1	0	1	0%	0.0
Related-Market	0	3	0	3	0%	1.4
Forward Integrators	0	1	0	1	0%	0.0
Total	0	12	3	15	0%	$236.7

New Technology — Emerging Market

Type of Firm	S	F	N	T	% Success	Sales ($millions)
Start-ups	3	4	1	8	37%	$16,379.3
Related-Technology	0	0	0	0	—	—
Related Market	0	0	0	0	—	—
Forward Integrators	0	0	0	0	—	—
Total	3	4	1	8	37%	$16,379.3

Proven Technology — Established Market

Type of Firm	S	F	N	T	% Success	Sales ($millions)
Start-ups	3	11	4	18	17%	$2,485.7
Related-Technology	0	4	0	4	0%	191.6
Related-Market	0	12	0	12	0%	361.2
Forward Integrators	0	3	0	3	0%	17.7
Total	3	30	4	37	8%	$3,056.2

Proven Technology — Emerging Market

Type of Firm	S	F	N	T	% Success	Sales ($millions)
Start-ups	4	7	2	13	31%	$32,043.7
Related-Technology	4	2	0	6	67%	11,461.0
Related-Market	1	4	0	5	20%	2,239.0
Forward Integrators	0	0	0	0	—	—
Total	9	13	2	24	36%	$45,743.7

Market Strategy at Entry — Established Market

	S	F	N	T	% Success	Sales ($millions)
Start-ups	3	18	7	28	11%	$2,721.0
Related-Technology	0	5	0	5	0%	191.6
Related-Market	0	15	0	15	0%	362.6
Forward Integrators	0	4	0	4	0%	17.7
Total	3	42	7	52	6%	$3,292.9

Statistics for all companies, regardless of technology strategy — Emerging Market

	S	F	N	T	% Success	Sales ($millions)
Start-ups	7	11	3	21	33%	$48,423.0
Related-Technology	4	2	0	6	67%	11,461.0
Related-Market	1	4	0	5	20%	2,239.0
Forward Integrators	0	0	0	0	—	—
Total	12	17	3	32	37%	$62,123.0

Source: Data are from various issues of *Disk/Trend Report.*

Note: S indicates success, F indicates failure, N indicates no, T indicates total.

initial products and those at the top using one or more new component technologies.[3] The horizontal axis charts *market* strategies, with firms at the left having entered already established value networks and those at the right having entered emerging value networks.[4] Another way to characterize this matrix is to note that companies that were agressive at entry in developing and adopting sustaining innovations appear in the two top boxes, left and right, while companies that led at entry in creating new value networks appear in the two right-hand boxes, top and bottom. The companies in the right boxes include *all* companies that attempted to create new value networks, even those networks that did not materialize into substantial markets (such as removable hard drives).

Each quadrant displays the number of companies that entered using the strategy represented. Under the *S* (for "success") are the number of firms that successfully generated $100 million in revenues in at least one year, even if the firm subsequently failed; *F* (for "failure") shows the number of firms that failed ever to reach the $100 million revenue threshold and that have subsequently exited the industry; *N* (for "no") indicates the number of firms for which there is as yet no verdict because, while still operating in 1994, they had not yet reached $100 million in sales; and *T* (for "total") lists the total number of firms that entered in each category.[5] The column labeled "% Success" indicates the percentage of the total number of firms that reached $100 million in sales. Finally, beneath the matrix are the sums of the data in the two quadrants above.

The numbers beneath the matrix show that only three of the fifty-one firms (6 percent) that entered established markets ever reached the $100 million revenue benchmark. In contrast, 37 percent of the firms that led in disruptive technological innovation—those entering markets that were less than two years old—surpassed the $100 million level, as shown on the right side of Table 6.1. Whether a firm was a start-up or a diversified firm had little impact on its success rate. What mattered appears not to have been its organizational form, but whether it was a leader in introducing disruptive products and creating the markets in which they were sold.[6]

Only 13 percent of the firms that entered attempting to lead in sustaining component technologies (the top half of the matrix) succeeded, while 20 percent of the firms that followed were successful. Clearly, the lower-right quadrant offered the most fertile ground for success.

The cumulative sales numbers in the right-most columns in each quadrant show the total, cumulative revenues logged by all firms pursuing each of the strategies; these are summarized below the matrix. The result is quite stunning. The firms that led in launching disruptive products together logged a cumulative total of $62 billion dollars in revenues between 1976 and 1994.[7] Those that followed into the markets later, after those markets had become established, logged only $3.3 billion in total revenue. It is, indeed, an innovator's dilemma. Firms that sought growth by entering small, emerging markets logged *twenty times* the revenues of the firms pursuing growth in larger markets. The difference in revenues per firm is even more striking: The firms that followed late into the markets enabled by disruptive technology, on the left half of the matrix, generated an average cumulative total of $64.5 million per firm. The *average* company that led in disruptive technology generated $1.9 *billion* in revenues. The firms on the left side seem to have made a sour bargain. They exchanged a *market risk,* the risk that an emerging market for the disruptive technology might not develop after all, for a *competitive risk,* the risk of entering markets against entrenched competition.[8]

COMPANY SIZE AND LEADERSHIP IN DISRUPTIVE TECHNOLOGIES

Despite evidence that leadership in disruptive innovation pays such huge dividends, established firms, as shown in the first four chapters of this book, often fail to take the lead. Customers of established firms can hold the organizations captive, working through rational, well-functioning resource allocation processes to keep them from commercializing disruptive technologies. One cruel *additional* disabling factor that afflicts established firms as they work to maintain their growth rate is that the larger and more successful they become, the more difficult it is to muster the rationale for entering an emerging market in its early stages, when the evidence above shows that entry is so crucial.

Good managers are driven to keep their organizations growing for many reasons. One is that growth rates have a strong effect on share prices. To the extent that a company's stock price represents the discounted present value of some consensus forecast of its future earnings stream, then the *level* of the stock price—whether it goes up or down—is driven by changes in the projected *rate of growth* in earnings.[9] In other words, if a company's current share price is predicated on a consensus growth forecast of 20 percent, and the market's consensus for growth is subsequently revised downward to 15 percent growth, then the company's share price will likely *fall*—even though its revenues and earnings will still be growing at a healthy rate. A strong and increasing stock price, of course, gives a company access to capital on favorable terms; happy investors are a great asset to a company.

Rising share prices make stock option plans an inexpensive way to provide incentive to and to reward valuable employees. When share prices stagnate or fall, options lose their value. In addition, company growth creates room at the top for high-performing employees to expand the scope of their responsibilities. When companies stop growing, they begin losing many of their most promising future leaders, who see less opportunity for advancement.

Finally, there is substantial evidence that growing companies find it much easier to justify investments in new product and process technologies than do companies whose growth has stopped.[10]

Unfortunately, companies that become large and successful find that maintaining growth becomes progressively more difficult. The math is simple: A $40 million company that needs to grow profitably at 20 percent to sustain its stock price and organizational vitality needs an additional $8 million in revenues the first year, $9.6 million the following year, and so on; a $400 million company with a 20 percent targeted growth rate needs new business worth $80 million in the first year, $96 million in the next, and so on; and a $4 billion company with a 20 percent goal needs to find $800 million, $960 million, and so on, in each successive year.

This problem is particularly vexing for big companies confronting disruptive technologies. Disruptive technologies facilitate the emergence of new markets, and there are no $800 million emerging markets. But it is precisely when emerging markets are small—when they are *least* attractive to large companies in search of big chunks of new revenue—that entry into them is so critical.

How can a manager of a large, successful company deal with these realities of size and growth when confronted by disruptive change? I have observed three approaches in my study of this problem:

1. Try to affect the growth rate of the emerging market, so that it becomes big enough, fast enough, to make a meaningful dent on the trajectory of profit and revenue growth of a large company.

2. Wait until the market has emerged and become better defined, and then enter after it "has become large enough to be interesting."

3. Place responsibility to commercialize disruptive technologies in organizations small enough that their performance will be mean-

ingfully affected by the revenues, profits, and small orders flowing from the disruptive business in its earliest years.

As the following case studies show, the first two approaches are fraught with problems. The third has its share of drawbacks too, but offers more evidence of promise.

CASE STUDY: PUSHING THE GROWTH RATE OF AN EMERGING MARKET

The history of Apple Computer's early entry into the hand-held computer, or personal digital assistant (PDA), market helps to clarify the difficulties confronting large companies in small markets.

Apple Computer introduced its Apple I in 1976. It was at best a preliminary product with limited functionality, and the company sold a total of 200 units at $666 each before withdrawing it from the market. But the Apple I wasn't a financial disaster. Apple had spent modestly on its development, and both Apple and its customers learned a lot about how desktop personal computers might be used. Apple incorporated this learning into its Apple II computer, introduced in 1977, which was highly successful. Apple sold 43,000 Apple II computers in the first two years they were on the market,[11] and the product's success positioned the company as the leader in the personal computer industry. On the basis of the Apple II's success Apple went public in 1980.

A decade after the release of the Apple II, Apple Computer had grown into a $5 billion company, and like all large and successful companies, it found itself having to add large chunks of revenue each year to preserve its equity value and organizational vitality. In the early 1990s, the emerging market for hand-held PDAs presented itself as a potential vehicle for achieving that needed growth. In many ways, this opportunity, analogous to that in 1978 when the Apple II computer helped shape its industry, was a great fit for Apple. Apple's distinctive design expertise was in user-friendly products, and user-friendliness and convenience were the basis of the PDA concept.

How did Apple approach this opportunity? Aggressively. It invested scores of millions of dollars to develop its product, dubbed the "Newton." The Newton's features were defined through one of the most thoroughly executed market research efforts in corporate history; focus groups and surveys of every type were used to determine what features consumers would want. The PDA had many of the characteristics of a disruptive computing technology, and recognizing the potential problems, Apple CEO John Sculley made the Newton's development a personal priority, promoting the product widely, and ensuring that the effort got the technical and financial resources it needed.

Apple sold 140,000 Newtons in 1993 and 1994, its first two years on the market. Most observers, of course, viewed the Newton as a big flop. Technically, its handwriting recognition capabilities were disappointing, and its wireless communications technologies had made it expensive. But what was most damning was that while Sculley had publicly positioned the Newton as a key product to sustain the company's growth, its first-year sales amounted to about 1 percent of Apple's revenues. Despite all the effort, the Newton made hardly a dent in Apple's need for new growth.

But was the Newton a failure? The timing of Newton's entry into the handheld market was akin to the timing of the Apple II into the desktop market. It was a market-creating, disruptive product targeted at an undefinable set of users whose needs were unknown to either themselves or Apple. On that basis, Newton's sales should have been a pleasant surprise to Apple's executives: It outsold the Apple II in its first two years by a factor of more than three to one. But while selling 43,000 units was viewed as an IPO-qualifying triumph in the smaller Apple of 1979, selling 140,000 Newtons was viewed as a failure in the giant Apple of 1994.

As chapter 7 will show, disruptive technologies often enable something to be done that previously had been deemed impossible. Because of this, when they initially emerge, neither manufacturers nor customers know how or why the products will be used, and hence do not know what specific features of the product will and will not ultimately be valued. Building such markets entails a process of mutual discovery by customers and manufacturers—and this simply takes time. In Apple's development of the desktop computer, for example, the Apple I failed, the first Apple II was lackluster, and the Apple II+ succeeded. The Apple III was a market failure because of quality problems, and the Lisa was a failure. The first two generations of the Macintosh computer also stumbled. It wasn't until the third iteration of the Macintosh that Apple and its customers finally found "it": the standard for convenient, user-friendly computing to which the rest of the industry ultimately had to conform.[12]

In launching the Newton, however, Apple was desperate to short-circuit this coalescent process for defining the ultimate product and market. It assumed that its customers knew what they wanted and spent very aggressively to find out what this was. (As the next chapter will show, this is impossible.) Then to give customers what they thought they wanted, Apple had to assume the precarious role of a sustaining technology leader in an emerging industry. It spent enormous sums to push mobile data communications and handwriting recognition technologies beyond the state of the art. And finally, it spent aggressively to convince people to buy what it had designed.

Because emerging markets are small by definition, the organizations competing in them must be able to become profitable at small scale. This is crucial because organizations or projects that are perceived as being profitable and successful can continue to attract financial and human resources both from their corporate parents and from capital markets. Initiatives perceived as failures have a difficult time attracting either. Unfortunately, the scale of the investments Apple made in its Newton in order to hasten the emergence of the PDA market made it very difficult to earn an attractive return. Hence, the Newton came to be broadly viewed as a flop.

As with most business disappointments, hindsight reveals the faults in Apple's Newton project. But I believe that the root cause of Apple's struggle was *not* inappropriate management. The executives' actions were a symptom of a deeper problem: Small markets cannot satisfy the near-term growth requirements of big organizations.

CASE STUDY: WAITING UNTIL A MARKET IS LARGE ENOUGH TO BE INTERESTING

A second way that many large companies have responded to the disruptive technology trap is to wait for emerging markets to "get large enough to be interesting" before they enter. Sometimes this works, as IBM's well-timed 1981 entry into the desktop PC business demonstrated. But it is a seductive logic that can backfire, because the firms creating new markets often forge capabilities that are closely attuned to the requirements of those markets and that later entrants find difficult to replicate. Two examples from the disk drive industry illustrate this problem.

Priam Corporation, which ascended to leadership of the market for 8-inch drives sold to minicomputer makers after its entry in 1978, had built the capability in that market to develop its drives on a two-year rhythm. This pace of new product introduction was consistent with the rhythm by which its customers, minicomputer makers, introduced their new products into the market.

Seagate's first 5.25-inch drive, introduced to the emerging desktop market in 1980, was disruptively slow compared to the performance of Priam's drives in the minicomputer market. But by 1983, Seagate and the other firms that led in implementing the disruptive 5.25-inch technology had developed a *one-year* product introduction rhythm in their market. Because Seagate and Priam achieved similar percentage improvements in speed with each new product generation, Seagate, by introducing new generations on a one-year rhythm, quickly began to converge on Priam's performance advantage.

Priam introduced its first 5.25-inch drive in 1982. But the rhythm by which it introduced its subsequent 5.25-inch models was the two-year capability it had honed in the minicomputer market—not the one-year cycle required to compete in the desktop marketplace. As a consequence, it was never able to secure a *single* major OEM order from a desktop computer manufacturer: It just couldn't hit their design windows with its new products. And Seagate, by taking many more steps forward than did Priam, was able to close the performance gap between them. Priam closed its doors in 1990.

The second example occurred in the next disruptive generation. Seagate Technology was the second in the industry to develop a 3.5-inch drive in 1984. Analysts at one point had speculated that Seagate might ship 3.5-inch drives as early as 1985; and indeed, Seagate showed a 10 MB model at the fall 1985 Comdex Show. When Seagate still had not shipped a 3.5-inch drive by late 1986, CEO Al Shugart explained, "So far, there just isn't a big enough market for it, as yet."[13] In 1987, when the 3.5-inch market at $1.6 billion had gotten "big enough to be interesting," Seagate finally launched its offering. By 1991, however, even though Seagate had by then built substantial volume in 3.5-inch drives, it had not yet succeeded in selling a single drive to a maker of portable computers: Its models were all sold into the desktop market, defensively cannibalizing its sales of 5.25-inch drives. Why?

One likely reason for this phenomenon is that Conner Peripherals, which pioneered and maintained the lead in selling 3.5-inch drives to portable computer makers, fundamentally changed the way drive makers had to approach the portables market. As one Conner executive described it,

From the beginning of the OEM disk drive industry, product development had proceeded in three sequential steps. First you designed the drive; then you made it; and then you sold it. We changed all that. We first *sell* the drives; then we design them; and then we build them.[14]

In other words, Conner set a pattern whereby drives for the portable computer market were custom-designed for major customers. And it refined a set of capabilities in its marketing, engineering, and manufacturing processes that were tailored to that pattern.[15] Said another Conner executive, "Seagate was never able to figure out how to sell drives in the portable market. They just never got it."[16]

CASE STUDY: GIVING SMALL OPPORTUNITIES TO SMALL ORGANIZATIONS

Every innovation is difficult. That difficulty is compounded immeasurably, however, when a project is embedded in an organization in which most people are continually questioning why the project is being done at all. Projects make sense to people if they address the needs of important customers, if they positively impact the organization's needs for profit and growth, and if participating in the project enhances the career opportunities of talented employees. When a project doesn't have these characteristics, its manager spends much time and energy justifying why it merits resources and cannot manage the project as effectively. Frequently in such circumstances, the best people do not want to be associated with the project—and when things get tight, projects viewed as nonessential are the first to be canceled or postponed.

Executives can give an enormous boost to a project's probability of success, therefore, when they ensure that it is being executed in an environment in which everyone involved views the endeavor as crucial to the organization's future growth and profitability. Under these conditions, when the inevitable disappointments, unforeseen problems, and schedule slippages occur, the organization will be more likely to find ways to muster whatever is required to solve the problem.

As we have seen, a project to commercialize a disruptive technology in a small, emerging market is very unlikely to be considered essential to success in a large company; small markets don't solve the growth problems of big companies. Rather than continually working to convince and remind everyone that the small, disruptive technology might *someday* be significant or that it is at least strategically important, large companies should seek to embed the project in an organization that is small enough to be motivated by the opportunity offered by a disruptive technology in its early years. This can be done either by spinning out an independent organization or by acquiring an appropriately small company. Expecting achievement-driven employees in a large organization to devote a critical mass of resources, attention, and energy to a disruptive project targeted at a small and poorly defined market is equivalent to flapping one's arms in an effort to fly: It denies an important tendency in the way organizations work.[17]

There are many success stories to the credit of this approach. Control Data, for example, which had essentially missed the 8-inch disk drive generation, sent a group to Oklahoma City to commercialize its 5.25-inch drive. In addition to CDC's need to escape the power of its mainstream customers, the firm explicitly wanted to create an organization whose size matched the opportunity. "We needed an organization," reflected one manager, "that could get excited about a $50,000 order. In Minneapolis [which derived nearly $1 billion from the sale of 14-inch drives in the mainframe market] you needed a million-dollar order just to turn anyone's head." CDC's Oklahoma City venture proved to be a significant success.

Another way of matching the size of an organization to the size of the opportunity is to acquire a small company within which to incubate the disruptive technology. This is how Allen Bradley negotiated its very successful disruptive transition from mechanical to electronic motor controls.

For decades the Allen Bradley Company (AB) in Milwaukee has been the undisputed leader in the motor controls industry, making heavy-duty, sophisticated switches that turn large electric motors off and on and protect them from overloads and surges in current. AB's customers were makers of machine tools and cranes as well as contractors who installed fans and pumps for industrial and commercial heating, ventilating, and air conditioning (HVAC) systems. Motor controls were electromechanical devices that operated on the same principle as residential light switches, although on a larger scale. In sophisticated machine tools and HVAC systems, electric motors and their controls were often linked, through systems of electromechanical relay switches, to turn on and off in particular sequences and under particular conditions. Because of the value of the equipment they controlled and the high cost of equipment downtime, controls were required to be rugged, capable of turning on and off millions of times and of withstanding the vibrations and dirt that characterized the environments in which they were used.

In 1968, a startup company, Modicon, began selling electronic programmable motor controls—a disruptive technology from the point of view of mainstream users of electromechanical controls. Texas Instruments (TI) entered the fray shortly thereafter with its own electronic controller. Because early electronic controllers lacked the real and perceived ruggedness and robustness for harsh environments of the hefty AB-type controllers, Modicon and TI were unable to sell their products to mainstream machine tool makers and HVAC contractors. As performance was measured in the mainstream markets, electronic products underperformed conventional controllers, and few mainstream customers needed the programmable flexibility offered by electronic controllers.

As a consequence, Modicon and TI were forced to cultivate an emerging market for programmable controllers: the market for factory automation. Customers in this emerging market were not equipment manufacturers, but equipment *users,* such as Ford and General Motors, who were just beginning their attempt to integrate pieces of automatic manufacturing equipment.

Of the five leading manufacturers of electromechanical motor controls—Allen Bradley, Square D, Cutler Hammer, General Electric, and Westinghouse—only Allen Bradley retained a strong market position as programmable electronic controls improved in ruggedness and began to invade the core motor control markets. Allen Bradley entered the electronic controller market just two years after Modicon and built a market-leading position in the new technology within a few years, even as it kept its strength in its old electromechanical products. It subsequently transformed itself into a major supplier of electronic controllers for factory automation. The other four companies, by contrast, introduced electronic controllers much later and subsequently either exited the controller business or were reduced to weak positions. From a capabilities perspective this is a surprising outcome, because General Electric and Westinghouse had much deeper expertise in microelectronics technologies at that time than did Allen Bradley, which had no institutional experience in the technology.

What did Allen Bradley do differently? In 1969, just one year after Modicon entered the market, AB executives bought a 25 percent interest in Information Instruments, Inc., a fledgling programmable controller start-up based in Ann Arbor, Michigan. The following year it purchased outright a nascent division of Bunker Ramo, which was focused on programmable electronic controls and their emerging markets. AB combined these acquisitions into a single unit and maintained it as a business separate from its mainstream electromechanical products operation in Milwaukee. Over time, the electronics products have significantly eaten into the electromechanical controller business, as one AB division attacked the other.[18] By contrast, each of the other four companies tried to manage its electronic controller businesses from within its mainstream electromechanical divisions, whose customers did not initially need or want electronic controls. Each failed to develop a viable position in the new technology.

Johnson & Johnson has with great success followed a strategy similar to Allen Bradley's in dealing with disruptive technologies such as endoscopic surgical equipment and disposable contact lenses. Though its total revenues amount to more than $20 billion, J&J comprises 160 autonomously operating companies, which range from its huge MacNeil and Janssen pharmaceuticals companies to small companies with annual revenues of less than $20 million. Johnson & Johnson's strategy is to launch products of disruptive technologies through very small companies acquired for that purpose.

SUMMARY

It is not crucial for managers pursuing growth and competitive advantage to be leaders in every element of their business. In sustaining technologies, in fact, evidence strongly suggests that companies which focus on extending the performance of conventional technologies, and choose to be followers in adopting new ones, can remain strong and competitive. This is not the case with disruptive technologies, however. There are enormous returns and significant first-mover advantages associated with early entry into the emerging markets in which disruptive technologies are initially used. Disk drive manufacturers that led in commercializing disruptive technology grew at vastly greater rates than did companies that were disruptive technology followers.

Despite the evidence that leadership in commercializing disruptive technologies is crucial, large, successful innovators encounter a significant dilemma in the pursuit of such leadership. In addition to dealing with the power of present customers as discussed in the last chapter, large, growth-oriented companies face the problem that small markets don't solve the near-term growth needs of large companies. The markets whose emergence is enabled by disruptive technologies all began as small ones. The first orders that the pioneering companies received in those markets were small ones. And the companies that cultivated those markets had to develop cost structures enabling them to become profitable at small scale. Each of these factors argues for a policy of implanting projects to commercialize disruptive innovations in small organizations that will view the projects as being on their critical path to growth and success, rather than as being distractions from the main business of the company.

This recommendation is not new, of course; a host of other management scholars have also argued that smallness and independence confer certain advantages in innovation. It is my hope that chapters 5 and 6 provide deeper insight about why and under what circumstances this strategy is appropriate.

NOTES

1. The benefits of persistently pursuing incremental improvements versus taking big strategic leaps have been capably argued by Robert Hayes in "Strategic Planning: Forward in Reverse?" *Harvard Business Review,* November–December, 1985, 190–197.

   I believe that there are some specific situations in which leadership in sustaining technology is crucial, however. In a private conversation, Professor Kim Clark characterized these situations as those affecting *knife-edge* businesses, that is, businesses in which the basis of competition is simple and unidimensional and there is little room for error. An example of such a knife-edge industry is the photolithographic aligner (PLA) industry, studied by Rebecca M. Henderson and Kim B. Clark, in "Architectural Innovation: The Reconfiguration of Existing Systems and the Failure of Established Firms," *Administrative Science Quarterly* (35), March, 1990, 9–30. In this case, aligner manufacturers failed when they fell behind technologically in the face of sustaining architectural changes. This is because the basis of competition in the PLA industry was quite straightforward even though the products themselves were very complex: products either made the narrowest line width on silicon wafers of any in the industry or no one bought them. This is because PLA customers, makers of integrated circuits, simply had to have the fastest and most capable photolithographic alignment equipment or they could not remain competitive in their own markets. The knife-edge existed because product functionality was the only basis of competition: PLA manufacturers would either fall off one side to rapid success or off the other side to failure. Clearly, such knife-edge situations make leadership in sustaining technology very important.

In most other sustaining situations, however, leadership is *not* crucial. This far more common situation is the subject of Richard S. Rosenbloom's study of the transition by National Cash Register from electro-mechanical to electronic technology. (See Richard S. Rosenbloom, "From Gears to Chips: The Transformation of NCR and Harris in the Digital Era," Working paper, Harvard Business School Business History Seminar, 1988). In this case, NCR was very late in its industry in developing and launching a line of electronic cash registers. So late was NCR with this technology, in fact, that its sales of new cash registers dropped essentially to zero for an entire year in the early 1980s. Nonetheless, the company had such a strong field service capability that it survived by serving its installed base for the year it took to develop and launch its electronic cash registers. NCR then leveraged the strength of its brand name and field sales presence to quickly recapture its share of the market.

Even though a cash register is a simpler machine than a photolithographic aligner, I would characterize its market as complex, in that there are multiple bases of competition, and hence multiple ways to survive. As a general rule, the more complex a market, the less important is leadership in sustaining technological innovations. It is in dealing with knife-edge markets or with disruptive technologies that leadership appears to be crucial. I am indebted to Professors Kim B. Clark and Robert Hayes for their contributions to my thinking on this topic.

2. This is not to say that firms whose product performance or product cost consistently lagged behind the competition were able to prosper. I assert that there is no evidence that leadership in sustaining technological innovation confers a discernible and enduring competitive advantage over companies that have adopted a follower strategy because there are numerous ways to "skin the cat" in improving the performance of a complex product such as a disk drive. Developing and adopting new component technologies, such as thin-film and magneto-resistive heads, is one way to improve performance, but there are innumerable other avenues for extending the performance of conventional technologies while waiting for new approaches to become better understood and more reliable. This argument is presented more fully in Clayton M. Christensen, "Exploring the Limits of the Technology S-Curve," *Production and Operations Management* (1), 1992, 334–366.

3. For the purposes of this analysis, a technology was classed as "new or unproven" if less than two years had elapsed from the time it had first

appeared in a product that was manufactured and sold by a company some-where in the world or if, even though it had been in the market for more than two years, less than 20 percent of the disk drive makers had used the technology in one of their products.

4. In this analysis, *emerging markets* or value networks were those in which two years or less had elapsed since the first rigid disk drive had been used with that class of computers; *established markets* or value networks were those in which more than two years had elapsed since the first drive was used.

5. Entry by acquisition was a rare route of entry in the disk drive industry. Xerox followed this strategy, acquiring Diablo, Century Data, and Shugart Associates. The performance of these companies after acquisition was so poor that few other companies followed Xerox's lead. The only other example of entry by acquisition was the acquisition of Tandon by Western Digital, a manufacturer of controllers. In the case of Xerox and Western Digital, the entry strategy of the firms they *acquired* is recorded in Table 6.1. Similarly, the start-up of Plus Development Corporation, a spin-out of Quantum, appears in Table 6.1 as a separate company.

6. The evidence summarized in this matrix may be of some use to venture capital investors, as a general way to frame the riskiness of proposed investments. It suggests that start-ups which propose to commercialize a breakthrough technology that is essentially sustaining in character have a far lower likeli-hood of success than start-ups whose vision is to use proven technology to disrupt an established industry with something that is simpler, more reliable, and more convenient. The established firms in an industry have every incentive to catch up with a supposed sustaining technological breakthrough, while they have strong disincentives to pursue disruptive initiatives.

7. Not all of the small, emerging markets actually became large ones. The market for removable drive modules, for example, remained a small niche for more than a decade, only beginning to grow to significant size in the mid-1990s. The conclusion in the text that emerging markets offer a higher probability for success reflects the average, not an invariant result.

8. The notions that one ought not accept the risks of innovating simultaneously along both market and technology dimensions are often discussed among venture capitalists. It is also a focus of chapter 5 in Lowell W. Steele, *Managing Technology* (New York: McGraw Hill, 1989). The study reported here of the posterior probabilities of success for different innovation strategies builds upon the concepts of Steele and Lyle Ochs (whom Steele cites). I was also stimulated by ideas presented in Allan N. Afuah and Nik Bahram, "The Hypercube of Innovation," *Research Policy* (21), 1992.

9. The simplest equation used by financial analysts to determine share price is

$P = D/(C\text{-}G)$, where P = price per share, D = dividends per share, C = the company's cost of capital, and G = projected long-term growth rate.

10. This evidence is summarized by Clayton M. Christensen in "Is Growth an *Enabler* of Good Management, or the *Result* of It?" Harvard Business School working paper, 1996.

11. Scott Lewis, "Apple Computer, Inc.," in Adele Hast, ed., *International Directory of Company Histories* (Chicago: St. James Press, 1991), 115–116.

12. An insightful history of the emergence of the personal computer industry appears in Paul Frieberger and Michael Swaine, *Fire in the Valley: The Making of the Personal Computer* (Berkeley, CA: Osborne-McGraw Hill, 1984).

13. "Can 3.5" Drives Displace 5.25s in Personal Computing?" *Electronic Business,* 1 August, 1986, 81–84.

14. Personal interview with Mr. William Schroeder, Vice Chairman, Conner Peripherals Corporation, November 19, 1991.

15. An insightful study on the linkage among a company's historical experience, its capabilities, and what it consequently can and cannot do, appears in Dorothy Leonard-Barton, "Core Capabilities and Core Rigidities: A Paradox in Managing New Product Development," *Strategic Management Journal* (13), 1992, 111–125.

16. Personal interview with Mr. John Squires, cofounder and Executive Vice President, Conner Peripherals Corporation, April 27, 1992.

17. See, for example, George Gilder, "The Revitalization of Everything: The Law of the Microcosm," *Harvard Business Review,* March–April, 1988, 49–62.

18. Much of this information about Allen Bradley has been taken from John Gurda, *The Bradley Legacy* (Milwaukee: The Lynde and Harry Bradley Foundation, 1992).

CHAPTER SEVEN

Discovering New and Emerging Markets

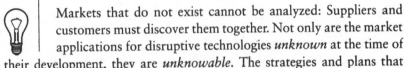Markets that do not exist cannot be analyzed: Suppliers and customers must discover them together. Not only are the market applications for disruptive technologies *unknown* at the time of their development, they are *unknowable*. The strategies and plans that managers formulate for confronting disruptive technological change, therefore, should be plans for learning and discovery rather than plans for execution. This is an important point to understand, because managers who believe they know a market's future will plan and invest very differently from those who recognize the uncertainties of a developing market.

Most managers learn about innovation in a *sustaining technology context* because most technologies developed by established companies are sustaining in character. Such innovations are, by definition, targeted at known markets in which customer needs are understood. In this environment, a planned, researched approach to evaluating, developing, and marketing innovative products is not only possible, it is critical to success.

What this means, however, is that much of what the best executives in successful companies have learned about managing innovation is not relevant to disruptive technologies. Most marketers, for example, have been schooled extensively, at universities and on the job, in the important art of listening to their customers, but few have any theoretical or practical training in how to discover markets that do not yet exist. The problem with this lopsided experience base is that when the same analytical and decision-making processes learned in the school of sustaining innovation are applied to enabling or disruptive technologies, the effect on the company can be paralyzing. These processes demand crisply quantified information when none exists, accurate estimates of financial returns when neither revenues nor costs can be known, and management according to detailed plans and budgets that cannot be formulated. Applying inappropriate marketing, investment, and management processes can render good companies incapable of creating the new markets in which enabling or disruptive technologies are first used.

In this chapter we shall see how experts in the disk drive industry were able to forecast the markets for sustaining technologies with stunning accuracy but had great difficulty in spotting the advent and predicting the size of new markets for disruptive innovations. Additional case histories in the motorcycle and microprocessor industries further demonstrate the uncertainty about emerging market applications for disruptive or enabling technologies, even those that, in retrospect, appear obvious.

FORECASTING MARKETS FOR SUSTAINING VERSUS DISRUPTIVE TECHNOLOGIES

An unusual amount of market information has been available about the disk drive industry from its earliest days—a major reason why studying it has yielded such rich insights. The primary source of data, *Disk/Trend Report,* published annually by Disk/Trend, Inc., of Mountain View, California, lists every model of disk drive that has ever been offered for sale by any company in the world, for each of the years from 1975 to the present. It shows the month and year in which each model was first shipped, lists the performance specifications of the drive, and details the component technologies used. In addition, every manufacturer in the world shares with *Disk/Trend* its sales by product type, with information about what types of customers bought which drive. Editors at *Disk/Trend* then aggregate this data to derive the size of each narrowly defined market segment and publish a listing of the major competitors' shares, carefully guarding all proprietary data. Manufacturers in the industry find the reports so valuable that they all continue to share their proprietary data with *Disk/Trend.*

In each edition, *Disk/Trend* publishes the actual unit volumes and dollar sales in each market segment for the year just past and offers its forecasts for each of the next four years in each category. Given its unparalleled access to industry data spanning two decades, this publication offers an unusual chance to test through unfolding market history the accuracy of past predictions. Over all, *Disk/Trend* has a remarkable track record in forecasting the future of established markets, but it has struggled to estimate accurately the size of new markets enabled by disruptive disk drive technologies.

The evidence is summarized in Figure 7.1, which compares the total unit volumes that *Disk/Trend Report* had forecast would be shipped in the first four years after commercial shipments of each new disk drive architecture began, to the total volumes that were actually shipped over

Figure 7.1 The Four Years after the First Commercial Shipments: Sustaining versus Disruptive Technologies

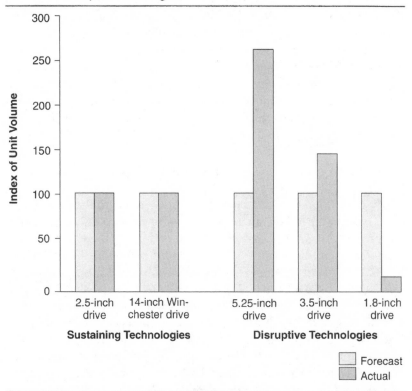

Source: Data are from various issues of *Disk/Trend Report*.

that four-year period. To facilitate comparison, the heights of the bars measuring forecast shipments were normalized to a value of 100, and the volumes actually shipped were scaled as a percentage of the forecast. Of the five new architectures for which *Disk/Trend*'s forecasts were available, the 14-inch Winchester and the 2.5-inch generation were sustaining innovations, which were sold into the same value networks as the preceding generation of drives. The other three, 5.25-, 3.5-, and 1.8-inch drives, were disruptive innovations that facilitated the emergence of new value networks. (*Disk/Trend* did not publish separate forecasts for 8-inch drives.)

Notice that *Disk/Trend*'s forecasts for the sustaining 2.5-inch and 14-inch Winchester technologies were within 8 percent and 7 percent, respectively, of what the industry actually shipped. But its estimates were off by 265 percent for 5.25-inch drives, 35 percent for 3.5-inch drives (really quite close), and 550 percent for 1.8-inch drives. Notably, the 1.8-inch drive, the forecast of which *Disk/Trend* missed so badly, was the first generation of drives with a primarily non-computer market.

The *Disk/Trend* staff used the same methods to generate the forecasts for sustaining architectures as they did for disruptive ones: interviewing leading customers and industry experts, trend analysis, economic modeling, and so on. The techniques that worked so extraordinarily well when applied to sustaining technologies, however, clearly failed badly when applied to markets or applications that did not yet exist.

IDENTIFYING THE MARKET FOR THE HP 1.3-INCH KITTYHAWK DRIVE

Differences in the forecastablity of sustaining versus disruptive technologies profoundly affected Hewlett-Packard's efforts to forge a market for its revolutionary, disruptive 1.3-inch Kittyhawk disk drive.[1] In 1991, Hewlett-Packard's Disk Memory Division (DMD), based in Boise, Idaho, generated about $600 million in disk drive revenues for its $20 billion parent company. That year a group of DMD employees conceived of a tiny, 1.3-inch 20 MB drive, which they code-named Kittyhawk. This was indeed a radical program for HP: The smallest drive previously made by DMD had been 3.5-inches, and DMD had been one of the last in the industry to introduce one. The 1.3-inch Kittyhawk represented a significant leapfrog for the company—and, most notably, was HP's first attempt to lead in a disruptive technology.

For the project to make sense in a large organization with ambitious growth plans, HP executives mandated that Kittyhawk's revenues had to ramp to $150 million within three years. Fortunately for Kittyhawk's proponents, however, a significant market for this tiny drive loomed on the horizon: hand-held palm-top computers, or personal digital assistants (PDAs). Kittyhawk's sponsors, after studying projections for this market, decided that they could scale the revenue ramp that had been set for them. They consulted a market research firm, which confirmed HP's belief that the market for Kittyhawk would indeed be substantial.

HP's marketers developed deep relationships with senior executives at major companies in the computer industry, for example, Motorola, ATT, IBM, Apple, Microsoft, Intel, NCR, and Hewlett-Packard itself, as well as at a host of lesser-known startup companies. All had placed substantial product development bets on the PDA market. Many of their products were designed with Kittyhawk's features in mind, and Kittyhawk's design in turn reflected these customers' well-researched needs.

The Kittyhawk team concluded that developing a drive that met these customers' requirements would be a demanding but feasible technological stretch, and they launched an aggressive twelve-month effort to develop the tiny device. The result, shown in Figure 7.2, was impressive. The first version packed 20 MB, and a second model, introduced a year later, stored 40 MB. To meet the ruggedness demanded in its target market of PDAs and electronic notebooks, Kittyhawk was equipped with an impact sensor similar to those used in automobile airbag crash sensors and could withstand a three-foot drop onto concrete without data loss. It was designed to sell initially at $250 per unit.

Although Kittyhawk's technical development went according to plan, the development of applications for it did not. The PDA market failed to materialize substantially, as sales of Apple's Newton and competing devices fell far short of aspirations. This surprised many of the computer industry experts whose opinions HP's marketers had worked so hard to synthesize. During its first two years on the market, Kittyhawk logged just a fraction of the sales that had been forecast. The sales achieved might have initially satisfied startup companies and venture capitalists, but for HP's management, the volumes were far below expectations and far too small to satisfy DMD's need to grow and gain overall market share. Even more surprising, the applications that contributed most significantly to Kittyhawk's sales were not in computers at all. They were Japanese-language portable word processors, miniature cash registers,

Figure 7.2 Hewlett-Packard's Kittyhawk Drive

Source: Hewlett Packard Company. Used by permission.

electronic cameras, and industrial scanners, none of which had figured in Kittyhawk's original marketing plans.

Even more frustrating, as the second anniversary of Kittyhawk's launch approached, were the inquiries received by HP marketers from companies making mass-market video game systems to buy very large volumes of Kittyhawk—if HP could make a version available at a lower price point. These companies had been aware of Kittyhawk for two years, but they reported that it had taken some time for them to see what could be done with a storage device so small.

To a significant extent, HP had designed Kittyhawk to be a sustaining technology for mobile computing. Along many of the metrics of value in that application—small size, low weight and power consumption, and ruggedness—Kittyhawk constituted a discontinuous sustaining improvement relative to 2.5- and 1.8-inch drives. Only in capacity (which HP had pushed as far as possible) was Kittyhawk deficient. The large inquiries and orders that finally began arriving for the Kittyhawk, however, were for a *truly* disruptive product: something priced at $50 per unit and with limited functionality. For these applications, a capacity of 10 MB would have been perfectly adequate.

Unfortunately, because HP had positioned the drive with the expensive features needed for the PDA market rather than designing it as a truly disruptive product, it simply could not meet the price required by home video game manufacturers. Having invested so aggressively to hit its original targets as defined by the PDA application, management had little patience and no money to redesign a simpler, defeatured 1.3-inch drive that fit the market applications that had finally become clear. HP withdrew Kittyhawk from the market in late 1994.

The HP project managers concede in retrospect that their most serious mistake in managing the Kittyhawk initiative was to act as if their forecasts about the market were right, rather than as if they were wrong. They had invested aggressively in manufacturing capacity for producing the volumes forecast for the PDA market and had incorporated design features, such as the shock sensor, that were crucial to acceptance in the PDA market they had so carefully researched. Such planning and investment is crucial to success in a sustaining technology, but, the managers reflected, it was not right for a disruptive product like Kittyhawk. If they had the opportunity to launch Kittyhawk all over again, they would assume that neither they nor anyone else knew for sure what kinds of customers would want it or in what volumes. This would lead them toward a much more exploratory, flexible approach toward product design and investment in manufacturing capacity; they would, given another chance, feel their way into the market, leaving enough resources to redirect their program if necessary and building upon what they learned on the way.

Hewlett-Packard's disk drive makers are not the only ones, of course, who behaved as if they knew what the market for a disruptive technology would be. They are in stellar company, as the following case histories show.

HONDA'S INVASION OF THE NORTH AMERICAN MOTORCYCLE INDUSTRY

Honda's success in attacking and dominating the North American and European motorcycle markets has been cited as a superb example of clear strategic thinking coupled with aggressive and coherent execution. According to these accounts, Honda employed a deliberate manufacturing strategy based on an experience curve in which it cut prices, built volume, aggressively reduced costs, cut prices some more, reduced costs further, and built an unassailable volume-based low-cost manufacturing position in the motorcycle market. Honda then used that base to move upmarket and ultimately blew all established motorcycle manufacturers out of the market except for Harley-Davidson and BMW, which barely survived.[2] Honda combined this manufacturing triumph with a clever product design, catchy advertising, and a convenient, broad-based distributor/retailer network tailored to the informal cyclists who constituted Honda's core customer base. Told in this manner, Honda's history is a tale of strategic brilliance and operational excellence that all managers dream will be told about them someday. The reality of Honda's achievement, as recounted by the Honda employees who were managing the business at the time, however, is quite different.[3]

During Japan's years of post-war reconstruction and poverty, Honda had emerged as a supplier of small, rugged motorized bicycles that were used by distributors and retailers in congested urban areas to make small deliveries to local customers. Honda developed considerable expertise in designing small, efficient engines for these bikes. Its Japanese market sales grew from an initial annual volume of 1,200 units in 1949 to 285,000 units in 1959.

Honda's executives were eager to exploit the company's low labor costs to export motorbikes to North America, but there was no equivalent market there for its popular Japanese "Supercub" delivery bike. Honda's research showed that Americans used motorcyles primarily for over-the-road distance driving in which size, power, and speed were the most highly valued product attributes. Accordingly, Honda engineers designed a fast, powerful motorcycle specifically for the American market, and in 1959 Honda dispatched three employees to Los Angeles to begin marketing efforts. To save living expenses, the three shared an apartment, and each brought with him a Supercub bike to provide cheap transportation around the city.

The venture was a frustrating experience from the beginning. Honda's products offered no advantage to prospective customers other than cost, and most motorcycle dealers refused to accept the unproven product line. When the team finally succeeded in finding some dealers and selling a few hundred units, the results were disastrous. Honda's understanding of engine design turned out not to be transferable to highway applications, in which bikes were driven at high speeds for extended periods: The engines sprung oil leaks and the clutches wore out. Honda's expenses in air-freighting the warrantied replacement motorcycles between Japan and Los Angeles nearly sunk the company.

Meanwhile, one Saturday, Kihachiro Kawashima, the Honda executive in charge of the North American venture, decided to vent his frustrations by taking his Supercub into the hills east of Los Angeles. It helped: He felt better after zipping around in the dirt. A few weeks later he sought relief dirt-biking again. Eventually he invited his two colleagues to join him on their Supercubs. Their neighbors and others who saw them zipping around the hills began inquiring where they could buy those cute little bikes, and the trio obliged by special-ordering Supercub models for them from Japan. This private use of what became known as off-road dirt bikes continued for a couple of years. At one point a Sears buyer tried to order Supercubs for the company's outdoor power equipment departments, but Honda ignored the opportunity, preferring to focus on selling large, powerful, over-the-road cycles, a strategy that continued to be unsuccessful.

Finally, as more and more people clamored for their own little Honda Supercubs to join their dirt-biking friends, the potential for a very different market dawned on Honda's U.S. team: Maybe there was an undeveloped off-the-road recreational motorbike market in North America for which—quite by accident—the company's little 50cc Supercub was nicely suited. Although it took much arguing and arm-twisting, the Los Angeles team ultimately convinced corporate management in Japan that while the company's large bike strategy was doomed to failure, another quite different opportunity to create a totally new market segment merited pursuit.

Once the small-bike strategy was formally adopted, the team found that securing dealers for the Supercub was an even more vexing challenge than it had been for its big bikes. There just weren't any retailers selling that class of product. Ultimately, Honda persuaded a few sporting goods dealers to take on its line of motorbikes, and as they began to promote the bikes successfully, Honda's innovative distribution strategy was born.

Honda had no money for a sophisticated advertising campaign. But a UCLA student who had gone dirt-biking with his friends came up with the advertising slogan, "You meet the nicest people on a Honda," for a paper he wrote in an advertising course. Encouraged by his teacher, he sold the idea to an advertising agency, which then convinced Honda to use it in what became an award-winning advertising campaign. These serendipitous events were, of course, followed by truly world-class design engineering and manufacturing execution, which enabled Honda to repeatedly lower its prices as it improved its product quality and increased its production volumes.

Honda's 50cc motorbike was a disruptive technology in the North American market. The rank-ordering of product attributes that Honda's customers employed in their product decision making defined for Honda a very different value network than the established network in which Harley-Davidson, BMW, and other traditional motorcycle makers had competed.

From its low-cost manufacturing base for reliable motorbikes, using a strategy reminiscent of the upmarket invasions described earlier in disk drives, steel, excavators, and retailing, Honda turned its sights upmarket, introducing between 1970 and 1988 a series of bikes with progressively more powerful engines.

For a time in the late 1960s and early 1970s, Harley attempted to compete head-on with Honda and to capitalize on the expanding low-end market by producing a line of small-engine (150 to 300 cc) bikes acquired from the Italian motorcycle maker Aeromecchania. Harley attempted to sell the bikes through its North American dealer network. Although Honda's manufacturing prowess clearly disadvantaged Harley in this effort, a primary cause of Harley's failure to establish a strong presence in the small-bike value network was the opposition of its dealer network. Their profit margins were far greater on high-end bikes, and many of them felt the small machines compromised Harley-Davidson's image with their core customers.

Recall from chapter 2 the finding that within a given value network, the disk drive companies and their computer-manufacturing customers had developed very similar economic models or cost structures, which determined the sorts of business that appeared profitable to them. We see the same phenomenon here. Within their value network, the economics of Harley's dealers drove them to favor the same type of business that Harley had come to favor. Their coexistence within the value network made it difficult for either Harley or its dealers to exit the network through its bottom. In the late 1970s Harley gave in and repositioned itself at the very high end of the motorcycle market—a strategy reminiscent of Seagate's repositioning in disk drives, and of the upmarket retreats of the cable excavator companies and the integrated steel mills.

Interestingly, Honda proved just as inaccurate in estimating *how large* the potential North American motorcycle market was as it had been in understanding *what* it was. Its initial aspirations upon entry in 1959 had been to capture 10 percent of a market estimated at 550,000 units per year with annual growth of 5 percent. By 1975 the market had grown 16 percent per year to 5,000,000 annual units—units that came largely from an application that Honda could not have foreseen.[4]

INTEL'S DISCOVERY OF THE MICROPROCESSOR MARKET

Intel Corporation, whose founders launched the company in 1969 based on their pioneering development of metal-on-silicon (MOS) technology to produce the world's first dynamic random access memory (DRAM) integrated circuits, had become by 1995 one of the world's most profitable major companies. Its storied success is even more remarkable because, when its initial leadership position in the DRAM market began crumbling between 1978 and 1986 under the onslaught of Japanese semiconductor manufacturers, Intel transformed itself from a second-tier DRAM company into the world's dominant microprocessor manufacturer. How did Intel do it?

Intel developed the original microprocessor under a contract development arrangement with a Japanese calculator manufacturer. When the project was over, Intel's engineering team persuaded company executives to purchase the microprocessor patent from the calculator maker, which owned it under the terms of its contract with Intel. Intel had no explicit strategy for building a market for this new microprocessor; the company simply sold the chip to whoever seemed to be able to use it.

Mainstream as they seem today, microprocessors were disruptive technologies when they first emerged. They were capable only of limited functionality, compared to the complex logic circuits that constituted the central processing units of large computers in the 1960s. But they were small and simple, and they enabled affordable logic and computation in applications where this previously had not been feasible.

Through the 1970s, as competition in the DRAM market intensified, margins began to decline on Intel's DRAM revenues while margins on its microprocessor product line, where there was less competition, stayed robust. Intel's system for allocating production capacity operated according to a formula whereby capacity was committed in proportion to the gross margins earned by each product line. The system therefore imperceptibly began diverting investment capital and manufacturing capacity away from the DRAM business and into microprocessors—without an explicit management decision to do so.[5] In fact, Intel senior management continued to focus most of its own attention and energy on DRAM, even while the company's resource allocation processes were gradually implementing an exit from that business.

This de facto strategy shift, driven by Intel's autonomously operating resource allocation process, was fortuitous. Because so little was known of the microprocessor market at that time, explicit analysis would have provided little justification for a bold move into microprocessors. Gordon Moore, Intel co-founder and chairman, for example, recalled that IBM's choice of the Intel 8088 microprocessor as the "brain" of its new personal computer was viewed within Intel as a "small design win."[6] Even after IBM's stunning success with its personal computers, Intel's internal forecast of the potential applications for the company's next-generation 286 chip did not include personal computers in its list of the fifty highest-volume applications.[7]

In retrospect, the application of microprocessors to personal computers is an obvious match. But in the heat of the battle, of the many applications in which microprocessors might have been used, even a management team as astute as Intel's could not know which would emerge as the most important and what volumes and profits it would yield.

UNPREDICTABILITY AND DOWNWARD IMMOBILITY IN ESTABLISHED FIRMS

The reaction of some managers to the difficulty of correctly planning the markets for disruptive technologies is to work harder and plan smarter. While this approach works for sustaining innovations, it denies the evidence about the nature of disruptive ones. Amid all the uncertainty surrounding disruptive technologies, managers can always count on one anchor: *Experts' forecasts will always be wrong.* It is simply impossible to predict with any useful degree of precision how disruptive products will be used or how large their markets will be. An important corollary is that, because markets for disruptive technologies are unpredictable, companies' initial strategies for entering these markets will generally be wrong.

How does this statement square with the findings presented in Table 6.1, which showed a stunning difference in the posterior probabilities of success between firms that entered new, emerging value networks (37 percent) and those that entered existing value networks (6 percent)? If markets cannot be predicted in advance, how can firms that target them be more successful? Indeed, when I have shown the matrix in Table 6.1 to managerial audiences, they are quite astonished by the differences in the magnitudes and probabilities of success. But it is clear that the managers don't believe that the results can be generalized to their own situations.

The findings violate their intuitive sense that creating new markets is a genuinely risky business.[8]

Failed Ideas versus Failed Businesses

The case studies reviewed in this chapter suggest a resolution to this puzzle. There is a big difference between the failure of an *idea* and the failure of a *firm*. Many of the ideas prevailing at Intel about where the disruptive microprocessor could be used were wrong; fortunately, Intel had not expended all of its resources implementing wrong-headed marketing plans while the right market direction was still unknowable. As a company, Intel survived many false starts in its search for the major market for microprocessors. Similarly, Honda's idea about how to enter the North American motorcycle market was wrong, but the company didn't deplete its resources pursuing its big-bike strategy and was able to invest aggressively in the winning strategy after it had emerged. Hewlett-Packard's Kittyhawk team was not as fortunate. Believing they had identified the winning strategy, its managers spent their budget on a product design and the manufacturing capacity for a market application that never emerged. When the ultimate applications for the tiny drive ultimately began to coalesce, the Kittyhawk team had no resources left to pursue them.

Research has shown, in fact, that the vast majority of successful new business ventures abandoned their original business strategies when they began implementing their initial plans and learned what would and would not work in the market.[9] The dominant difference between successful ventures and failed ones, generally, is not the astuteness of their original strategy. Guessing the right strategy at the outset isn't nearly as important to success as conserving enough resources (or having the relationships with trusting backers or investors) so that new business initiatives get a second or third stab at getting it right. Those that run out of resources or credibility before they can iterate toward a viable strategy are the ones that fail.

Failed Ideas and Failed Managers

In most companies, however, individual managers don't have the luxury of surviving a string of trials and errors in pursuit of the strategy that works. Rightly or wrongly, individual managers in most organizations believe that they *cannot* fail: If they champion a project that fails because the initial marketing plan was wrong, it will constitute a blotch on their track record, blocking their rise through the organization. Because failure is intrinsic to the process of finding new markets for disruptive technologies, the inability or unwillingness of individual managers to put their careers at risk acts as a powerful deterrent to the movement of established firms into the value networks created by those technologies. As Joseph Bower observed in his classic study of the resource allocation process at a major chemical company, "Pressure from the market reduces both the probability and the cost of being wrong.[10]

Bower's observation is consistent with the findings in this book about the disk drive industry. When demand for an innovation was assured, as was the case with sustaining technologies, the industry's established leaders were capable of placing huge, long, and risky bets to develop whatever technology was required. When demand was not assured, as was the case in disruptive technologies, the established firms could not even make the technologically straightforward bets required to commercialize such innovations. That is why 65 percent of the companies entering the disk drive industry attempted to do so in an established, rather than emerging market. Discovering markets for emerging technologies inherently involves failure, and most individual decision makers find it very difficult to risk backing a project that might fail because the market is not there.

Plans to Learn versus Plans to Execute

Because failure is intrinsic to the search for initial market applications for disruptive technologies, managers need an approach very different from what they would take toward a sustaining technology. In general, for sustaining technologies, plans must be made before action is taken, forecasts can be accurate, and customer inputs can be reasonably reliable. Careful planning, followed by aggressive execution, is the right formula for success in sustaining technology.

But in disruptive situations, action must be taken before careful plans are made. Because much less can be known about what markets need or how large they can become, plans must serve a very different purpose: They must be plans for *learning* rather than plans for implementation. By approaching a disruptive business with the mindset that they can't know where the market is, managers would identify what critical information about new markets is most necessary and in what sequence that information is needed. Project and business plans would mirror those priorities, so that key pieces of information would be created, or important uncertainties resolved, before expensive commitments of capital, time, and money were required.

Discovery-driven planning, which requires managers to identify the assumptions upon which their business plans or aspirations are based,[11] works well in addressing disruptive technologies. In the case of Hewlett-Packard's Kittyhawk disk drive, for example, HP invested significant sums with its manufacturing partner, the Citizen Watch Company, in building and tooling a highly automated production line. This commitment was based on an assumption that the volumes forecast for the drive, built around forecasts by HP customers of PDA sales, were accurate. Had HP's managers instead assumed that nobody knew in what volume PDAs would sell, they might have built small modules of production capacity rather than a single, high-volume line. They could then have held to capacity or added or reduced capacity as key events confirmed or disproved their assumptions.

Similarly, the Kittyhawk product development plan was based on an assumption that the dominant application for the little drive was in PDAs, which demanded high ruggedness. Based on this assumption, the Kittyhawk team committed to components and a product architecture that made the product too expensive to be sold to the price-sensitive video game makers at the emerging low end of the market. Discovery-driven planning would have forced the team to test its market assumptions *before* making commitments that were expensive to reverse—in this case, possibly by creating a modularized design that easily could be reconfigured or defeatured to address different markets and price points, as events in the marketplace clarified the validity of their assumptions.

Philosophies such as *management by objective* and *management by exception* often impede the discovery of new markets because of where they focus management attention. Typically, when performance falls short of plan, these systems encourage management to close the gap between what was planned and what happened. That is, they focus on unanticipated failures. But as Honda's experience in the North American motorcycle market illustrates, markets for disruptive technologies often emerge from unanticipated successes, on which many planning systems do not focus the attention of senior management.[12] Such discoveries often come by watching how people use products, rather than by listening to what they say.

I have come to call this approach to discovering the emerging markets for disruptive technologies *agnostic marketing,* by which I mean marketing under an explicit assumption that *no one*—not us, not our customers—can know whether, how, or in what quantities a disruptive product can or will be used before they have experience using it. Some managers, faced with such uncertainty, prefer to wait until others have defined the market. Given the powerful first-mover advantages at stake, however, managers confronting disruptive technologies need to get out of their laboratories and focus groups and directly create knowledge about new customers and new applications through discovery-driven expeditions into the marketplace.

NOTES

1. What follows is a summary of the fuller history recounted in "Hewlett-Packard: The Flight of the Kittyhawk," Harvard Business School, Case No. 9-697-060, 1996.
2. Examples of such histories of Honda's success include the Harvard Business School case study, "A Note on the Motorcycle Industry—1975," No. 9-578-210, and a report published by The Boston Consulting Group, "Strategy Alternatives for the British Motorcycle Industry," 1975.
3. Richard Pascale and E. Tatum Christiansen, "Honda (A)," Harvard Business School Teaching, Case No. 9-384-049, 1984, and "Honda (B)," Harvard Business School, Teaching Case No. 9-384-050, 1984.
4. *Statistical Abstract of the United States* (Washington, D.C.: United States Bureau of the Census, 1980), 648.
5. Intel's exit from the DRAM business and entry into microprocessors has been chronicled by Robert A. Burgelman in "Fading Memories: A Process Theory of Strategic Business Exit in Dynamic Environments," *Administrative Science Quarterly* (39), 1994, 24–56. This thoroughly researched and compellingly written study of the process of strategy evolution is well worth reading.
6. George W. Cogan and Robert A. Burgelman, "Intel Corporation (A): The DRAM Decision," Stanford Business School, Case PS-BP-256.
7. Robert A. Burgelman, "Fading Memories: A Process Theory of Strategic Business Exit in Dynamic Environments," *Administrative Science Quarterly* (39) 1994.
8. Studies of how managers define and perceive risk can shed significant light on this puzzle. Amos Tversky and Daniel Kahneman, for example, have shown that people tend to regard propositions that they do not understand as more risky, regardless of their intrinsic risk, and to regard things they *do* understand as *less* risky, again without regard to intrinsic risk. (Amos Tversky and Daniel Kahneman, "Judgment Under Uncertainty: Heuristics and Biases," *Science* [185], 1974, 1124–1131.) Managers, therefore, may view creation

of new markets as risky propositions, in the face of contrary evidence, because they do not understand non-existent markets; similarly, they may regard investment in sustaining technologies, even those with high intrinsic risk, as safe because they understand the market need.

9. Among the excellent studies in this tradition are Myra M. Hart, *Founding Resource Choices: Influences and Effects,* DBA thesis, Harvard University Graduate School of Business Administration, 1995; Amar Bhide, "How Entrepreneurs Craft Strategies that Work," *Harvard Business Review,* March–April, 1994, 150–163; Amar Bhide, "Bootstrap Finance: The Art of Start-Ups," *Harvard Business Review,* November–December 1992, 109–118; "Hewlett-Packard's Kittyhawk," Harvard Business School, Case No. 9-697-060; and "Vallourec's Venture into Metal Injection Molding," Harvard Business School, Case No. 9-697-001.

10. Joseph Bower, *Managing the Resource Allocation Process* (Homewood, IL: Richard D. Irwin, 1970), 254.

11. Rita G. McGrath and Ian C. MacMillan, "Discovery-Driven Planning," *Harvard Business Review,* July–August, 1995, 4–12.

12. This point is persuasively argued in Peter F. Drucker, *Innovation and Entrepreneurship* (New York: Harper & Row, 1985). Below, in chapter 9, I recount how software maker Intuit discovered that many of the people buying its *Quicken* personal financial management software were, in fact, using it to keep the books of their small businesses. Intuit had not anticipated this application, but it consequently adapted the product more closely to small business needs and launched *Quickbooks,* which captured more than 70 percent of the small business accounting software market within two years.

CHAPTER EIGHT

How to Appraise Your Organization's Capabilities and Disabilities

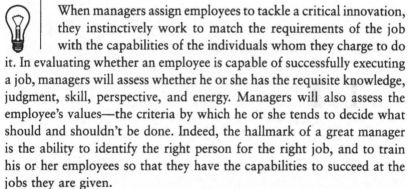

When managers assign employees to tackle a critical innovation, they instinctively work to match the requirements of the job with the capabilities of the individuals whom they charge to do it. In evaluating whether an employee is capable of successfully executing a job, managers will assess whether he or she has the requisite knowledge, judgment, skill, perspective, and energy. Managers will also assess the employee's values—the criteria by which he or she tends to decide what should and shouldn't be done. Indeed, the hallmark of a great manager is the ability to identify the right person for the right job, and to train his or her employees so that they have the capabilities to succeed at the jobs they are given.

Unfortunately, some managers don't think as rigorously about whether their *organizations* have the capability to successfully execute jobs that may be given to them. Frequently, they assume that if the people working on a project individually have the requisite capabilities to get the job done well, then the organization in which they work will also have the same capability to succeed. This often is not the case. One could take two sets of identically capable people and put them to work in two different organizations, and what they accomplish would likely be significantly different. This is because organizations themselves, independent of the people and other resources in them, have capabilities. To succeed consistently, good managers need to be skilled not just in choosing, training, and motivating the right people for the right job, but in choosing, building, and preparing the right *organization* for the job as well.

The purpose of this chapter is to describe the theory that lies behind the empirical observations made in chapters 5, 6, and 7—in particular, the observation that the only companies that succeeded in addressing disruptive technology were those that created independent organizations whose size matched the size of the opportunity. The notion that organizations have "core competencies" has been a popular one for much of the last decade.[1] In practice, however, most managers have found that the concept is sufficiently vague that some supposed "competence" can be cited in support of a bewildering variety of innovation proposals. This chapter brings greater precision to the core competence concept, by presenting a framework to help managers understand, when they are confronted with a necessary change, whether the organizations over which they preside are competent or incompetent of tackling the challenges that lie ahead.

AN ORGANIZATIONAL CAPABILITIES FRAMEWORK

Three classes of factors affect what an organization can and cannot do: its resources, its processes, and its values. When asking what sorts of innovations their organizations are and are not likely to be able to implement successfully, managers can learn a lot about capabilities by disaggregating their answers into these three categories.[2]

Resources

Resources are the most visible of the factors that contribute to what an organization can and cannot do. Resources include people, equipment, technology, product designs, brands, information, cash, and relationships with suppliers, distributors, and customers. Resources are usually *things*, or *assets*—they can be hired and fired, bought and sold, depreciated or enhanced. They often can be transferred across the boundaries of organizations much more readily than can processes and values. Without doubt, access to abundant and high-quality resources enhances an organization's chances of coping with change.

Resources are the things that managers most instinctively identify when assessing whether their organizations can successfully implement changes that confront them. Yet resource analysis clearly does not tell a sufficient story about capabilities. Indeed, we could deal identical sets of resources to two different organizations, and what they created from those resources would likely be very different—because the capabilities to transform inputs into goods and services of greater value reside in the organization's processes and values.

Processes

Organizations create value as employees transform inputs of resources— people, equipment, technology, product designs, brands, information, energy, and cash—into products and services of greater worth. The patterns of interaction, coordination, communication, and decision-making through which they accomplish these transformations are *processes*.[3] Processes include not just manufacturing processes, but those by which product development, procurement, market research, budgeting, planning, employee development and compensation, and resource allocation are accomplished.

Processes differ not only in their purpose, but also in their visibility. Some processes are "formal," in the sense that they are explicitly defined, visibly documented, and consciously followed. Other processes are "informal," in that they are habitual routines or ways of working that have evolved over time, which people follow simply because they work—or because "That's the way we do things around here." Still other methods of working and interacting have proven so effective for so long that people unconsciously follow them—they constitute the culture of the organization. Whether they are formal, informal, or cultural, however, processes define how an organization transforms the sorts of inputs listed above into things of greater value.

Processes are defined or evolve *de facto* to address specific tasks. This means that when managers use a process to execute the tasks for which it was designed, it is likely to perform efficiently. But when the same, seemingly efficient process is employed to tackle a very different task, it is likely to seem slow, bureaucratic, and inefficient. In other words, a process that defines a *capability* in executing a certain task concurrently defines *disabilities* in executing other tasks.[4] The reason good managers strive for focus in their organizations is that processes and tasks can be readily aligned.[5]

One of the dilemmas of management is that, by their very nature, processes are established so that employees perform recurrent tasks in a consistent way, time after time. To ensure consistency, they are meant *not* to change—or if they must change, to change through tightly controlled procedures. *This means that the very mechanisms through which organizations create value are intrinsically inimical to change.*

Some of the most crucial processes to examine as capabilities or disabilities aren't the obvious value-adding processes involved in logistics, development, manufacturing, and customer service. Rather, they are the enabling or background processes that support investment decision-making. As we saw in chapter 7, the processes that render good companies incapable of responding to change are often those that define how market research is habitually done; how such analysis is translated into financial projections; how plans and budgets are negotiated and how those numbers are delivered; and so on. These typically inflexible processes are where many organizations' most serious disabilities in coping with change reside.

Values

The third class of factors that affect what an organization can or cannot accomplish is its values. The values of an organization are the criteria by which decisions about priorities are made. Some corporate values are ethical in tone, such as those that guide decisions to ensure patient well-being at Johnson & Johnson or that guide decisions about plant safety at Alcoa. But within the Resources-Processes-Values (RPV) framework, values have a broader meaning. An organization's values are the standards by which employees make prioritization decisions—by which they judge whether an order is attractive or unattractive; whether a customer is more important or less important; whether an idea for a new product is attractive or marginal; and so on. Prioritization decisions are made by employees at every level. At the executive tiers, they often take the form of decisions to invest or not invest in new products, services, and processes. Among salespeople, they consist of on-the-spot, day-to-day decisions about which products to push with customers and which not to emphasize.

The larger and more complex a company becomes, the more important it is for senior managers to train employees at every level to make independent decisions about priorities that are consistent with the strategic direction and the business model of the company. A key metric of good management, in fact, is whether such clear and consistent values have permeated the organization.[6]

Clear, consistent, and broadly understood values, however, also define what an organization cannot do. A company's values, by necessity, must reflect its cost structure or its business model, because these define the rules its employees must follow in order for the company to make money. If, for example, the structure of a company's overhead costs requires it to achieve gross profit margins of 40 percent, a powerful value or decision rule will have evolved that encourages middle managers to kill ideas that promise gross margins below 40 percent. This means that such an organization would be *incapable* of successfully commercializing projects targeting low-margin markets. At the same time, another organization's values, driven by a very different cost structure, might enable or facilitate the success of the very same project.

The values of successful firms tend to evolve in a predictable fashion in at least two dimensions. The first relates to acceptable gross margins. As companies add features and functionality to their products and services in order to capture more attractive customers in premium tiers of their markets, they often add overhead cost. As a result, gross margins that at one point were quite attractive, at a later point seem unattractive. Their values change. For example, Toyota entered the North American market with its Corona model—a product targeting the lowest-priced tiers of the market. As the entry tier of the market became crowded with look-alike models from Nissan, Honda, and Mazda, competition among equally low-cost competitors drove down profit margins. Toyota developed more sophisticated cars targeted at higher tiers of the market in order to improve its margins. Its Corolla, Camry, Previa, Avalon, and Lexus families of cars have been introduced in response to the same competitive pressures—it kept its margins healthy by migrating up-market. In the process, Toyota has had to add costs to its operation to design, build, and support cars of this caliber. It progressively deemphasized the entry-level tiers of the market, having found the margins it could earn there to be unattractive, given its changed cost structure.

Nucor Steel, the leading minimill that led the up-market charge against the integrated mills that was recounted in chapter 4, likewise has experienced a change in values. As it has managed the center of gravity in its product line up-market from re-bar to angle iron to structural beams and finally to sheet steel, it has begun to decidedly deemphasize re-bar—the product that had been its bread and butter in its earlier years.

The second dimension along which values predictably change relates to how big a business has to be in order to be interesting. Because a company's stock price represents the discounted present value of its projected earnings stream, most managers typically feel compelled not just to maintain growth, but to maintain a constant *rate* of growth. In order for a $40 million company to grow 25 percent, it needs to find $10 million in new business the next year. For a $40 *billion* company to grow 25 percent, it needs to find $10 billion in new business the next year. The size of market opportunity that will solve each of these companies' needs for growth is very different. As noted in chapter 6, an opportunity that excites a small organization isn't big enough to be interesting to a very large one. One of the bittersweet rewards of success is, in fact, that as companies become large, they literally lose the capability to enter small emerging markets. This disability is not because of a change in the resources within the companies—their resources typically are vast. Rather, it is because their values change.

Executives and Wall Street financiers who engineer megamergers among already huge companies in order to achieve cost savings need to account for the impact of these actions on the resultant companies' values. Although their merged organizations might have more resources to throw at innovation problems, their commercial organizations tend to lose their appetites for all but the biggest blockbuster opportunities. Huge size constitutes a very real *disability* in managing innovation. In many ways, Hewlett-Packard's recent decision to split itself into two companies is rooted in its recognition of this problem.

THE RELATIONSHIP BETWEEN PROCESSES AND VALUES, AND SUCCESS IN ADDRESSING SUSTAINING VS. DISRUPTIVE TECHNOLOGIES

The resources-processes-values (RPV) framework has been a useful tool for me to understand the findings from my research relating to the differences in companies' track records in sustaining and disruptive technologies. Recall that we identified 116 new technologies that were introduced in the industry's history. Of these, 111 were sustaining technologies, in that their impact was to improve the performance of disk drives. Some of these were incremental improvements while others, such as magneto-resistive heads, represented discontinuous leaps forward in performance. In all 111 cases of sustaining technology, the companies that led in developing and introducing the new technology were the companies that had led in the old technology. The success rate of the established firms in developing and adopting sustaining technologies was 100 percent.

The other five of these 116 technologies were disruptive innovations—in each case, smaller disk drives that were slower and had lower capacity than those used in the mainstream market. There was no new technology involved in these disruptive products. Yet *none* of the industry's leading companies remained atop the industry after these disruptive innovations entered the market—their batting average was *zero*.

Why such markedly different batting averages when playing the sustaining versus disruptive games? The answer lies in the RPV framework of organizational capabilities. The industry leaders developed and introduced sustaining technologies over and over again. Month after month, year after year, as they introduced new and improved products in order to gain an edge over the competition, the leading companies developed processes for evaluating the technological potential and assessing their customers' needs for alternative sustaining technologies. In the parlance of this chapter, the organizations developed a *capability* for doing these things, which resided in their processes. Sustaining technology investments also fit the values of the leading companies, in that they promised higher margins from better products sold to their leading-edge customers.

On the other hand, the disruptive innovations occurred so intermittently that no company had a routinized process for handling them. Furthermore, because the disruptive products promised lower profit margins per unit sold and could not be used by their best customers, these innovations were inconsistent with the leading companies' values. The leading disk drive companies had the *resources*—the people, money, and technology—required to succeed at both sustaining and disruptive technologies. But their processes and values constituted disabilities in their efforts to succeed at disruptive technologies.

Large companies often surrender emerging growth markets because smaller, disruptive companies are actually more *capable* of pursuing them. Though start-ups lack resources, it doesn't matter. Their values can embrace small markets, and their cost structures can accommodate lower margins. Their market research and resource allocation processes allow managers to proceed intuitively rather than having to be backed up by careful research and analysis, presented in PowerPoint. All of these advantages add up to enormous opportunity or looming disaster—depending upon your perspective.

Managers who face the need to change or innovate, therefore, need to do more than assign the right resources to the problem. They need to be sure that the organization in which those resources will be working is itself capable of succeeding—and in making that assessment, managers must scrutinize whether the organization's processes and values fit the problem.

THE MIGRATION OF CAPABILITIES

In the start-up stages of an organization, much of what gets done is attributable to its *resources*—its people. The addition or departure of a few key people can have a profound influence on its success. Over time, however, the locus of the organization's capabilities shifts toward its processes and values. As people work together successfully to address recurrent tasks, processes become defined. And as the business model takes shape and it becomes clear which types of business need to be accorded highest priority, values coalesce. In fact, one reason that many soaring young companies flame out after they go public based upon a hot initial product is that whereas their initial success was grounded in resources— the founding group of engineers—they fail to create *processes* that can create a *sequence* of hot products.

An example of such flame out is the story of Avid Technology, a producer of digital editing systems for television. Avid's technology removed tedium from the video editing process. Customers loved it, and on the back of its star product, Avid stock rose from $16 at its 1993 IPO to $49 in mid-1995. However, the strains of being a one-trick pony soon surfaced as Avid was faced with a saturated market, rising inventories and receivables, and increased competition. Customers loved the product, but Avid's lack of effective processes to consistently develop new products and to control quality, delivery, and service ultimately tripped the company and sent its stock back down.

In contrast, at highly successful firms such as McKinsey and Company, the processes and values have become so powerful that it almost doesn't matter which people get assigned to which project teams. Hundreds of new MBAs join the firm every year, and almost as many leave. But the company is able to crank out high-quality work year after year because its core capabilities are rooted in its processes and values rather than in its resources. I sense, however, that these capabilities of McKinsey also constitute its disabilities. The rigorously analytical, data-driven processes that help it create value for its clients in existing, relatively stable markets render it much less capable of building a strong client base among the rapidly growing companies in dynamic technology markets.

In the formative stages of a company's processes and values, the actions and attitudes of the company's founder have a profound impact. The founder often has strong opinions about the way employees ought to work together to reach decisions and get things done. Founders similarly impose their views of what the organization's priorities need to be. If the founder's methods are flawed, of course, the company will likely fail. But if those methods are useful, employees will collectively experience for themselves the validity of the founder's problem-solving methodologies and criteria for decision-making. As they successfully use those methods of working together to address recurrent tasks, processes become defined. Likewise, if the company becomes financially successful by prioritizing various uses of its resources according to criteria that reflect the founder's priorities, the company's values begin to coalesce.

As successful companies mature, employees gradually come to assume that the priorities they have learned to accept, and the ways of doing things and methods of making decisions that they have employed so successfully, are the right way to work. Once members of the organization begin to adopt ways of working and criteria for making decisions by assumption, rather than by conscious decision, then those processes and values come to constitute the organization's *culture*.[7] As companies grow from a few employees to hundreds and thousands, the challenge of getting all employees to agree on what needs to be done and how it should be done so that the right jobs are done repeatedly and consistently can be daunting for even the best managers. Culture is a powerful management tool in these situations. Culture enables employees to act autonomously and causes them to act consistently.

Hence, the location of the most powerful factors that define the capabilities and disabilities of organizations migrates over time —from resources toward visible, conscious processes and values, and then toward culture. As long as the organization continues to face the same sorts of problems that its processes and values were designed to address, managing the organization is relatively straightforward. But because these factors also define what an organization *cannot* do, they constitute disabilities when the problems facing the company change. When the organization's capabilities reside primarily in its people, changing to address new problems is relatively simple. But when the capabilities have come to reside in processes and values and *especially* when they have become embedded in culture, change can become extraordinarily difficult.

A case in point: Did Digital Equipment have the capability to succeed in personal computers?

Digital Equipment Corporation (DEC) was a spectacularly successful maker of minicomputers from the 1960s through the 1980s. One might have been tempted to assert, when the personal computer market began to coalesce in the early 1980s, that DEC's "core competence" was in building computers. But if computers were DEC's competence, why did the company stumble?

Clearly, DEC had the *resources* to succeed in personal computers. Its engineers were routinely designing far more sophisticated computers than PCs. DEC had plenty of cash, a great brand, and strong technology. But did DEC have the *processes* to succeed in the personal computer business? No. The processes for designing and manufacturing minicomputers involved designing many of the key components of the computer internally and then integrating the components into proprietary configurations. The design process itself consumed two to three years for a new product model. DEC's manufacturing processes entailed making most components and assembling them in a batch mode. It sold direct to corporate engineering organizations. These processes worked extremely well in the minicomputer business.

The personal computer business, in contrast, required processes through which the most cost-effective components were outsourced from the best suppliers around the globe. New computer designs, comprised of modular components, had to be completed in six- to twelve-month cycles. The computers were manufactured in high-volume assembly lines, and sold through retailers to consumers and businesses. None of these processes required to compete successfully in the personal computer business existed within DEC. In other words, although the *people* working at DEC, as individuals, had the abilities to design, build, and sell personal computers profitably, they were working in an organization that was incapable of doing this because its processes had been designed and had evolved to do *other* tasks well. The very processes that made the company capable of succeeding in one business rendered it incapable of succeeding in another.

And what about DEC's *values*? Because of the overhead costs that were required to succeed in the minicomputer business, DEC had to adopt a set of values that essentially dictated, "If it generates 50 percent gross margins or more, it's good business. If it generates less than 40 percent margins, it's not worth doing." Management had to ensure that all employees prioritized projects according to this criterion, or the company couldn't make money. Because personal computers generated lower margins, they did not "fit" with DEC's values. The company's criteria for prioritization placed higher-performance minicomputers ahead of personal computers in the resource allocation process. And any attempts that the company made to enter the personal computer business had to target the highest-margin tiers of that market—because the financial results that might be earned in those tiers were the only ones that the company's values would tolerate. But because of the patterns noted in chapter 4—the strong tendency for competitors with low-overhead business models to migrate up-market—Digital's values rendered it incapable of pursuing a winning strategy.

As we saw in chapter 5, Digital Equipment could have owned *another* organization whose processes and values were tailored to those required to play in the personal computer game. But the particular organization in Maynard, Massachusetts, whose extraordinary capabilities had carried the company to such success in the minicomputer business, was simply incapable of succeeding in the personal computer world.

CREATING CAPABILITIES TO COPE WITH CHANGE

If a manager determined that an employee was incapable of succeeding at a task, he or she would either find someone else to do the job or carefully train the employee to be able to succeed. Training often works, because individuals can become skilled at multiple tasks.

Despite beliefs spawned by popular change-management and reengineering programs, processes are not nearly as flexible or "trainable" as are resources—and values are even less so. The processes that make an organization good at outsourcing components cannot simultaneously make it good at developing and manufacturing components in-house. Values that focus an organization's priorities on high-margin products cannot simultaneously focus priorities on low-margin products. This is why focused organizations perform so much better than unfocused ones: their processes and values are matched carefully with the set of tasks that need to be done.

For these reasons, managers who determine that an organization's capabilities aren't suited for a new task, are faced with three options through which to create new capabilities. They can:

- Acquire a different organization whose processes and values are a close match with the new task
- Try to change the processes and values of the current organization
- Separate out an independent organization and develop within it the new processes and values that are required to solve the new problem

Creating Capabilities Through Acquisitions

Managers often sense that acquiring rather than developing a set of capabilities makes competitive and financial sense. The RPV model can be a useful way to frame the challenge of integrating acquired organizations. Acquiring managers need to begin by asking, "What is it that really created the value that I just paid so dearly for? Did I justify the price because of its resources—its people, products, technology, market position, and so on? Or, was a substantial portion of its worth created by processes and values—unique ways of working and decision-making that have enabled the company to understand and satisfy customers, and develop, make, and deliver new products and services in a timely way?

If the acquired company's processes and values are the real driver of its success, then the last thing the acquiring manager wants to do is to integrate the company into the new parent organization. Integration will vaporize many of the processes and values of the acquired firm as its managers are required to adopt the buyer's way of doing business and have their proposals to innovate evaluated according to the decision criteria of the acquiring company. If the acquiree's processes and values were the reason for its historical success, a better strategy is to let the business stand alone, and for the parent to infuse its resources into the acquired firm's processes and values. This strategy, in essence, truly constitutes the acquisition of new capabilities.

If, on the other hand, the company's *resources* were the primary rationale for the acquisition, then integrating the firm into the parent can make a lot of sense—essentially plugging the acquired people, products, technology, and customers into the parent's processes, as a way of leveraging the parent's existing capabilities.

The perils of the DaimlerChrysler merger that began in the late 1990s, for example, can be better understood through the RPV model. Chrysler had few resources that could be considered unique in comparison to its competitors. Its success in the market of the 1990s was rooted in its processes—particularly in its rapid, creative product design processes, and in its processes of integrating the efforts of its subsystem suppliers. What would be the best way for Daimler to leverage the capabilities that Chrysler brought to the table? Wall Street exerted nearly inexorable pressure on management to consolidate the two organizations in order to cut costs. However, integrating the two companies would likely vaporize the key processes that made Chrysler such an attractive acquisition in the first place.

This situation is reminiscent of IBM's 1984 acquisition of Rolm. There wasn't anything in Rolm's pool of resources that IBM didn't already have. It was Rolm's processes for developing PBX products and for finding new markets for them that was really responsible for its success. In 1987 IBM decided to fully integrate the company into its corporate structure. Trying to push Rolm's resources—its products and its customers—through the same processes that were honed in its large computer business, caused the Rolm business to stumble badly. And inviting executives of a computer company whose values had been whetted on operating profit margins of 18 percent to get excited about prioritizing products with operating margins below 10 percent was impossible. IBM's decision to integrate Rolm actually destroyed the very source of the original worth of the deal. As this chapter is being written in February 2000, DaimlerChrysler, bowing to the investment community's drumbeat for efficiency savings, now stands on the edge of the same precipice.

Often, it seems, financial analysts have a better intuition for the value of resources than for processes.

In contrast, Cisco Systems' acquisitions process has worked well—because its managers seem to have kept resources, processes, and values in the right perspective. Between 1993 and 1997 it acquired primarily small companies that were less than two years old: early-stage organizations whose market value was built primarily upon their resources—particularly engineers and products. Cisco has a well-defined, deliberate process by which it essentially plugs these resources into the parent's processes and systems, and it has a carefully cultivated method of keeping the engineers of the acquired company happily on the Cisco payroll. In the process of integration, Cisco throws away whatever nascent processes and values came with the acquisition—because those weren't what Cisco paid for. On a couple of occasions when the company acquired a larger, more mature organization—notably its 1996 acquisition of StrataCom—Cisco did *not* integrate. Rather, it let StrataCom stand alone, and infused its substantial resources into the organization to help it grow at a more rapid rate.[8]

On at least three occasions, Johnson & Johnson has used acquisitions to establish a position in an important wave of disruptive technology. Its businesses in disposable contact lenses, endoscopic surgery, and diabetes blood glucose meters were all acquired when they were small, were allowed to stand alone, and were infused with resources. Each has become a billion-dollar business. Lucent Technologies and Nortel followed a similar strategy for catching the wave of routers, based upon packet-switching technology, that were disrupting their traditional circuit-switching equipment. But they made these acquisitions late and the firms they acquired, Ascend Communications and Bay Networks, respectively, were extraordinarily expensive because they had already created the new market application, data networks, along with the much larger Cisco Systems—and they were right on the verge of attacking the voice network.

Creating New Capabilities Internally

Companies that have tried to develop new capabilities within established organizational units also have a spotty track record, unfortunately. Assembling a beefed-up set of resources as a means of changing what an existing organization can do is relatively straightforward. People with new skills can be hired, technology can be licensed, capital can be raised, and product lines, brands, and information can be acquired. Too often, however, resources such as these are then plugged into fundamentally unchanged processes—and little change results. For example, through the 1970s and 1980s Toyota upended the world automobile industry through its innovation in development, manufacturing, and supply-chain *processes*—without investing aggressively in resources such as advanced manufacturing or information-processing technology. General Motors responded by investing nearly $60 billion in manufacturing *resources*—computer-automated equipment that was designed to reduce cost and improve quality. Using state-of-the-art resources in antiquated processes, however, made little difference in General Motors' performance, because it is in its processes and values that the organization's most fundamental capabilities lie. Processes and values define how resources—many of which can be bought and sold, hired and fired—are combined to create value.

Unfortunately, processes are very hard to change—for two reasons. The first is that organizational boundaries are often drawn to facilitate the operation of present processes. Those boundaries can impede the creation of new processes that cut across those boundaries. When new challenges require different people or groups to interact differently than they habitually have done—addressing different challenges with different timing than historically had been required—managers need to pull the relevant people out of the existing organization and draw a new boundary around a new group. New team boundaries enable or facilitate new patterns of working together that ultimately can coalesce as new processes—new capabilities for transforming inputs into outputs. Professors Steven C. Wheelwright and Kim B. Clark have called these structures heavyweight teams.[9]

The second reason new process capabilities are hard to develop is that, in some cases, managers don't *want* to throw the existing processes out—the methods work perfectly well in doing what they were designed to do. As noted above, while resources tend to be flexible and can be used in a variety of situations, processes and values are by their very nature *inflexible*. Their very *raison d'être* is to cause the same thing to be done consistently, over and over again. Processes are meant *not* to change.

When disruptive change appears on the horizon, managers need to assemble the capabilities to confront the change *before* it has affected the mainstream business. In other words, they need an organization that is geared toward the new challenge before the old one, whose processes are tuned to the existing business model, has reached a crisis that demands fundamental change.

Because of its task-specific nature, it is impossible to ask one process to do two fundamentally different things. Consider the examples presented in chapter 7, for instance. The market research and planning processes that are appropriate for the launch of new products into existing markets simply aren't capable of guiding a company into emerging, poorly defined markets. And the processes by which a company would experimentally and intuitively feel its way into emerging markets would constitute suicide if employed in a well-defined existing business. If a company needs to do both types of tasks simultaneously, then it needs two very different processes. And it is very difficult for a single organizational unit to employ fundamentally different, opposing processes. As shown below, this is why managers need to create different teams, within which different processes to address new problems can be defined and refined.

Creating Capabilities Through a Spin-out Organization

The third mechanism for new capability creation—spawning them within spin-out ventures—is currently *en vogue* among many managers as they wrestle with how to address the Internet. When are spin-outs a crucial step in building new capabilities to exploit change, and what are the guidelines by which they should be managed? A separate organization is required when the mainstream organization's *values* would render it incapable of focusing resources on the innovation project. Large organizations cannot be expected to allocate freely the critical financial and human resources needed to build a strong position in small, emerging markets. And it is very difficult for a company whose cost structure is tailored to compete in high-end markets to be profitable in low-end markets as well. When a threatening disruptive technology requires a different cost structure in order to be profitable and competitive, or when the current size of the opportunity is insignificant relative to the growth needs of the mainstream organization, then—and only then—is a spin-out organization a required part of the solution.

How separate does the effort need to be? The primary requirement is that the project cannot be forced to compete with projects in the mainstream organization for resources. Because values are the criteria by which prioritization decisions are made, projects that are inconsistent with a company's mainstream values will naturally be accorded lowest priority. Whether the independent organization is physically separate is less important than is its independence from the normal resource allocation process.

In our studies of this challenge, we have never seen a company succeed in addressing a change that disrupts its mainstream values absent the personal, attentive oversight of the CEO—precisely because of the power of processes and values and particularly the logic of the normal resource allocation process. Only the CEO can ensure that the new organization gets the required resources and is free to create processes and values that are appropriate to the new challenge. CEOs who view spin-outs as a tool to get disruptive threats off of their personal agendas are almost certain to meet with failure. We have seen no exceptions to this rule.

The framework summarized in Figure 8.1 can help managers exploit the capabilities that reside in their current processes and values when that is possible, and to create new ones, when the present organization is incapable. The left axis in Figure 8.1 measures the extent to which the existing processes—the patterns of interaction, communication, coordination, and decision-making currently used in the organization—are the ones that will get the new job done effectively. If the answer is yes (toward the lower end of the scale), the project manager can exploit the organization's existing processes and organizational structure to succeed. As depicted in the corresponding position on the right axis, functional or lightweight teams, as described by Clark and Wheelwright,[10] are useful

Figure 8.1   Fitting an Innovation's Requirements with the Organization's Capabilities

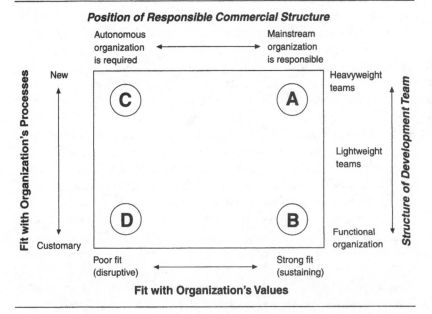

Note: The left and bottom axes reflect the questions the manager needs to ask about the existing situation. The notes at the right side represent the appropriate response to the situation on the left axis. The notes at the top represent the appropriate response to the manager's answer to the bottom axis.

structures for exploiting existing capabilities. In such teams, the role of the project manager is to facilitate and coordinate work that is largely done within functional organizations.

On the other hand, if the ways of getting work done and of decision-making in the mainstream business would impede rather than facilitate the work of the new team—because different people need to interact with different people about different subjects and with different timing than has habitually been necessary—then a heavyweight team structure is necessary. Heavyweight teams are tools to create new processes—new ways of working together that constitute new capabilities. In these teams, members do not simply represent the interests and skills of their function. They are charged to act like general managers, and reach decisions and make trade-offs for the good of the *project*. They typically are dedicated and colocated.

The horizontal axis of Figure 8.1 asks managers to assess whether the organization's values will allocate to the new initiative the resources it will need in order to become successful. If there is a poor, disruptive fit, then the mainstream organization's values will accord low priority to the project. Therefore, setting up an autonomous organization within which development and commercialization can occur will be absolutely essential to success. At the other extreme, however, if there is a strong, sustaining fit, then the manager can expect that the energy and resources of the mainstream organization will coalesce behind it. There is no reason for a skunk works or a spin-out in such cases.

Region A in Figure 8.1 depicts a situation in which a manager is faced with a breakthrough but sustaining technological change—it fits the organization's values. But it presents the organization with different types of problems to solve and therefore requires new types of interaction and coordination among groups and individuals. The manager needs a heavyweight development team to tackle the new task, but the project can be executed within the mainstream company. This is how Chrysler, Eli Lilly, and Medtronic accelerated their product development cycles so dramatically.[11] Heavyweight teams are the organizational mechanism that the managers of IBM's disk drive division used to learn how to integrate components more effectively in their product designs, in order to wring 50 percent higher performance out of the components they used. Microsoft's project to develop and launch its Internet browser was located in the Region A corner of this framework. It represented an extraordinary, difficult managerial achievement that required different people to work together in patterns different than any ever used before within Microsoft. But it was a *sustaining* technology to the company. Its customers wanted the product, and it strengthened the company's integral business model. There was, therefore, no need to spin the project out into a completely different organization.

When in Region B, where the project fits the company's processes and values, a lightweight development team can be successful. In such teams coordination across functional boundaries occurs within the mainstream organization.

Region C denotes an area in which a manager is faced with a disruptive technological change that doesn't fit the organization's existing processes and values. To ensure success in such instances, managers should create an autonomous organization and commission a heavyweight development team to tackle the challenge. In addition to the examples cited in chapters 5, 6, and 7, many companies' efforts to address the distribution channel conflicts created by the Internet should be managed in this manner. In 1999 Compaq Computer, for example, launched a business to market its computers direct to customers over the Internet, so that it could compete more effectively with Dell Computer. Within a few weeks its retailers had protested so loudly that Compaq had to back away from the strategy. This was *very* disruptive to the values, or profit model, of the company and its retailers. The only way it could manage this conflict would be to launch the direct business through an independent company. It might even need a different brand in order to manage the tension.

Some have suggested that Wal-Mart's strategy of managing its on-line retailing operation through an independent organization in Silicon Valley is foolhardy, because the spin-out organization can't leverage Wal-Mart's extraordinary logistics management processes and infrastructure. I believe the spin-out was wise, however, based upon Figure 8.1. The on-line venture actually needs very different logistics processes than those of its bricks-and-mortar operations. Those operations transport goods by the truck-load. On-line retailers need to pick individual items from inventory and ship small packages to diverse locations. The venture is not only disruptive to Wal-Mart's values, but it needs to create its own logistics processes as well. It needed to be spun out separately.

Region D typifies projects in which products or services similar to those in the mainstream need to be sold within a fundamentally lower overhead cost business model. Wal-Mart's Sam's Clubs would fit in this region. These, in fact, can leverage similar logistics management processes as the main company; but budgeting, management, and P&L responsibility needs to be different.

Functional and lightweight teams are appropriate vehicles for exploiting established capabilities, whereas heavyweight teams are tools for creating new ones. Spin-out organizations, similarly, are tools for forging new values. Unfortunately, most companies employ a one-size-fits-all organizing strategy, using lightweight teams for programs of every size and character. Among those few firms that have accepted the "heavyweight gospel," many have attempted to organize all of their development teams in a heavyweight fashion. Ideally, each company should tailor the team structure and organizational location to the process and values required by each project.

In many ways, the disruptive technologies model is a theory of relativity, because what is disruptive to one company might have a sustaining impact on another. For example, Dell Computer began by selling computers over the telephone. For Dell, the initiative to begin selling and accepting orders over the Internet was a *sustaining* innovation. It helped it make more money in the way it was already structured. For Compaq, Hewlett-Packard, and IBM, however, marketing direct to customers over the Internet would have a powerfully disruptive impact. The same is true in stock brokerage. For discount brokers such as Ameritrade and Charles Schwab, which accepted most of their orders by telephone, trading securities on-line simply helped them discount more cost-effectively—and even offer enhanced service relative to their former capabilities. For full-service firms with commissioned brokers such as Merrill Lynch, however, on-line trading represents a powerful disruptive threat.

SUMMARY

Managers whose organizations are confronting change must first determine that they have the resources required to succeed. They then need to ask a separate question: does the organization have the processes and values to succeed? Asking this second question is not as instinctive for most managers because the processes by which work is done and the values by which employees make their decisions have served them well. What I hope this framework adds to managers' thinking, however, is that the very capabilities of their organizations also define their disabilities. A little time spent soul-searching for honest answers to this issue will pay off handsomely. Are the processes by which work habitually gets done in the organization appropriate for this new problem? And will the values of the organization cause this initiative to get high priority, or to languish?

If the answer to these questions is no, it's okay. Understanding problems is the most crucial step in solving them. Wishful thinking about this issue can set teams charged with developing and implementing an innovation on a course fraught with roadblocks, second-guessing, and frustration. The reasons why innovation often seems to be so difficult for established firms is that they employ highly capable people, and then set them to work within processes and values that weren't designed to facilitate success with the task at hand. Ensuring that capable people are ensconced in capable organizations is a major management responsibility in an age such as ours, when the ability to cope with accelerating change has become so critical.

NOTES

1. See C. K. Prahalad, and Gary Hamel, "The Core Competence of the Corporation," *Harvard Business Review,* 1990.
2. Many of these ideas emerged from wonderful, stimulating discussions with doctoral students in the Business Policy seminar at the Harvard Business School between 1993 and 1999. I wish to thank all of those students, but in particular Don Sull, Tom Eisenmann, Tomoyoshi Noda, Michael Raynor, Michael Roberto, Deborah Sole, Clark Gilbert, and Michael Overdorf for their contributions to these ideas.
3. The most logical, comprehensive characterization of processes that we have seen is in David Garvin, "The Processes of Organization and Management," *Sloan Management Review,* Summer, 1998. When we use the term "processes," we mean for it to include all of the types of processes that Garvin has defined.
4. See Dorothy Leonard-Barton, "Core Capabilities and Core Rigidities: A Paradox in Managing New Product Development," *Strategic Management Journal* (13), 1992, 111–125. Professor Leonardi's work on this topic, in my opinion, constitutes the fundamental paradigm upon which much subsequent research is being built.
5. See Wickham Skinner, "The Focused Factory," *Harvard Business Review,* 1974.
6. See, for example, Thomas Peters and Robert Waterman, *In Search of Excellence* (New York: Harper & Row Publishers, 1982).
7. See Edgar Schein, *Organizational Culture and Leadership* (San Francisco: Jossey-Bass Publishers, 1988). This description of the development of an organization's culture draws heavily from Schein's research.

8. See Nicole Tempest, "Cisco Systems, Inc. Post-Acquisition Manufacturing Integration," a teaching case published jointly by the Stanford University Graduate School of Business and the Harvard Business School, 1998.

9. Steven C. Wheelwright and Kim B. Clark, *Revolutionizing Product Development* (New York: The Free Press, 1992).

10. See Kim B. Clark and Steven C. Wheelwright, "Organizing and Leading Heavyweight Development Teams," *California Management Review* (34), Spring, 1992, 9–28. The concepts described in this article are extremely important. We highly recommend that managers interested in these problems study it thoughtfully. They define a heavyweight team as one in which team members typically are dedicated and colocated. The charge of each team member is not to represent their functional group on the team, but to act as a *general manager*—to assume responsibility for the success of the entire project, and to be actively involved in the decisions and work of members who come from each functional area. As they work together to complete their project, they will work out new ways of interacting, coordinating, and decision-making that will come to comprise the new processes, or new capabilities, that will be needed to succeed in the new enterprise on an ongoing basis. These ways of getting work done then get institutionalized as the new business or product line grows.

11. See Jeff Dyer, "How Chrysler Created an American Keiretsu," *Harvard Business Review,* July-August, 1996, 42–56; Clayton M. Christensen, "We've Got Rhythm! Medtronic Corporation's Cardiac Pacemaker Business," Harvard Business School, Case No. 698-004; and Steven C. Wheelwright, "Eli Lilly: The Evista Project," Harvard Business School, Case No. 699-016.

CHAPTER **NINE**

Performance Provided, Market Demand, and the Product Life Cycle

 The graphs in this book showing the intersecting technology and market trajectories have proven useful in explaining how leading firms can stumble from positions of industry leadership. In each of the several industries explored, technologists were able to provide rates of performance improvement that have exceeded the rates of performance improvement that the market has needed or was able to absorb. Historically, when this *performance oversupply* occurs, it creates an opportunity for a disruptive technology to emerge and subsequently to invade established markets from below.

As it creates this threat or opportunity for a disruptive technology, performance oversupply also triggers a fundamental change in the basis of competition in the product's market: The rank-ordering of the criteria by which customers choose one product or service over another will change, signaling a transition from one phase (variously defined by management theorists) to the next of the product life cycle. In other words, the intersecting trajectories of performance supplied and performance demanded are fundamental triggers behind the phases in the product life cycle. Because of this, trajectory maps such as those used in this book usefully characterize how an industry's competitive dynamics and its basis of competition are likely to change over time.

As with past chapters, this discussion begins with an analysis from the disk drive industry of what can happen when the performance supplied exceeds the market's demands. After seeing the same phenomenon played out in the markets for accounting software and for diabetes care products, the link between this pattern and the phases of the product life cycle will be clear.

PERFORMANCE OVERSUPPLY AND CHANGING BASES OF COMPETITION

The phenomenon of performance oversupply is charted in Figure 9.1, an extract from Figure 1.7. It shows that by 1988, the capacity of the average 3.5-inch drive had finally increased to equal the capacity demanded in the mainstream desktop personal computer market, and that the capacity of the average 5.25-inch drive had by that time surpassed what the mainstream desktop market demanded by nearly 300 percent. At this point, for the first time since the desktop market emerged, computer makers had a choice of drives to buy: The 5.25- and 3.5-inch drives *both* provided perfectly adequate capacity.

What was the result? The desktop personal computer makers began switching to 3.5-inch drives in droves. Figure 9.2 illustrates this, using a substitution curve format in which the vertical axis measures the ratio of new- to old-technology units sold. In 1985 this measure was .007, meaning that less than 1 percent (.0069) of the desktop market had switched to the 3.5-inch format. By 1987, the ratio had advanced 0.20, meaning that 16.7 percent of the units sold into this market that year were 3.5-inch drives. By 1989, the measure was 1.5, that is, only four years after the 3.5-inch product had appeared as a faint blip on the radar screen of the market, it accounted for 60 percent of drive sales.

Why did the 3.5-inch drive so decisively conquer the desktop PC market? A standard economic guess might be that the 3.5-inch format represented a more cost-effective architecture: If there were no longer any meaningful differentiation between two types of products (both had adequate capacity), price competition would intensify. This was not the case here, however. Indeed, computer makers had to pay, on average, 20 percent more per megabyte to use 3.5-inch drives, and yet they *still* flocked to the product. Moreover, computer manufacturers opted for the costlier drive while facing fierce price competition in their own product markets. Why?

Performance oversupply triggered a change in the basis of competition.

Figure 9.1 Intersecting Trajectories of Capacity Demanded versus Capacity
Supplied in Rigid Disk Drives

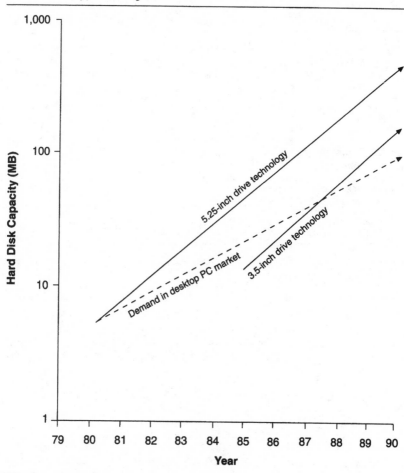

Source: Data are from various issues of *Disk/Trend Report.*

Once the demand for capacity was satiated, other attributes, whose performance had not yet satisfied market demands, came to be more highly valued and to constitute the dimensions along which drive makers sought to differentiate their products. In concept, this meant that the most important attribute measured on the vertical axis of figures such as 8.1 changed, and that new trajectories of product performance, compared to market demands, took shape.

Figure 9.2 Substitution of 8-, 5.25-, and 3.5-Inch Drives of 30 to 100 MB

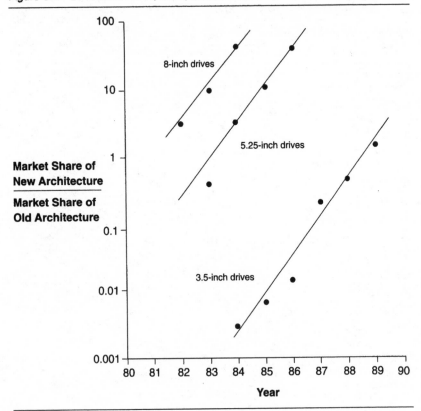

Source: Data are from various issues of *Disk/Trend Report.*

Specifically, in the desktop personal computer marketplace between 1986 and 1988, the smallness of the drive began to matter more than other features. The smaller 3.5-inch drive allowed computer manufacturers to reduce the size, or desktop footprint, of their machines. At IBM, for example, the large XT/AT box gave way to the much smaller PS1/PS2 generation machines.

For a time, when the availability of small drives did not satisfy market demands, desktop computer makers continued to pay a hefty premium for 3.5-inch drives. In fact, using the hedonic regression analysis described in chapter 4, the 1986 shadow price for a one-cubic-inch reduction in the volume of a disk drive was $4.72. But once the computer makers had configured their new generations of desktop machines to use the smaller drive, their demand for even more smallness was satiated. As a result, the 1989 shadow price, or the price premium accorded to smaller drives, diminished to $0.06 for a one-cubic-inch reduction.

Generally, once the performance level demanded of a particular attribute has been achieved, customers indicate their satiation by being less willing to pay a premium price for continued improvement in that attribute. Hence, performance oversupply triggers a shift in the basis of competition, and the criteria used by customers to choose one product over another changes to attributes for which market demands are not yet satisfied.

Figure 9.3 summarizes what seems to have happened in the desktop PC market: The attribute measured on the vertical axis repeatedly changed. Performance oversupply in capacity triggered the first redefinition of the vertical axis, from capacity to physical size. When performance on this new dimension satisfied market needs, the definition of performance on the vertical axis changed once more, to reflect demand for reliability. For a time, products offering competitively superior shock resistance and mean time between failure (MTBF) were accorded a significant price premium, compared to competitive offerings. But as MTBF values approached one million hours,[1] the shadow price accorded to an increment of one hundred hours MTBF approached zero, suggesting performance oversupply on that dimension of product performance. The subsequent and current phase is an intense price-based competition, with gross margins tumbling below 12 percent in some instances.

WHEN DOES A PRODUCT BECOME A COMMODITY?

The process of commoditization of disk drives was defined by the interplay between the trajectories of what the market demanded and what the technology supplied. The 5.25-inch drive had become a price-driven commodity in the desktop market by about 1988, when the 3.5-inch drive was still at a premium price. The 5.25-inch drive, in addition, even though priced as a commodity in desktop applications, was at the same time, relative to 8-inch drives, achieving substantial price premiums in higher-tier markets. As described in chapter 4, this explains the aggressive moves upmarket made by established companies.

A product becomes a commodity within a specific market segment when the repeated changes in the basis of competition, as described above, completely play themselves out, that is, when market needs on each attri-

Figure 9.3 Changes in the Basis of Competition in the Disk Drive Industry

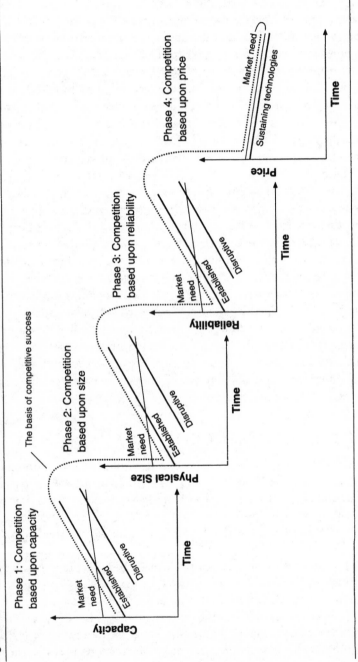

bute or dimension of performance have been fully satisfied by more than one available product. The performance oversupply framework may help consultants, managers, and researchers to understand the frustrated comments they regularly hear from salespeople beaten down in price negotiations with customers: "Those stupid guys are just treating our product like it was a commodity. Can't they see how much better our product is than the competition's?" It may, in fact, be the case that the product offerings of competitors in a market continue to be differentiated from each other. But differentiation loses its meaning when the features and functionality have exceeded what the market demands.

PERFORMANCE OVERSUPPLY AND THE EVOLUTION OF PRODUCT COMPETITION

The marketing literature provides numerous descriptions of the product life cycle and of the ways in which the characteristics of products within given categories evolve over time.[2] The findings in this book suggest that, for many of these models, performance oversupply is an important factor driving the transition from one phase of the cycle to the next.

Consider, for example, the product evolution model, called the *buying hierarchy* by its creators, Windermere Associates of San Francisco, California, which describes as typical the following four phases: functionality, reliability, convenience, and price. Initially, when no available product satisfies the functionality requirements the market, the basis of competition, or the criteria by which product choice is made, tends to be product *functionality*. (Sometimes, as in disk drives, a market may cycle through several different functionality dimensions.) Once two or more products credibly satisfy the market's demand for functionality, however, customers can no longer base their choice of products on functionality, but tend to choose a product and vendor based on *reliability*. As long as market demand for reliability exceeds what vendors are able to provide, customers choose products on this basis—and the most reliable vendors of the most reliable products earn a premium for it.

But when two or more vendors improve to the point that they more than satisfy the reliability demanded by the market, the basis of competition shifts to *convenience*. Customers will prefer those products that are the most convenient to use and those vendors that are most convenient to deal with. Again, as long as the market demand for convenience exceeds what vendors are able to provide, customers choose products on this basis and reward vendors with premium prices for the convenience they offer. Finally, when multiple vendors offer a package of convenient products and services that fully satisfies market demand, the basis of competition shifts to *price*. The factor driving the transition from one phase of the buying hierarchy to the next is performance oversupply.

Another useful conception of industry evolution, formulated by Geoffrey Moore in his book *Crossing the Chasm*,[3] has a similar underlying logic, but articulates the stages in terms of the user rather than the product. Moore suggests that products are initially used by innovators and *early adopters* in an industry—customers who base their choice solely on the product's functionality. During this phase the top-performing products command significant price premiums. Moore observes that markets then expand dramatically after the demand for functionality in the mainstream market has been met, and vendors begin to address the need for reliability among what he terms *early majority* customers. A third wave of growth occurs when product and vendor reliability issues have been resolved, and the basis of innovation and competition shifts to convenience, thus pulling in the *late majority* customers. Underlying Moore's model is the notion that technology can improve to the point that market demand for a given dimension of performance can be satiated.

This evolving pattern in the basis of competition—from functionality, to reliability and convenience, and finally to price—has been seen in many of the markets so far discussed. In fact, a key characteristic of a disruptive technology is that it heralds a change in the basis of competition.

OTHER CONSISTENT CHARACTERISTICS OF DISRUPTIVE TECHNOLOGIES

Two additional important characteristics of disruptive technologies consistently affect product life cycles and competitive dynamics: First, the attributes that make disruptive products worthless in mainstream markets typically become their strongest selling points in emerging markets; and second, disruptive products tend to be simpler, cheaper, and more reliable and convenient than established products. Managers must understand these characteristics to effectively chart their own strategies for designing, building, and selling disruptive products. Even though the specific market applications for disruptive technologies cannot be known in advance, managers can bet on these two regularities.

1. The Weaknesses of Disruptive Technologies Are Their Strengths

The relation between disruptive technologies and the basis of competition in an industry is complex. In the interplay among performance oversupply, the product life cycle, and the emergence of disruptive technologies, it is often the very attributes that render disruptive technologies useless in mainstream markets that constitute their value in new markets.

In general, companies that have succeeded in disruptive innovation initially took the characteristics and capabilities of the technology for granted and sought to find or create a new market that would value or accept those attributes. Thus, Conner Peripherals created a market for small drives in portable computers, where smallness was valued; J. C. Bamford and J. I. Case built a market for excavators among residential contractors, where small buckets and tractor mobility actually created value; and Nucor found a market that didn't mind the surface blemishes on its thin-slab-cast sheet steel.

The companies toppled by these disruptive technologies, in contrast, each took the established market's *needs* as given, and did not attempt to market the technology until they felt it was good enough to be valued in the mainstream market. Thus, Seagate's marketers took the firm's early 3.5-inch drives to IBM for evaluation, rather than asking, "Where is the market that would actually value a smaller, lower-capacity drive?" When Bucyrus Erie acquired its Hydrohoe hydraulic excavator line in 1951, its managers apparently did not ask, "Where is the market that actually *wants* a mobile excavator that can only dig narrow trenches?" They assumed instead that the market needed the largest possible bucket size and the longest possible reach; they jury-rigged the Hydrohoe with cables, pulleys, clutches, and winches and attempted to sell it to general excavation contractors. When U.S. Steel was evaluating continuous thin-slab casting, they did not ask, "Where is the market for low-priced sheet steel with poor surface appearance?" Rather, they took it for granted that the market needed the highest-possible quality of surface finish and invested more capital in a conventional caster. They applied to a disruptive innovation a way of thinking appropriate to a sustaining technology.

In the instances studied in this book, established firms confronted with disruptive technology typically viewed their primary development challenge as a *technological* one: to improve the disruptive technology enough that it suits known markets. In contrast, the firms that were most successful in commercializing a disruptive technology were those framing their primary development challenge as a *marketing* one: to build or find a market where product competition occurred along dimensions that favored the disruptive attributes of the product.[4]

It is critical that managers confronting disruptive technology observe this principle. If history is any guide, companies that keep disruptive technologies bottled up in their labs, working to improve them until they suit mainstream markets, will not be nearly as successful as firms that find markets that embrace the attributes of disruptive technologies as they initially stand. These latter firms, by creating a commercial base and then moving upmarket, will ultimately address the mainstream market much more effectively than will firms that have framed disruptive technology as a laboratory, rather than a marketing, challenge.

2. Disruptive Technologies Are Typically Simpler, Cheaper, and More Reliable and Convenient than Established Technologies

When performance oversupply has occurred and a disruptive technology attacks the underbelly of a mainstream market, the disruptive technology often succeeds both because it satisfies the market's need for functionality, in terms of the buying hierarchy, and because it is simpler, cheaper, and more reliable and convenient than mainstream products. Recall, for example, the attack of hydraulic excavation technology into the mainstream sewer and general excavation markets recounted in chapter 3. Once hydraulically powered excavators had the strength to handle buckets of 2 to 4 cubic yards of earth (surpassing the performance demanded in mainstream markets), contractors rapidly switched to these products even though the cable-actuated machines were capable of moving even more earth per scoop. Because both technologies provided adequate bucket capacity for their needs, contractors opted for the technology that was most reliable: hydraulics.

Because established companies are so prone to push for high-performance, high-profit products and markets, they find it very difficult not to overload their first disruptive products with features and functionality. Hewlett-Packard's experience in designing its 1.3-inch Kittyhawk disk drive teaches just this lesson. Unable to design a product that was truly simple and cheap, Kittyhawk's champions pushed its capacity to the limits of technology and gave it levels of shock resistance and power consumption that would make it competitive as a sustaining product. When very high volume applications for a cheap, simple, single-function, 10 MB drive began to emerge, HP's product was not disruptive enough to catch that wave. Apple committed a similar error in stretching the functionality of its Newton, instead of initially targeting simplicity and reliability.

PERFORMANCE OVERSUPPLY IN THE ACCOUNTING SOFTWARE MARKET

Intuit, the maker of financial management software, is known primarily for its extraordinarily successful personal financial software package, *Quicken. Quicken* dominates its market because it is easy and convenient. Its makers pride themselves on the fact that the vast majority of *Quicken* customers simply buy the program, boot it up on their computers, and begin using it without having to read the instruction manual. Its developers made it so convenient to use, and continue to make it simpler and more convenient, by watching how customers *use* the product, not by listening to what they or the "experts" say they need. By watching for small hints of where the product might be difficult or confusing to use, the developers direct their energies toward a progressively simpler, more convenient product that provides adequate, rather than superior, functionality.[5]

Less well known is Intuit's commanding 70 percent share of the North American small business accounting software market.[6] Intuit captured that share as a late entrant when it launched *Quickbooks,* a product based on three simple insights. First, previously available small business accounting packages had been created under the close guidance of certified public accountants and required users to have a basic knowledge of accounting (debits and credits, assets and liabilities, and so on) and to make every journal entry twice (thus providing an audit trail for each transaction). Second, most existing packages offered a comprehensive and sophisticated array of reports and analyses, an array that grew ever more complicated and specialized with each new release as developers sought to differentiate their products by offering greater functionality. And third, 85 percent of all companies in the United States were too small to employ an accountant: The books were kept by the proprietors or by family members, who had no need for or understanding of most of the entries and reports available from mainstream accounting software. They did not know what an audit trail was, let alone sense a need to use one.

Scott Cook, Intuit's founder, surmised that most of these small companies were run by proprietors who relied more on their intuition and direct knowledge of the business than on the information contained in accounting reports. In other words, Cook decided that the makers of accounting software for small businesses had overshot the functionality required by that market, thus creating an opportunity for a disruptive software technology that provided adequate, not superior functionality and was simple and more convenient to use. Intuit's disruptive *Quickbooks* changed the basis of product competition from functionality to convenience and captured 70 percent of its market within two years of its introduction.[7] In fact, by 1995 *Quickbooks* accounted for a larger share of Intuit's revenues than did *Quicken*.

The response of established makers of small business accounting software to Intuit's invasion, quite predictably, has been to move upmarket, continuing to release packages loaded with greater functionality; these focus on specific market subsegments, targeted at sophisticated users of information systems at loftier tiers of the market. Of the three leading suppliers of small business accounting software (each of which claimed about 30 percent of the market in 1992), one has disappeared and one is languishing. The third has introduced a simplified product to counter the success of *Quickbooks,* but it has claimed only a tiny portion of the market.

PERFORMANCE OVERSUPPLY IN THE PRODUCT LIFE CYCLE OF INSULIN

Another case of performance oversupply and disruptive technology precipitating a change in the basis of competition—and threatening a change in industry leadership—is found in the worldwide insulin business. In 1922, four researchers in Toronto first successfully extracted insulin from the pancreases of animals and injected it, with miraculous results, into humans with diabetes. Because insulin was extracted from the ground-up pancreases of cows and pigs, improving the purity of insulin (measured in impure parts per million, or ppm) constituted a critical trajectory of performance improvement. Impurities dropped from 50,000 ppm in 1925 to 10,000 ppm in 1950 to 10 ppm in 1980, primarily as the result of persistent investment and effort by the world's leading insulin manufacturer, Eli Lilly and Company.

Despite this improvement, animal insulins, which are slightly different from human insulin, caused a fraction of a percent of diabetic patients to build up resistance in their immune systems. Thus, in 1978, Eli Lilly contracted with Genentech to create genetically altered bacteria that could produce insulin proteins that were the structural equivalent of human insulin proteins and 100 percent pure. The project was technically success-ful, and in the early 1980s, after a nearly $1 billion investment, Lilly introduced its Humulin-brand insulin to the market. Priced at a 25 percent premium over insulins of animal extraction, because of its human equiva-lence and its purity, Humulin was the first commercial-scale product for human consumption to emerge from the biotechnology industry.

The market's response to this technological miracle, however, was tepid. Lilly found it very difficult to sustain a premium price over animal insulin, and the growth in the sales volume of Humulin was disappointingly slow. "In retrospect," noted a Lilly researcher, "the market was not terribly dissatisfied with pork insulin. In fact, it was pretty happy with it."[8] Lilly had spent enormous capital and organizational energy overshooting the market's demand for product purity. Once again, this was a differentiated product to which the market did not accord a price premium because the performance it provided exceeded what the market demanded.

Meanwhile, Novo, a much smaller Danish insulin maker, was busy developing a line of insulin *pens,* a more convenient way for taking insulin. Conventionally, people with diabetes carried a separate syringe, inserted its needle into one glass insulin vial, pulled its plunger out to draw slightly more than the desired amount of insulin into the syringe, and held up the needle and flicked the syringe several times to dislodge any air bubbles that clung to the cylinder walls. They generally then had to repeat this process with a second, slower acting type of insulin. Only after squeezing the plunger slightly to force any remaining bubbles—and, inevitably, some insulin—out of the syringe could they inject themselves with the insulin. This process typically took one to two minutes.

Novo's pen, in contrast, held a cartridge containing a couple of weeks' supply of insulin, usually mixtures of both the fast-acting and the gradually released types. People using the Novo pen simply had to turn a small dial to the amount of insulin they needed to inject, poke the pen's needle under the skin, and press a button. The procedure took less than ten seconds. In contrast to Lilly's struggle to command a premium price for Humulin, Novo's convenient pens easily sustained a 30 percent price premium per unit of insulin. Through the 1980s, propelled largely by the success of its line of pens and pre-mixed cartridges, Novo increased its share of the worldwide insulin market substantially—and profitably. Lilly's and Novo's experiences offer further proof that a product whose performance exceeds market demands suffers commodity-like pricing, while disruptive products that redefine the basis of competition command a premium.

Teaching the Harvard Business School case to executives and MBA students about Lilly overshooting the market demand for insulin purity has been one of my most interesting professional experiences. In every class, the majority of students quickly pounce on Lilly for having missed something so obvious—that only a fraction of a percent of people with diabetes develop insulin resistance—and that the differentiation between highly purified pork insulin at 10 ppm and perfectly pure Humulin was not significant. Surely, they assert, a few simple focus groups in which patients and doctors were asked whether they wanted purer insulin would have given Lilly adequate guidance.

In every discussion, however, more thoughtful students soon begin to sway class opinion toward the view that (as we have seen over and over) what is obvious in retrospect might not be at all obvious in the thick of battle. Of all the physicians to whom Lilly's marketers listened, for example, which ones tended to carry the most credibility? Endocrinologists whose practices focused on diabetes care, the leading customers in this business. What sorts of patients are most likely to consume the professional interests of these specialists? Those with the most advanced and intractable problems, among which insulin resistance was prominent. What, therefore, were these leading customers likely to tell Lilly's marketers when they asked what should be done to improve the next-generation insulin product? Indeed, the power and influence of leading customers is a major reason why companies' product development trajectories overshoot the demands of mainstream markets.

Furthermore, thoughtful students observe that it would not even occur to most marketing managers to ask the question of whether a 100 percent pure human insulin might exceed market needs. For more than fifty years in a very successful company with a very strong culture, greater purity was the very definition of a better product. Coming up with purer insulins had *always* been the formula for staying ahead of the competition. Greater purity had *always* been a catching story that the salesforce could use to attract the time and attention of busy physicians. What in the company's history would cause its culture-based assumptions suddenly to change and its executives to begin asking questions that never before had needed to be answered?[9]

CONTROLLING THE EVOLUTION OF PRODUCT COMPETITION

Figure 9.4 summarizes the model of performance oversupply, depicting a multi-tiered market in which the trajectory of performance improvement demanded by the market is shallower than the trajectory of improvement supplied by technologists. Hence, each tier of the market progresses through an evolutionary cycle marked by a shifting basis for product choice. Although other terms for product life cycles would yield similar results, this diagram uses the buying hierarchy devised by Windermere Associates, in which competition centers first on functionality, followed by relia-

Figure 9.4 Managing Changes in the Basis of Competition

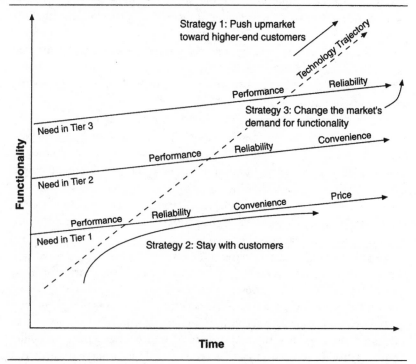

bility, convenience, and, finally, price. In each of the cases reviewed in this chapter, the products heralding shifts in the basis of competition and progression to the next product life cycle phase were disruptive technologies.

The figure shows the strategic alternatives available to companies facing performance oversupply and the consequent likelihood that disruptive approaches will change the nature of competition in their industry. The first general option, labeled strategy 1 and the one most commonly pursued in the industries explored in this book, is to ascend the trajectory of sustaining technologies into ever-higher tiers of the market, ultimately abandoning lower-tier customers when simpler, more convenient, or less costly disruptive approaches emerge.

A second alternative, labeled strategy 2, is to march in lock-step with the needs of customers in a given tier of the market, catching successive waves of change in the basis of competition. Historically, this appears to have been difficult to do, for all of the reasons described in earlier chapters. In the personal computer industry, for example, as the functionality of desktop machines came to satiate the demands of the lower tiers of the market, new entrants such as Dell and Gateway 2000 entered with value propositions centered on convenience of purchase and use. In the face of this, Compaq responded by actively pursuing this second approach, aggressively fighting any upmarket drift by producing a line of computers with low prices and modest functionality targeted to the needs of the lower tiers of the market.

The third strategic option for dealing with these dynamics is to use marketing initiatives to steepen the slopes of the market trajectories so that customers demand the performance improvements that the technologists provide. Since a necessary condition for the playing out of these dynamics is that the slope of the technology trajectory be steeper than the market's trajectory, when the two slopes are parallel, performance oversupply—and the progression from one stage of the product life cycle to the next—does not occur or is at least postponed.

Some computer industry observers believe that Microsoft, Intel, and the disk drive companies have pursued this last strategy very effectively. Microsoft has used its industry dominance to create and successfully market software packages that consume massive amounts of disk memory and require ever-faster microprocessors to execute. It has, essentially, increased the slopes of the trajectories of improvement in functionality demanded by their customers to parallel the slope of improvement provided by their technologists. The effect of this strategy is described in

Figure 9.5, depicting recent events in the disk drive industry. (This chart
updates through 1996 the disk drive trajectory map in Figure 1.7.) Notice
how the trajectories of capacity demanded in the mid-range, desktop, and
notebook computer segments kinked upward in the 1990s along a path
that essentially paralleled the capacity path blazed by the makers of 3.5-
inch and 2.5-inch disk drives. Because of this, these markets have not

Figure 9.5 Changed Performance Demand Trajectories and the Deferred Impact
of Disruptive Technologies

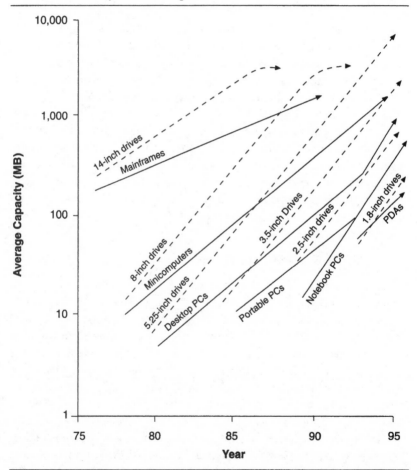

Source: An earlier version of this figure was published in Clayton M. Christensen, "The Rigid Disk
Drive Industry: A History of Commercial and Technological Turbulence," *Business History Review*
67, no. 4 (Winter 1993): 559.

experienced performance oversupply in recent years. The 2.5-inch drive remains locked within the notebook computer market because capacity demanded on the desktop is increasing at too brisk a pace. The 3.5-inch drive remains solidly ensconced in the desktop market, and the 1.8-inch drive has penetrated few notebook computers, for the same reasons. In this situation, the companies whose products are positioned closest to the top of the market, such as Seagate and IBM, have been the most profitable, because in the absence of technology oversupply, a shift in the stages of the product life cycle at the high end of the market has been held at bay.

It is unclear how long the marketers at Microsoft, Intel, and Seagate can succeed in creating demand for whatever functionality their technologists can supply. Microsoft's *Excel* spreadsheet software, for example, required 1.2 MB of disk storage capacity in its version 1.2, released in 1987. Its version 5.0, released in 1995, required 32 MB of disk storage capacity. Some industry observers believe that if a team of developers were to watch typical users, they would find that functionality has substantially overshot mainstream market demands. If true, this could create an opportunity for a disruptive technology—applets picked off the internet and used in simple internet appliances rather than in full-function computers, for example—to invade this market from below.

RIGHT AND WRONG STRATEGIES

Which of the strategies illustrated in Figure 9.4 is best? This study finds clear evidence that there is no one best strategy. Any of the three, consciously pursued, can be successful. Hewlett-Packard's pursuit of the first strategy in its laser jet printer business has been enormously profitable. In this instance, it has been a safe strategy as well, because HP is attacking its own position with disruptive ink-jet technology. Compaq Computer and the trinity of Intel, Microsoft, and the disk drive makers have successfully—at least to date—implemented the second and third strategies, respectively.

These successful practitioners have in common their apparent understanding—whether explicit or intuitive—of both their customers' trajectories of need and their own technologists' trajectories of supply. Understanding these trajectories is the key to their success thus far. But the list of firms that have consistently done this is disturbingly short. Most well-run companies migrate unconsciously to the northeast, setting themselves up to be caught by a change in the basis of competition and an attack from below by disruptive technology.

NOTES

1. In disk drive industry convention, a mean time between failure measure of one million hours means that if one million disk drives were turned on simultaneously and operated continuously for one hour, one of those drives would fail within the first hour.
2. Three of the earliest and most influential papers that proposed the existence of product life cycles were Jay W. Forrester, "Industrial Dynamics," *Harvard Business Review,* July–August, 1958, 9–14; Arch Patton, "Stretch Your Products' Earning Years—Top Management's Stake in the Product Life Cycle," *Management Review* (38), June, 1959, 67–79; and William E. Cox, "Product Life Cycles as Marketing Models," *Journal of Business* (40), October, 1967, 375. Papers summarizing the conceptual and empirical problems surrounding the product life cycle concept include Nariman K. Dhalla and Sonia Yuspeh, "Forget the Product Life Cycle Concept!" *Harvard Business Review,* January–February, 1976, 102–112; David R. Rink and John E. Swan, "Product Life Cycle Research: A Literature Review," *Journal of Business Research,* 1979, 219; and George S. Day, "The Product Life Cycle: Analysis and Applications Issues," *Journal of Marketing* (45), Fall, 1981, 60–67. A paper by Gerard J. Tellis and C. Merle Crawford, "An Evolutionary Approach to Product Growth Theory," *Journal of Marketing* (45), Fall, 1981, 125–132, contains a cogent critique of the product life cycle concept, and presents a theory of product evolution that presages many of the ideas presented in this section.
3. Geoffrey A. Moore, *Crossing the Chasm* (New York: HarperBusiness, 1991).
4. The same behavior characterized the emergence of portable radios. In the early 1950s, Akio Morita, the chairman of Sony, took up residence in an inexpensive New York City hotel in order to negotiate a license to AT&T's patented transistor technology, which its scientists had invented in 1947. Morita found AT&T to be a less-than-willing negotiator and had to visit the company repeatedly badgering AT&T to grant the license. Finally AT&T relented. After the meeting ended in which the licensing documents were signed, an AT&T official asked Morita what Sony planned to do with the license. "We will build small radios," Morita replied. "Why would anyone care about smaller radios?" the official queried. "We'll see," was Morita's answer. Several months later Sony introduced to the U.S. market the first

portable transistor radio. According to the dominant metrics of radio performance in the mainstream market, these early transistor radios were really bad, offering far lower fidelity and much more static than the vacuum tube–based tabletop radios that were the dominant design of the time. But rather than work in his labs until his transistor radios were performance-competitive in the major market (which is what most of the leading electronics companies did with transistor technology), Morita instead found a market that valued the attributes of the technology as it existed at the time—the portable personal radio. Not surprisingly, none of the leading makers of tabletop radios became a leading producer of portable radios, and all were subsequently driven from the radio market. (This story was recounted to me by Dr. Sheldon Weinig, retired vice chairman for manufacturing and technology of Sony Corporation.)

5. John Case, "Customer Service: The Last Word," *Inc. Magazine,* April, 1991, 1–5.

6. This information in this section was given to the author by Scott Cook, the founder and chairman of Intuit Corporation, and by Jay O'Connor, marketing manager for *Quickbooks.*

7. Cook recounts that in the process of designing a simple and convenient accounting software package, Intuit's developers arrived at a profound insight. The double-entry accounting system originally developed by Venetian merchants to catch arithmetical mistakes continued to be used in every available package of accounting software—even though computers typically do not make mistakes in addition and subtraction. Intuit was able to greatly simplify its product by eliminating this unneeded dimension of product functionality.

8. See "Eli Lilly & Co.: Innovation in Diabetes Care," Harvard Business School, Case No. 9-696-077. This case notes that although Lilly was not able to achieve premium pricing for its Humulin insulin, it benefited from the investment. Humulin protected Lilly against a possible shortfall in the pancreas supply, threatened by declining red meat consumption, and it gave Lilly a very valuable experience and asset base in the volume manufacturing of bioengineered drugs.

9. Once such minority opinions have been raised in class, many students then begin to see that institutions widely regarded as among the best-managed and most successful in the world may have overshot what their mainstream markets demand. Intel, for example, has always measured the speed of its microprocessors on the vertical axis of its performance graphs. It has always assumed that the market demands ever-faster microprocessors, and evidence to the tune of billions of dollars in profit has certainly confirmed that belief. Certainly some leading-edge customers need chips that process instructions at rates of 200, 400, and 800 MHz. But what about the mainstream market? Is it possible that sometime soon the speed and cost of Intel's new microprocessors might

overshoot market demands? And if technology oversupply is possible, how will thousands of Intel employees be able to recognize when this has occurred, accepting the change with enough conviction to completely alter the trajectory of their development efforts? Discerning technology oversupply is difficult. Doing something about it is even more so.

CHAPTER **TEN**

Managing Disruptive Technological Change: A Case Study

As we approach the end of this book, we should better understand why great companies can stumble. Incompetence, bureaucracy, arrogance, tired executive blood, poor planning, and short-term investment horizons obviously have played leading roles in toppling many companies. But we have learned here that even the best managers are subject to certain laws that make disruptive innovation difficult. It is when great managers haven't understood or have attempted to fight these forces that their companies have stumbled.

This chapter uses the forces and principles described in earlier chapters to illustrate how managers can succeed when faced with disruptive technology change. To do so, I employ a case study format, using a personal voice, to suggest how I, as a hypothetical employee of a major automaker, might manage a program to develop and commercialize one of the most vexing innovations of our day: the electric vehicle. My purpose here is explicitly *not* to offer any so-called right answer to this particular challenge, nor to predict whether or how electric vehicles may become commercially successful. Rather, it is to suggest in a familiar but challenging context how managers might structure their thinking about a similar problem by proposing a sequence of questions that, if asked, can lead to a sound and useful answer.

HOW CAN WE KNOW IF A TECHNOLOGY IS DISRUPTIVE?

Electric-powered vehicles have hovered at the fringe of legitimacy since the early 1900s, when they lost the contest for the dominant vehicle design to gasoline power. Research on these vehicles accelerated during the 1970s, however, as policy makers increasingly looked to them as a way to reduce urban air pollution. The California Air Resources Board (CARB) forced an unprecedented infusion of resources into the effort in the early 1990s when it mandated that, starting in 1998, no automobile manufacturer would be allowed to sell *any* cars in California if electric vehicles did not constitute at least 2 percent of its unit sales in the state.[1]

In my hypothetical responsibility for managing an automaker's program, my first step would be to ask a series of questions: How much do we need to worry about electric cars? That is, aside from California's mandate, does the electric car pose a legitimate disruptive threat to companies making gasoline-powered automobiles? Does it constitute an opportunity for profitable growth?

To answer these questions, I would graph the trajectories of performance improvement demanded in the market versus the performance improvement supplied by the technology; in other words, I would create for electric vehicles a trajectory map similar to those in Figures 1.7 or 9.5. Such charts are the best method I know for identifying disruptive technologies.

The first step in making this chart involves defining current mainstream market needs and comparing them with the current capacity of electric vehicles. To measure market needs, I would watch carefully what customers *do*, not simply listen to what they *say*. Watching how customers actually use a product provides much more reliable information than can be gleaned from a verbal interview or a focus group.[2] Thus, observations indicate that auto users today require a minimum cruising range (that is, the distance that can be driven without refueling) of about 125 to 150 miles; most electric vehicles only offer a minimum cruising range of 50 to 80 miles. Similarly, drivers seem to require cars that accelerate from 0 to 60 miles per hour in less than 10 seconds (necessary primarily to merge safely into high-speed traffic from freeway entrance ramps); most electric vehicles take nearly 20 seconds to get there. And, finally, buyers in the mainstream market demand a wide array of options, but it would be impossible for electric vehicle manufacturers to offer a similar variety within the small initial unit volumes that will characterize that business.[3] According to almost any definition of functionality used for the vertical axis of our proposed chart, the electric vehicle will be deficient compared to a gasoline-powered car.

This information is not sufficient to characterize electric vehicles as disruptive, however. They will only be disruptive if we find that they are also on a trajectory of improvement that might someday make them competitive in parts of the mainstream market. To assess this possibility, we need to project trajectories measuring the performance improvement demanded in the market versus the performance improvement that electric vehicle technology may provide. If these trajectories are parallel, then electric vehicles are unlikely to become factors in the mainstream market; but if the technology will progress faster than the pace of improvement demanded in the market, then the threat of disruption is real.

Figure 10.1 shows that the trajectories of performance improvement demanded in the market—whether measured in terms of required acceleration, cruising range, or top cruising speed—are relatively flat. This is because traffic laws impose a limit on the usefulness of ever-more-powerful cars, and demographic, economic, and geographic considerations limit the increase in commuting miles for the average driver to less than 1 percent per year.[4] At the same time, the performance of electric vehicles is improving at a faster rate—between 2 and 4 percent per year—suggesting that sustaining technological advances might indeed carry electric vehicles from their position today, where they cannot compete in mainstream markets, to a position in the future where they might.[5]

In other words, as an automotive company executive, I would worry about the electric vehicle, not just because it is politically correct to be investing in environmentally friendly technologies, but because electric vehicles have the smell of a disruptive technology. They can't be used in mainstream markets; they offer a set of attributes that is orthogonal to those that command attention in the gasoline-powered value network; and the technology is moving ahead at a faster rate than the market's trajectory of need.

Because electric vehicles are not sustaining innovations, however, mainstream automakers naturally doubt that there is a market for them—another symptom of a disruptive innovation. Consider this statement by the director of Ford's electric vehicle program: "The electric Ranger will sell at approximately $30,000 and have a lead-acid battery that will give it a range of 50 miles . . . . The 1998 electric vehicle will be a difficult sell. The products that will be available will not meet customer expectations in terms of range, cost or utility."[6] Indeed, given their present performance

Figure 10.1 The Electric Car

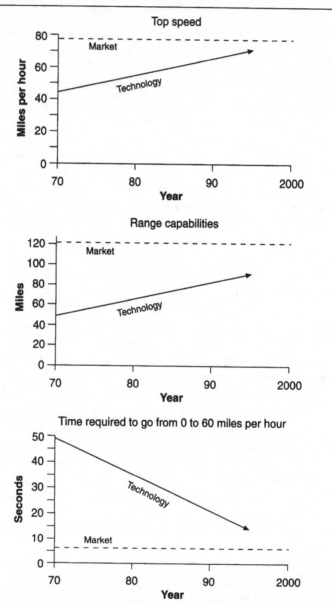

Source: Data are from Dr. Paul J. Miller, Senior Energy Fellow, W. Alton Jones Foundation and from numerous articles about electric vehicles.

along these parameters, it will be about as easy to sell electric vehicles into the mainstream car market as it was to sell 5.25-inch disk drives to mainframe computer makers in 1980.

In evaluating these trajectories, I would be careful to keep asking the right question: Will the trajectory of electric vehicle performance ever intersect the trajectory of *market* demands (as revealed in the way customers *use* cars)? Industry experts may contend that electric vehicles will never perform as well as gasoline-powered cars, in effect comparing the trajectories of the two *technologies*. They are probably correct. But, recalling the experience of their counterparts in the disk drive industry, they will have the right answer to the wrong question. I also would note, but not be deterred by, the mountain of expert opinion averring that without a major technological breakthrough in battery technology, there will never be a substantial market for electric vehicles. The reason? If electric vehicles are viewed as a *sustaining technology* for established market value networks, they are clearly right. But because the track records of experts predicting the nature and size of markets for disruptive technologies is very poor, I would be particularly skeptical of the experts' skepticism, even as I remain uncertain about my own conclusions.

WHERE IS THE MARKET FOR ELECTRIC VEHICLES?

Having decided that electric vehicles are a potentially disruptive technology, my next challenge would be to define a marketing strategy that could lead my company to a legitimate, unsubsidized market in which electric cars might first be used. In formulating this marketing strategy, I would apply three findings from earlier chapters in this book.

First, I would acknowledge that, by definition, *electric vehicles cannot initially be used in mainstream applications* because they do not satisfy the basic performance requirements of that market. I would therefore be sure that *everybody* having *anything* to do with my program understands this point: Although we don't have a clue about where the market is, the one thing we know for certain is that it *isn't* in an established automobile market segment. Ironically, I would expect most automakers to focus precisely and myopically on the mainstream market because of the principle of resource dependence and the principle that small markets don't solve the growth and profit needs of big companies. I would not, therefore, follow the lead of other automakers in my search for customers, because

I would recognize that their instincts and capabilities are likely to be trained on the wrong target.[7]

Nonetheless, my task is to find a market in which the vehicles can be used, because the early entrants into disruptive technology markets develop capabilities that constitute strong advantages over later entrants. They're the ones that, from a profitable business base in this beachhead market, will most successfully throw impetus behind the sustaining innovations required to move the disruptive technology upmarket, toward the mainstream. Holding back from the market, waiting for laboratory researchers to develop a breakthrough battery technology, for example, is the path of least resistance for managers. But this strategy has *rarely* proven to be a viable route to success with a disruptive innovation.

Historically, as we have seen, the very attributes that make disruptive technologies uncompetitive in mainstream markets actually count as *positive* attributes in their emerging value network. In disk drives, the smallness of 5.25-inch models made them unusable in large computers but very useful on the desktop. While the small bucket capacity and short reach of early hydraulic excavators made them useless in general excavation, their ability to dig precise, narrow trenches made them useful in residential construction. Odd as it sounds, therefore, I would direct my marketers to focus on uncovering *somewhere* a group of buyers who have an undiscovered need for a vehicle that accelerates relatively slowly and can't be driven farther than 100 miles!

The second point on which I would base my marketing approach is that *no one can learn from market research what the early market(s) for electric vehicles will be.* I can hire consultants, but the only thing I can know for sure is that their findings will be wrong. Nor can customers tell me whether or how they might use electric vehicles, because *they* will discover how they might use the products at the same time as *we* discover it—just as Honda's Supercub opened an unforeseen new application for motorbiking. The only useful information about the market will be what I create through expeditions into the market, through testing and probing, trial and error, by selling real products to real people who pay real money.[8] Government mandates, incidentally, are likely to distort rather than solve the problem of finding a market. I would, therefore, force my organization to live by its wits rather than to rely on capricious subsidies or non-economic–based California regulation to fuel my business.

The third point is that my business plan must be a plan for *learning*, not one for executing a preconceived strategy. Although I will do my best to hit the right market with the right product and the right strategy the first time out, there is a high probability that a better direction will emerge as the business heads toward its initial target. I must therefore plan to be wrong and to learn what is right as fast as possible.[9] I cannot spend all of my resources or all of my organizational credibility on an all-or-nothing first-time bet, as Apple did with its Newton or Hewlett-Packard did with its Kittyhawk. I need to conserve resources to get it right on the second or third try.

These three concepts would constitute the foundation of my marketing strategy.

Potential Markets: Some Speculation

What might emerge as the initial value network for electric vehicles? Again, though it is impossible to predict, it almost surely will be one in which the weaknesses of the electric vehicle will be seen as strengths. One of my students has suggested that the parents of high school students, who buy their children cars for basic transportation to and from school, friends' homes, and school events, might constitute a fertile market for electric vehicles.[10] Given the option, these parents might see the product simplicity, slow acceleration, and limited driving range of electric vehicles as very *desirable* attributes for their teenagers' cars—especially if they were styled with teenagers in mind. Given the right marketing approach, who knows what might happen? An earlier generation met a lot of nice people on their Hondas.

Another possible early market might be taxis or small-parcel delivery vehicles destined for the growing, crowded, noisy, polluted cities of Southeast Asia. Vehicles can sit on Bangkok's roads all day, mostly idling in traffic jams and never accelerating above 30 miles per hour. Electric motors would not need to run and hence would not drain the battery while idling. The maneuverability and ease of parking of these small vehicles would be additional attractions.

These or similar market ideas, whether or not they ultimately prove viable, are at least consistent with the way disruptive technologies develop and emerge.

How Are Today's Automobile Companies Marketing Electric Vehicles?

The strategy proposed here for finding and defining the initial market for electric vehicles stands in stark contrast to the marketing approaches being used by today's major automakers, each of which is struggling to sell electric vehicles into its mainstream market in the time-honored tradition of established firms mishandling disruptive technologies. Consider this statement made in 1995 by William Glaub, Chrysler general sales manager, discussing his company's planned offering for 1998.[11]

> Chrysler Corporation is preparing to provide an electric powered version of our slick new minivan in time for the 1998 model year. After an in-depth study of the option between a purpose-built vehicle and modification of an existing platform, the choice of the minivan to use as an electric powered platform, in retrospect, is an obvious best choice for us. Our experience shows that fleets will likely be the best opportunity to move any number of these vehicles . . . . The problem that we face is *not* in creating an attractive package. The new minivan is an attractive package. The problem is that sufficient energy storage capacity is not available on board the vehicle.[12]

To position its offering in the mainstream market, Chrysler has had to pack its minivan with 1,600 *pounds* of batteries. This, of course, makes its acceleration much slower, its driving range shorter, and its braking distance longer than other available gasoline-powered automobiles. Because of the way Chrysler has positioned its electric vehicle, industry analysts naturally compare it to gasoline-powered minivans, using the metrics paramount in the mainstream value network. At an estimated cost of $100,000 (compared with $22,000 for the gasoline-powered model), nobody in their right mind would consider buying Chrysler's product.

Chrysler's marketers are, naturally enough, very pessimistic about their ability to sell *any* electric minivans in California, despite the government's mandate that they do so. William Glaub, for example, continued the remarks cited above with the following observation:

> Markets are developed with fine products that customers desire to own. No salesman can take marginal product into the marketplace and have any hope of establishing a sustainable consumer base. Consumers will not be forced into a purchase that they do not want. Mandates will not work in a consumer-driven, free market economy. For electric vehicles to find a place in the market, respectable products comparable to today's gasoline-powered cars must be available.[13]

Chrysler's conclusion is absolutely correct, given the way its marketers have framed their challenge.[14] Mainstream customers can *never* use a disruptive technology at its outset.

WHAT SHOULD BE OUR PRODUCT, TECHNOLOGY, AND DISTRIBUTION STRATEGIES?

Product Development for Disruptive Innovations

Guiding my engineers in designing our initial electric vehicle will be a challenge, because of the classic chicken-and-egg problem: Without a market, there is no obvious or reliable source of customer input; without a product that addresses customers' needs, there can be no market. How can we design a product in such a vacuum? Fortunately, the principles described in this book give us some help.

The most valuable guidance comes from chapter 9, which indicated that the basis of competition will change over a product's life cycle and that the cycle of evolution itself is driven by the phenomenon of performance oversupply, that is, the condition in which the performance provided by a technology exceeds the actual needs of the market. Historically, performance oversupply opens the door for simpler, less expensive, and more convenient—and almost always disruptive—technologies to enter.

Performance oversupply indeed seems to have occurred in autos. There are practical limits to the size of auto bodies and engines, to the value of going from 0 to 60 in fewer seconds, and to the consumer's ability to cope with overchoice in available options. Thus, we can safely predict that the basis of product competition and customer choice will shift away from these measures of functionality toward other attributes, such as reliability and convenience. This is borne out by the nature of the most successful entrants into the North American market during the past thirty years; they have succeeded not because they introduced products with superior functionality, but because they competed on the basis of reliability and convenience.

Toyota, for example, entered the U.S. market with its simple, reliable Corona, establishing a low-end market position. Then, consistent with the inexorable attraction to migrate upmarket, Toyota introduced models, such as Camry, Previa, and Lexus, with added features and functionality, creating a vacuum at the low end of the market into which entrants such as Saturn and Hyundai have entered. Saturn's strategy has been to characterize the customer's entire experience of buying and owning the vehicle as reliable and convenient, but it, too, judging by recent reports,[15] will soon take its turn moving upmarket, creating a new vacuum at the low end for even simpler, more convenient transportation.

In all likelihood, therefore, the winning design in the first stages of the electric vehicle race will be characterized by simplicity and convenience and will be incubated in an emerging value network in which these attributes are important measures of value. Each of the disruptive technologies studied in this book has been smaller, simpler, and more convenient than preceding products. Each was initially used in a new value network in which simplicity and convenience were valued. This was true for smaller, simpler disk drives; desktop and portable computers; hydraulic backhoes; steel minimills as opposed to integrated mills; insulin-injecting pens as opposed to syringes.[16]

Using these qualities as my guiding principles, I would instruct my design engineers to proceed according to the following three criteria.

First, this vehicle must be *simple, reliable, and convenient.* That probably means, for example, that figuring out a way to recharge its batteries quickly, using the commonly available electrical service, would be an immutable technological objective.

Second, because no one knows the ultimate market for the product or how it will ultimately be used, we must design a product platform in which *feature, function, and styling changes can be made quickly and at low cost.* Assuming, for example, that the initial customers for electric vehicles will be parents who buy them for their teenaged children to drive to and from school, friends' homes, and activities, the first model would have features and styling appropriate and appealing to teenagers. But, although we may target this market first, there's a high probability that our initial concept will prove wrong. So we've got to get the first models done fast and on a shoestring—leaving ample budget to get it right once feedback from the market starts coming in.[17]

Third, we must *hit a low price point.* Disruptive technologies typically have a lower *sticker* price per unit than products that are used in the mainstream, even though their cost in use is often higher. What enabled the use of disk drives in desktop computers was not just their smaller size; it was their low unit price, which fit within the overall price points that personal computer makers needed to hit. The price *per megabyte* of the smaller disk drives was always higher than for the larger drives. Similarly, in excavators the price *per excavator* was lower for the early hydraulic models than for the established cable-actuated ones, but their total cost per cubic yard of earth moved per hour was much higher. Accordingly, our electric vehicle must have a lower sticker price than the prevailing price for gasoline-powered cars, even if the operating cost per mile driven is higher. Customers have a long track record of paying price premiums for convenience.

Technology Strategy for Disruptive Innovations

Our technology plan cannot call for any technological breakthroughs on the path critical for the project's success. Historically, disruptive technologies involve no new technologies; rather, they consist of components built around proven technologies and put together in a novel product architecture that offers the customer a set of attributes never before available.

The major automakers engaged in electric vehicle development today all maintain that a breakthrough in battery technology is absolutely essential before electric vehicles can be commercially viable. John R. Wallace, of Ford, for example, has stated the following:

> The dilemma is that today's batteries cannot satisfy these consumer needs. As anybody who is familiar with today's battery technology will tell you, electric vehicles are not ready for prime time. All of the batteries expected to be available in 1998 fall short of the 100-mile range [required by consumers]. The only solution for the problems of range and cost is improved battery technology. To ensure a commercially successful electric vehicle market, the focus of our resources should be on the development of battery technology. Industry efforts such as those through the U.S. Advanced Battery consortium, along with cooperative efforts among all electric vehicle stakeholders—such as utilities, battery companies, environmentalists, regulators and converters—are the most effective way to ensure the marketability of electric vehicles.[18]

William Glaub, of Chrysler, takes a similar position: "The advanced lead-acid batteries that will be used will provide less than the fuel storage equivalent of two gallons of gasoline. This is like leaving home every day with the 'low fuel' light on. In other words, the battery technology is simply not ready."[19]

The reason these companies view a breakthrough in battery technology as the critical bottleneck to the commercial success of electric vehicles, of course, is that their executives have positioned their minds and their products in the mainstream market. For Chrysler, this means an electric minivan; for Ford, an electric Ranger. Given this position, they must deliver a sustaining technological impact from what is inherently a disruptive technology. They need a breakthrough in battery technology because they made the choice to somehow position electric vehicles as a sustaining technology. A battery breakthrough is *not* likely to be required of companies whose executives choose to harness or account for the basic laws of disruptive technology by creating a market in which the weaknesses of the electric vehicle become its strengths.

Where will advances in battery technology eventually come from? Looking at the historical record, we can assert the following. The companies that ultimately achieve the advances in battery technology required to power cars for 150-mile cruises (if they are ever developed) will be those that pioneer the creation of a new value network using proven technology and then develop the sustaining technologies needed to carry them upward into more attractive markets.[20] Our finding that well-managed companies are generally upwardly mobile and downwardly immobile, therefore, suggests that the impetus to find the battery breakthrough will indeed be strongest among the disruptive innovators, which will have built a low-end market for electric vehicles before trying to move upmarket toward the larger, more profitable mainstream.

Distribution Strategy for Disruptive Innovations

It has almost always been the case that disruptive products redefine the dominant distribution channels, because dealers' economics—their models for how to make money—are powerfully shaped by the mainstream value network, just as the manufacturer's are. Sony's disruptive introduction of convenient and reliable portable transistorized radios and televisions shifted the dominant retail channel from appliance and department stores with expensive sales support and field service networks (required for sets built with vacuum tubes) to volume-oriented, low-overhead discount retailers. Honda's disruptive motorbikes were rejected by mainstream motorcycle dealers, forcing the company to create a new channel among sporting goods retailers. We saw, in fact, that a major reason why Harley-Davidson's small-bike initiative failed is that its dealers rejected it: The image and economics of the small Italian bikes Harley had acquired did not fit its dealer network.

The reason disruptive technologies and new distribution channels frequently go hand-in-hand is, in fact, an economic one. Retailers and distributors tend to have very clear formulas for making money, as the histories of Kresge and Woolworth in chapter 4 showed. Some make money by selling low volumes of big-ticket products at high margins; others make money by selling large volumes at razor-thin margins that cover minimal operating overheads; still others make their money servicing products already sold. Just as disruptive technologies don't fit the models of established firms for improving profits, they often don't fit the models of their *distributors,* either.

My electric vehicle program would, therefore, have as a basic strategic premise the need to find or create new distribution channels for electric vehicles. Unless proven otherwise, I'd bet that mainstream dealers of gasoline-powered automobiles would not view the sorts of disruptive electric vehicles we have in mind as critical to their success.

WHAT ORGANIZATION BEST SERVES DISRUPTIVE INNOVATIONS?

After identifying the electric vehicle as a potentially disruptive technology; setting realistic bearings for finding its potential markets; and establishing strategic parameters for the product's design, technology, and distribution network, as program manager I would next turn to organization. Creating an organizational context in which this effort can prosper will be crucial, because rational resource allocation processes in established companies consistently deny disruptive technologies the resources they need to survive, regardless of the commitment senior management may ostensibly have made to the program.

Spinning Off an Independent Organization

As we saw in the discussion of resource dependence in chapter 5, established firms that successfully built a strong market position in a disruptive technology were those that spun off from the mainstream company an independent, autonomously operated organization. Quantum, Control Data, IBM's PC Division, Allen Bradley, and Hewlett-Packard's desk-jet initiative all succeeded because they created organizations whose survival was predicated upon successful commercialization of the disruptive technology: These firms embedded a dedicated organization squarely within the emerging value network.

As program manager, therefore, I would strongly urge corporate management to create an independent organization to commercialize electric vehicle technology, either an autonomous business unit, such as GM's Saturn Division or the IBM PC Division, or an independent company whose stock is largely owned by the corporation. In an independent organization, my best employees would be able to focus on electric vehicles without being repeatedly withdrawn from the project to solve pressing problems for customers who pay the present bills. Demands from our own customers, on the other hand, would help us to focus on and lend impetus and excitement to our program.

An independent organization would not only make resource dependence work for us rather than against us, but it would also address the principle that small markets cannot solve the growth or profit problems of large companies. For many years into the future, the market for electric vehicles will be so small that this business is unlikely to contribute significantly to the top or bottom lines of a major automaker's income statement. Thus, since senior managers at these companies cannot be expected to focus either their priority attention or their priority resources on electric vehicles, the most talented managers and engineers would be unlikely to want to be associated with our project, which must inevitably be seen as a financially insignificant effort: To secure their own futures within the company, they naturally will want to work on mainstream programs, not peripheral ones.

In the early years of this new business, orders are likely to be denominated in hundreds, not tens of thousands. If we are lucky enough to get a few wins, they almost surely will be small ones. In a small, independent organization, these small wins will generate energy and enthusiasm. In the mainstream, they would generate skepticism about whether we should even be in the business. I want my organization's *customers* to answer the question of whether we should be in the business. I don't want to spend my precious managerial energy constantly defending our existence to efficiency analysts in the mainstream.

Innovations are fraught with difficulties and uncertainties. Because of this, I want *always* to be sure that the projects that I manage are positioned directly on the path everyone believes the organization must take to achieve higher growth and greater profitability. If my program is widely viewed as being on that path, then I have confidence that when the inevitable problems arise, somehow the organization will work with me to muster whatever it takes to solve them and succeed. If, on the other hand, my program is viewed by key people as nonessential to the organization's growth and profitability, or even worse, is viewed as an idea that might *erode* profits, then even if the technology is simple, the project will fail.

I can address this challenge in one of two ways: I could convince everyone in the mainstream (in their heads *and* their guts) that the disruptive technology is profitable, or I could create an organization that is small enough, with an appropriate cost structure, that my program can be viewed as being on its critical path to success. The latter alternative is a far more tractable management challenge.

In a small, independent organization I will more likely be able to create an appropriate attitude toward failure. Our initial stab into the market is not likely to be successful. We will, therefore, need the flexibility to fail, but to fail on a *small* scale, so that we can try again without having destroyed our credibility. Again, there are two ways to create the proper tolerance toward failure: change the values and culture of the mainstream organization or create a new organization. The problem with asking the mainstream organization to be more tolerant of risk-taking and failure is that, in general, we don't *want* to tolerate marketing failure when, as is most often the case, we are investing in sustaining technology change. The mainstream organization is involved in taking sustaining technological innovations into existing markets populated by known customers with researchable needs. Getting it wrong the first time is not an intrinsic part of these processes: Such innovations are amenable to careful planning and coordinated execution.

Finally, I don't want my organization to have pockets that are too deep. While I don't want my people to feel pressure to generate significant profit for the mainstream company (this would force us into a fruitless search for an instant large market), I want them to feel *constant* pressure to find some way—*some* set of customers *somewhere*—to make our small organization cash-positive as fast as possible. We need a strong motivation to accelerate through the trials and errors inherent in cultivating a new market.

Of course, the danger in making this unequivocal call for spinning out an independent company is that some managers might apply this remedy indiscriminately, viewing skunkworks and spinoffs as a blanket solution—an industrial-strength aspirin that cures all sorts of problems. In reality, spinning out is an appropriate step only when confronting disruptive innovation. The evidence is *very* strong that large, mainstream organizations can be extremely creative in developing and implementing *sustaining* innovations.[21] In other words, the degree of disruptiveness inherent in an innovation provides a fairly clear indication of when a mainstream organization might be capable of succeeding with it and when it might be expected to fail.

In terms of the framework presented in Figure 5.6, the electric vehicle is not only a disruptive innovation, but it involves massive architectural reconfiguration as well, a reconfiguration that must occur not only within the product itself but across the entire value chain. From procurement through distribution, functional groups will have to interface differently than they have ever before. Hence, my project would need to be managed as a heavyweight team in an organization independent of the mainstream company. This organizational structure cannot guarantee the success of our electric vehicle program, but it would at least allow my team to work in an environment that accounts for, rather than fights, the principles of disruptive innovation.

NOTES

1. In 1996, the state government delayed implementation of this requirement until the year 2002, in response to motor vehicle manufacturers' protests that, given the performance and cost of the vehicles they had been able to design, there was no demand for electric vehicles.
2. An excellent study on this subject is summarized in Dorothy Leonard-Barton, *Wellsprings of Knowledge* (Boston: Harvard Business School Press, 1995).
3. This information was taken from an October 1994 survey conducted by The Dohring Company and quoted by the Toyota Motor Sales Company at the CARB (California Air Resources Board) Workshop on Electric Vehicle Consumer Marketability held in El Monte, California, on June 28, 1995.
4. This information was provided by Dr. Paul J. Miller, Senior Energy Fellow, W. Alton Jones Foundation, Inc., Charlottesville, Virginia. It was augmented with information from the following sources: Frank Keith, Paul Norton, and Dana Sue Potestio, *Electric Vehicles: Promise and Reality* (California State Legislative Report [19], No. 10, July, 1994); W. P. Egan, *Electric Cars* (Canberra, Australia: Bureau of Transport Economics, 1974); Daniel Sperling, *Future Drive: Electric Vehicles and Sustainable Transportation* (Washington, D.C.: Island Press, 1995); and William Hamilton, *Electric Automobiles* (New York: McGraw Hill Company, 1980).
5. Based on the graphs in Figure 10.1, it will take a long time for disruptive electric vehicle technology to become competitive in mainstream markets if future rates of improvement resemble those of the past. The historical rate of performance improvement is, of course, no guarantee that the future rate can be maintained. Technologists very well might run into insurmountable technological barriers. What we *can* say for sure, however, is that the incentive of disruptive technologists to find some way to engineer around such barriers will be just as strong as the disincentive that established car makers will feel to move down-market. If present rates of improvement continue, however,

we would expect the cruising range of electric cars, for example, to intersect with the average range demanded in the mainstream market by 2015, and electric vehicle acceleration to intersect with mainstream demands by 2020. Clearly, as will be discussed below, it will be crucial for electric vehicle innovators to find markets that value the attributes of the technology as it currently is capable, rather than waiting until the technology improves to the point that it can be used in the mainstream market.

6. This statement was made by John R. Wallace, Director of Electric Vehicle Programs, Ford Motor Company, at the CARB Workshop on Electric Vehicle Consumer Marketability held at El Monte, California, on June 28, 1995.

7. It is remarkable how instinctively and consistently good companies try to force innovations toward their existing base of customers, regardless of whether they are sustaining or disruptive in character. We have seen this several times in this book: for example, in mechanical excavators, where Bucyrus Erie tried with its "Hydrohoe" to make hydraulic excavation technology work for mainstream excavation contractors; in motorcycles, where Harley-Davidson tried to launch low-end brand name bikes through its dealer network; and in the electric vehicle case described here, in which Chrysler packed nearly a ton of batteries into a minivan. Charles Ferguson and Charles Morris, in their book *Computer Wars,* recount a similar story about IBM's efforts to commercialize Reduced Instruction Set Computing (RISC) microprocessor technology. RISC was invented at IBM, and its inventors built computers with RISC chips that were "screamingly fast." IBM subsequently spent massive amounts of time, money, and manpower trying to make the RISC chip work in its main line of minicomputers. This required so many design compromises, however, that the program was never successful. Several key members of IBM's RISC team left in frustration, subsequently playing key roles in establishing the RISC chipmaker MIPS and Hewlett-Packard's RISC chip business. These efforts were successful because, having accepted the attributes of the product for what they were, they found a market, in engineering workstations, that valued those attributes. IBM failed because it tried to force the technology into a market it had already found. Interestingly, IBM ultimately built a successful business around a RISC-architecture chip when it launched its own engineering workstation. See Charles Ferguson and Charles Morris, *Computer Wars* (New York: Time Books, 1994).

8. The notion that non-existent markets are best researched through action, rather than through passive observation, is explored in Gary Hamel and C. K. Prahalad, "Corporate Imagination and Expeditionary Marketing," *Harvard Business Review,* July-August, 1991, 81–92.

9. The concept that business plans dealing with disruptive innovations should be plans for learning rather than plans for executing a preconceived strategy is taught clearly by Rita G. McGrath and Ian MacMillan in "Discovery-Driven Planning," *Harvard Business Review,* July-August, 1995, 44–54.

10. Jeffrey Thoresen Severts, "Managing Innovation: Electric Vehicle Development at Chrysler," Harvard Business School MBA student paper, 1996. A
copy of this paper is available on request from Clayton Christensen, Harvard
Business School.

11. Glaub's remarks were made in the context of the California Air Resources
Board mandate that by 1998 all companies selling gasoline-powered vehicles
in the state must, in order to sell any cars at all, sell enough electric-powered
vehicles to constitute 2 percent of their total vehicle unit sales in the state.
As already noted, the state government, in 1996, delayed implementation of
that requirement until 2002.

12. This statement was made by William Glaub, General Sales Manager, Field
Sales Operations, Chrysler Corporation, at the CARB Workshop on Electric
Vehicle Consumer Marketability held in El Monte, California, on June 28,
1995; see p. 5 of the company's press release about the workshop.

13. Ibid.

14. It is important to note that these statistics for Chrysler's offering were determined by Chrysler's efforts to commercialize the disruptive technology; they
are not intrinsic to electrically powered vehicles *per se*. Electric vehicles
designed for different, lighter-duty applications, such as one by General
Motors, have driving ranges of up to 100 miles. (See Jeffrey Thoresen Severts,
"Managing Innovation: Electric Vehicle Development at Chrysler," Harvard
Business School student paper, 1996.)

15. See, for example, Gabriella Stern and Rebecca Blumenstein, "GM Is Expected
to Back Proposal for Midsize Version of Saturn Car," *The Wall Street Journal*,
May 24, 1996, B4.

16. This list of smaller, simpler, more convenient disruptive technologies could
be extended to include a host of others whose histories could not be squeezed
into this book: tabletop photocopiers; surgical staplers; portable, transistorized radios and televisions; helican scan VCRs; microwave ovens; bubble jet
printers. Each of these disruptive technologies has grown to dominate both
its initial and its mainstream markets, having begun with simplicity and
convenience as their primary value propositions.

17. The notion that it takes time, experimentation, and trial and error to achieve
a dominant product design, a very common pattern with disruptive technologies, is discussed later in this chapter.

18. This statement was made by John R. Wallace, of Ford, at the CARB Workshop
on Electric Vehicle Consumer Marketability held in El Monte, California,
on June 28, 1995; see p. 5 of the company's press release.

19. Glaub, statement made at the CARB Workshop.

20. Two excellent articles in which the relative roles of product development
and incremental versus radical technology development are researched and
discussed are Ralph E. Gomory, "From the 'Ladder of Science' to the Product

Development Cycle," *Harvard Business Review,* November-December, 1989, 99–105, and Lowell Steele, "Managers' Misconceptions About Technology," *Harvard Business Review,* 1983, 733–740.

21. In addition to the findings from the disk drive study summarized in chapters 1 and 2 that established firms were able to muster the wherewithal to lead in extraordinarily complex and risky sustaining innovations, there is similar evidence from other industries; see, for example, Marco Iansiti, "Technology Integration: Managing Technological Evolution in a Complex Environment," *Research Policy* 24, 1995, 521–542.

CHAPTER ELEVEN

The Dilemmas of Innovation: A Summary

One of the most gratifying outcomes of the research reported in this book is the finding that managing better, working harder, and not making so many dumb mistakes is not the answer to the innovator's dilemma. This discovery is gratifying because I have never met a group of people who are smarter or work harder or are as right so often as the managers I know. If finding better people than these were the answer to the problems posed by disruptive technologies, the dilemma would indeed be intractable.

We have learned in this book that in their straightforward search for profit and growth, some very capable executives in some extraordinarily successful companies, using the best managerial techniques, have led their firms toward failure. Yet companies must not throw out the capabilities, organizational structures, and decision-making processes that have made them successful in their mainstream markets just because they don't work in the face of disruptive technological change. The vast majority of the innovation challenges they will face are sustaining in character, and these are just the sorts of innovations that these capabilities are designed to tackle. Managers of these companies simply need to recognize that these capabilities, cultures, and practices are valuable only in certain conditions.

I have found that many of life's most useful insights are often quite simple. In retrospect, many of the findings of this book fit that mold: Initially they seemed somewhat counterintuitive, but as I came to understand them, the insights were revealed as simple and sensible. I review them here, in the hope that they will prove useful to those readers who may be wrestling with the innovator's dilemmas.

First, the pace of progress that markets demand or can absorb may be different from the progress offered by technology. This means that products that do not appear to be useful to our customers today (that is, disruptive technologies) may squarely address their needs tomorrow. Recognizing this possibility, we cannot expect our customers to lead us toward innovations that they do not now need. Therefore, while keeping close to our customers is an important management paradigm for handling sustaining innovations, it may provide misleading data for handling disruptive ones. Trajectory maps can help to analyze conditions and to reveal which situation a company faces.

Second, managing innovation mirrors the resource allocation process: Innovation proposals that get the funding and manpower they require may succeed; those given lower priority, whether formally or de facto, will starve for lack of resources and have little chance of success. One major reason for the difficulty of managing innovation is the complexity of managing the resource allocation process. A company's executives may seem to make resource allocation decisions, but the implementation of those decisions is in the hands of a staff whose wisdom and intuition have been forged in the company's mainstream value network: They understand what the company should do to improve profitability. Keeping a company successful requires that employees continue to hone and exercise that wisdom and intuition. This means, however, that until other alternatives that appear to be financially more attractive have disappeared or been eliminated, managers will find it extraordinarily difficult to keep resources focused on the pursuit of a disruptive technology.

Third, just as there is a resource allocation side to every innovation problem, matching the market to the technology is another. Successful companies have a practiced capability in taking sustaining technologies to market, routinely giving their customers more and better versions of what they say they want. This is a valued capability for handling sustaining innovation, but it will not serve the purpose when handling disruptive technologies. If, as most successful companies try to do, a company stretches or forces a disruptive technology to fit the needs of current, mainstream customers—as we saw happen in the disk drive, excavator, and electric vehicle industries—it is almost sure to fail. Historically, the more successful approach has been to find a new market that values the current characteristics of the disruptive technology. Disruptive technology should be framed as a marketing challenge, not a technological one.

Fourth, the capabilities of most organizations are far more specialized and context-specific than most managers are inclined to believe. This is because capabilities are forged within value networks. Hence, organizations have capabilities to take certain new technologies into certain markets. They have disabilities in taking technology to market in other ways. Organizations have the capability to tolerate failure along some dimensions, and an incapacity to tolerate other types of failure. They have the capability to make money when gross margins are at one level, and an inability to make money when margins are at another. They may have the capability to manufacture profitably at particular ranges of volume and order size, and be unable to make money with different volumes or sizes of customers. Typically, their product development cycle times and the steepness of the ramp to production that they can negotiate are set in the context of their value network.

All of these capabilities—of organizations and of individuals—are defined and refined by the types of problems tackled in the past, the nature of which has also been shaped by the characteristics of the value networks in which the organizations and individuals have historically competed. Very often, the new markets enabled by disruptive technologies require very different capabilities along each of these dimensions.

Fifth, in many instances, the information required to make large and decisive investments in the face of disruptive technology simply does not exist. It needs to be created through fast, inexpensive, and flexible forays into the market and the product. The risk is very high that any particular idea about the product attributes or market applications of a disruptive technology may not prove to be viable. Failure and interative learning are, therefore, intrinsic to the search for success with a disruptive technology. Successful organizations, which ought not and cannot tolerate failure in sustaining innovations, find it difficult simultaneously to tolerate failure in disruptive ones.

Although the mortality rate for ideas about disruptive technologies is high, the overall business of creating new markets for disruptive technologies need not be inordinately risky. Managers who don't bet the farm on their first idea, who leave room to try, fail, learn quickly, and try again, can succeed at developing the understanding of customers, markets, and technology needed to commercialize disruptive innovations.

Sixth, it is not wise to adopt a blanket technology strategy to be always a leader or always a follower. Companies need to take distinctly different postures depending on whether they are addressing a disruptive or a sustaining technology. Disruptive innovations entail significant first-mover advantages: Leadership is important. Sustaining situations, however, very often do not. The evidence is quite strong that companies whose strategy is to extend the performance of conventional technologies through consistent incremental improvements do about as well as companies whose strategy is to take big, industry-leading technological leaps.

Seventh, and last, the research summarized in this book suggests that there are powerful barriers to entry and mobility that differ significantly from the types defined and historically focused on by economists. Economists have extensively described barriers to entry and mobility and how they work. A characteristic of almost all of these formulations, however, is that they relate to *things,* such as assets or resources, that are difficult to obtain or replicate.[1] Perhaps the most powerful protection that small entrant firms enjoy as they build the emerging markets for disruptive technologies is that they are doing something that it simply does not make sense for the established leaders to do. Despite their endowments in technology, brand names, manufacturing prowess, management experience, distribution muscle, and just plain cash, successful companies populated by good managers have a genuinely hard time doing what does not fit their model for how to make money. Because disruptive technologies rarely make sense during the years when investing in them is most important, conventional managerial wisdom at established firms constitutes an entry and mobility barrier that entrepreneurs and investors can bank on. It is powerful and pervasive.

Established companies *can* surmount this barrier, however. The dilemmas posed to innovators by the conflicting demands of sustaining and disruptive technologies can be resolved. Managers must first understand what these intrinsic conflicts are. They then need to create a context in which each organization's market position, economic structure, developmental capabilities, and values are sufficiently aligned with the power of their customers that they assist, rather than impede, the very different work of sustaining and disruptive innovators. I hope this book helps them in this effort.

NOTES

1. By *things* I mean barriers such as proprietary technology; ownership of expensive manufacturing plants with large minimum efficient manufacturing scales; pre-emption of the most powerful distributors in major markets; exclusive control of key raw materials or unique human resources; the credibility and reputation that comes from strong brand names; cumulative production experience and/or the presence of steep economies of scale; and so on. The seminal work on entry barriers from an economist's perspective is Joseph Bain, *Barriers to New Competition* (Cambridge, MA: Harvard University Press, 1956); see also Richard Caves and Michael Porter, "From Entry Barriers to Mobility Barriers," *Quarterly Journal of Economics* (91), May, 1977, 241–261.

The Innovator's Dilemma Book Group Guide

The summary and questions in this guide are designed to stimulate thinking and discussion about The Innovator's Dilemma, how its findings are
manifest in many industries today, and the implications of those findings
for the future.

Thesis of the Book

In *The Innovator's Dilemma,* Professor Clayton Christensen asks the
question: Why do well-managed companies fail? He concludes that they
often fail because the very management practices that have allowed them
to become industry leaders also make it extremely difficult for them
to develop the disruptive technologies that ultimately steal away their
markets.

Well-managed companies are excellent at developing the sustaining
technologies that improve the performance of their products in the ways
that matter to their customers. This is because their management practices
are biased toward:

Listening to customers

Investing aggressively in technologies that give those customers what
they say they want

Seeking higher margins

Targeting larger markets rather than smaller ones

Disruptive technologies, however, are distinctly different from sustaining technologies.*Disruptive technologies change the value proposition in a market. When they first appear, they almost always offer lower performance in terms of the attributes that mainstream customers care about. In computer disk drives, for example, disruptive technologies have always had less capacity than the old technologies. But disruptive technologies have other attributes that a few fringe (generally new) customers value. They are typically cheaper, smaller, simpler, and frequently more convenient to use. Therefore, they open new markets. Further, because with experience and sufficient investment, the developers of disruptive technologies will always improve their products' performance, they eventually are able to take over the older markets. This is because they are able to deliver sufficient performance on the old attributers, and they add some new ones.

The Innovator's Dilemma describes both the processes through which disruptive technologies supplant older technologies and the powerful forces within well-managed companies that make them unlikely to develop those technologies themselves. Professor Christensen offers a framework of four Principles of Disruptive Technology to explain why the management practices that are the most productive for exploiting existing technologies are antiproductive when it comes to developing disruptive ones. And, finally, he suggests ways that managers can harness these principles so that their companies can become more effective at developing for themselves the new technologies that are going to capture their markets in the future.

Principles of Disruptive Technology

1. Companies Depend on Customers and Investors for Resources
   In order to survive, companies must provide customers and investors with the products, services, and profits that they require. The highest performing companies, therefore, have well-developed systems for killing ideas that their customers don't want. As a result, these companies find it very difficult to invest adequate resources in disruptive technologies—lower-margin opportunities

that their customers don't want—until their customers want them. And by then, it is too late.

2. **Small Markets Don't Solve the Growth Needs of Large Companies**
To maintain their share prices and create internal opportunities for their employees, successful companies need to grow. It isn't necessary that they increase their growth rates, but they must maintain them. And as they get larger, they need increasing amounts of new revenue just to maintain the same growth rate. Therefore, it becomes progressively more difficult for them to enter the newer, smaller markets that are destined to become the large markets of the future. To maintain their growth rates, they must focus on large markets.

3. **Markets That Don't Exist Can't Be Analyzed**
Sound market research and good planning followed by execution according to plan are the hallmarks of good management. But companies whose investment processes demand quantification of market size and financial returns before they can enter a market get paralyzed when faced with disruptive technologies because they demand data on markets that don't yet exist.

4. **Technology Supply May Not Equal Market Demand**
Although disruptive technologies can initially be used only in small markets, they eventually become competitive in mainstream markets. This is because the pace of technological progress often exceeds the rate of improvement that mainstream customers want or can absorb. As a result, the products that are currently in the mainstream eventually will overshoot the performance that mainstream markets demand, while the disruptive technologies that underperform relative to customer expectations in the mainstream market today may become directly competitive tomorrow. Once two or more products are offering adequate performance, customers will find other criteria for choosing. These criteria tend to move toward reliability, convenience, and price, all of which are areas in which the newer technologies often have advantages.

A big mistake that managers make in dealing with new technologies is that they try to fight or overcome the Principles of Disruptive Technology. Applying the traditional management practices that lead to success with sustaining technologies always leads to failure with disruptive technolo-

234 | *The Innovator's Dilemma* Book Group Guide

gies, says Professor Christensen. The more productive route, which often leads to success, he says, is to understand the natural laws that apply to disruptive technologies and to use them to create new markets and new products. Only by recognizing the dynamics of how disruptive technologies develop can managers respond effectively to the opportunities that they present.

Specifically, he advises managers faced with disruptive technologies to:

1. Give responsibility for disruptive technologies to organizations whose customers need them so that resources will flow to them.

2. Set up a separate organization small enough to get excited by small gains.

3. Plan for failure. Don't bet all your resources on being right the first time. Think of your initial efforts at commercializing a disruptive technology as learning opportunities. Make revisions as you gather data.

4. Don't count on breakthroughs. Move ahead early and find the market for the current attributes of the technology. You will find it outside the current mainstream market. You will also find that the attributes that make disruptive technologies unattractive to mainstream markets are the attributes on which the new markets will be built.

Questions for Discussion

1. The characteristics of a disruptive technology are:

They are simpler and cheaper and lower performing.

They generally promise lower margins, not higher profits.

Leading firms' most profitable customers generally can't use and don't want them.

They are first commercialized in emerging or insignificant markets.

The Innovator's Dilemma discusses disruptive innovations in the disk-drive, excavator, steel, and auto industries. Looking back through history, can you identify some disruptive technologies that eventually replaced older products and industries? Can you think of others that are emerging today, maybe even ones that could threaten your business?

2. There is a tendency in all markets for companies to move upmarket toward more complicated products with higher prices. Why is it difficult for companies to enter markets for simpler, cheaper products? Can you think of companies that have upscaled themselves out of business? How might they have avoided that?

3. The same tendency for companies to move upmarket that can be fatal for established companies also accounts for the eventual development of emerging markets into mainstream markets. Besides the examples in the book, can you think of companies that have upscaled themselves to success?

4. In attempting to commercialize a disruptive technology, why is it important to begin investing on the assumption that your expectations will be wrong? Besides the motorcycle, excavator, and disk-drive examples in the book, can you think of other examples in which a company began marketing a product for one application but the big market turned out to be for another application?

5. One of the hallmarks of disruptive technologies is that initially they underperform the current technology on the attributes that matter most to mainstream customers. The companies that succeed in commercializing them, therefore, must find different customers for whom the new technology's attributes are most valuable. Can you think of any markets that are emerging today based on attributes or qualities that seemed unimportant to the mainstream markets when they were introduced? What older, mainstream products or companies are threatened?

6. When two or more products meet the minimum specifications for the functionality of a product, customers begin to look for other deciding factors. According to a Windermere Associates study cited in the book, the progression usually is from functionality to reliability to convenience to price. What are some current markets that have recently moved one or more steps along this progression?

7. Most people think that senior executives make the important decisions about where a company will go and how it will invest its resources, but the real power lies with the people deeper in the organization who decide which proposals will be presented to senior management. What are the corporate factors that lead

midlevel employees to ignore or kill disruptive technologies? Should well-managed companies change these practices and policies?

8. What are the personal career considerations that lead ambitious employees in large corporations to ignore or kill disruptive technologies? Should well-managed companies change the policies that encourage employees to think this way?

9. What do the findings in this book suggest about how companies will be organized in the future? Should large organizations with structures created around functionalities redesign themselves into interconnected teams, as some management theorists currently believe? Or, recognizing that different technologies and different markets have differing needs, should they try to have distinct organizational structures and management practices for different circumstances? Is this realistically possible?

10. The CEO of a disk-drive maker is quoted in chapter 4 as saying that "We got way ahead of the market" in explaining why his company failed to commercialize a 1.8-inch disk drive that it had developed. At the time, however, there was a burgeoning market for 1.8-inch drives among new users that his company hadn't discovered. Professor Christensen argues that "disruptive technology should be framed as a marketing challenge, not a technological one." Do you think there is a market somewhere for all technologies? If not, how would you as a manager go about figuring out which technologies to shelve and which ones to pursue aggressively?

11. Similarly, Professor Christensen argues that companies should not wait for new breakthroughs to improve a technology's performance. Instead, they need to find customers who value the very attributes that others consider to be shortcomings. As a manager, how do you decide when a technology—or idea—needs more development and when it's time to aggressively put it on the market?

12. The primary thesis of *The Innovator's Dilemma* is that the management practices that allow companies to be leaders in mainstream markets are the same practices that cause them to miss the opportunities offered by disruptive technologies. In other words, well-managed companies fail *because* they are well man-

aged. Do you think that the definition of what constitutes "good management" is changing? In the future, will listening to customers, investing aggressively in producing what those customers say they want, and carefully analyzing markets become "bad management"? What kind of system might combine the best of both worlds?

Index

About the Author

Clayton M. Christensen is the Kim B. Clark Professor of Business Administration at Harvard Business School. In addition to his most recent book, *How Will You Measure Your Life?*, he is the author or coauthor of many critically acclaimed books, including several *New York Times* bestsellers—*The Innovator's Dilemma*, *The Innovator's Solution*, and most recently, *Disrupting Class*. Christensen is the cofounder of Innosight, a management consultancy; Rose Park Advisors, an investment firm; and the Clayton Christensen Institute for Disruptive Innovation, a nonprofit think tank. In 2011 he was named the winner of the global Thinkers50 Innovation Award.